D1240924

A THEORY OF CHARACTER IN NEW TESTAMENT NARRATIVE

A THEORY OF CHARACTER IN NEW TESTAMENT NARRATIVE

CORNELIS BENNEMA

Fortress Press
Minneapolis

A THEORY OF CHARACTER IN NEW TESTAMENT NARRATIVE

Cover design: Tory Herman

Library of Congress Cataloging-in-Publication Data is available

Print ISBN: 978-1-4514-7221-9

eBook ISBN: 978-1-4514-8430-4

The paper used in this publication meets the minimum requirements of American National Standard for Information Sciences — Permanence of Paper for Printed Library Materials, ANSI Z329.48-1984.

Manufactured in the U.S.A.

This book was produced using PressBooks.com, and PDF rendering was done by PrinceXML.

For Max

Contents

Foreword by R. Alan Culpepper   ix
Preface   xi
Abbreviations   xv

1. Introduction—Identifying a Dominant Pattern/Paradigm   1
    1.1. The Current State of Affairs   4
    1.2. Identifying a Pattern or Paradigm of Character Reconstruction   24
    1.3. The Plan and Approach of the Book   27
2. Character in Antiquity and Modernity—Deconstructing the Dominant
  Pattern/Paradigm   31
    2.1. Character in Ancient Hebrew Literature   33
    2.2. Character in Ancient Greco-Roman Literature   35
    2.3. Character in Modern Literature   44
    2.4. Deconstructing the Dominant Pattern/Paradigm of Character
        Reconstruction   49
    2.5. Conclusion   59
3. A Theory of Character in New Testament Narrative—Constructing
  a New Paradigm   61
    3.1. Character in Text and Context   62
    3.2. Character Analysis and Classification   72
    3.3. Character Evaluation and Significance   90
    3.4. Revisiting Ancient Characterization   106
    3.5. Conclusion   110
4. Application of the Theory—Validating the New Paradigm   113
    4.1. Characters in the Gospel of Mark   114
    4.2. Characters in the Gospel of John   133
    4.3. Characters in the Acts of the Apostles   164
    4.4. Conclusion   182
5. Conclusion   185

Bibliography   191
Index of Modern Authors   213

Foreword

R. Alan Culpepper

Cornelis Bennema has tackled one of the most difficult challenges facing New Testament narrative critics: the construction of a comprehensive theory of characterization that interpreters can use to understand the subtleties of the roles of the characters in New Testament narratives. Developing a framework for the interpretation of biblical characters is challenging for several reasons. (1) There is not a readymade theory of characterization in ancient or modern literary theory that is adequate for this purpose. For example, are characters defined by traits or plot functions, and how can interpreters analyze the construction, roles, and functions of characters without being reductionistic? (2) Biblical interpreters have not settled the issue of whether theories of characterization drawn from modern literary criticism can or should be used in the interpretation of ancient narratives. (3) Studies of characterization in the Gospels and Acts have proceeded (at least since the demise of the Literary Aspects of the Gospels and Acts group in the Society of Biblical Literature) in provincial conversations, with interpreters of each of the Gospels (and Acts) talking only to each other. And, (4) while there has been what might be described as a burst of interest in characterization in the past five years, with fascinating interpretations of individual characters, this work has proceeded largely without corollary advances in the theory of characterization. Interpreters, in the main, are therefore still using, modifying, or reacting against the theoretical frameworks used by those of us involved in the first wave of narrative criticism thirty years ago.

Bennema has stepped into this gap, and this volume is not his first move toward a theory of characterization. In *Encountering Jesus: Character Studies in the Gospel of John* (2009) Bennema set forth a framework for locating characters along various continua (see the Preface). I applauded *Encountering Jesus* as "a book I have been waiting for" because it was the first effort I had seen to develop an adequate theoretical model and apply it to all the characters in the Gospel of John. This current volume represents a significant advance over *Encountering Jesus*, refining rather than abandoning his earlier work. In this volume Bennema engages the study of characterization in Mark and Acts as well as John (examining both current scholarship and selected characters in these three NT books), surveys and critiques current literature on characterization, examines both ancient constructions and modern theories of characterization, and makes the case for the legitimacy of using modern literary theory in the study of characterization in the NT narratives.

Bennema identifies three features of "the dominant paradigm" in current study: (1) the contrast between Hebraic and Hellenic characterization, (2) the contrast between ancient and modern characterization, and (3) the practice of applying modern literary methods developed for the study of fiction to the ancient historical sources. In response, he concludes that "there is no consensus on how to analyze, classify, and evaluate characters," and "many scholars tend to oversimplify most New Testament characters," using fixed, reductionist categories. The conclusion is obvious: "we need a comprehensive, nonreductionist theoretical framework in which we can analyze, classify, and evaluate the New Testament characters and determine their possible significance."

Bennema challenges the commonly accepted notions of the sharp contrasts between characters in Greco-Roman and Hebraic literature as well as the accepted dichotomy between ancient and modern characters, arguing that "the differences in characterization in the Hebrew Bible, ancient Greek literature, and modern narrative are differences in emphases rather than kind." He therefore advocates (1) the value of locating characters along continua of complexity, development, and penetration into the characters' inner life; (2) the legitimacy of using modern literary methods and models; and (3) the importance of this model of inference and classification for interpreting New Testament characters and their roles.

Following this discussion of theory and other approaches to characterization, Bennema develops the elements that define a "plausible historically informed modern reader" and applies his model to selected characters in Mark, John, and Acts. These character studies are insightful on their own, quite apart from the theoretical discussion that precedes them. The theoretical discussion, however, is the heart of the book. Bennema's engagement with the debates about New Testament characters and current approaches to the study of characters and characterization sets the stage now for the debates and refinements that will no doubt follow.

Scholarship advances by means of creative, original proposals and careful assessments and engagement with others' work—and this book offers both.

R. Alan Culpepper
McAfee School of Theology, Mercer University

Preface

This book proposes a paradigm shift in the study of character in New Testament narrative (or a new paradigm if one thinks there was not one to begin with). There is currently no consensus on how to study character in either literary theory or biblical studies. Nor is there a comprehensive theory of character. Many New Testament scholars appear to operate with a pattern or paradigm that has three assumptions: (i) characters in the Greco-Roman literature are "Aristotelian," that is, "flat" or "types"; (ii) characters in the Gospels (and Acts) are not like characters in modern fiction (round, individualistic, psychologized) but resemble Greco-Roman characters ("flat," one-dimensional); (iii) it is acceptable to use insights from modern literary methods to study ancient characters. While these scholars rarely justify this paradigm and sometimes overlook its inherent inconsistency, other scholars argue that modern theories of character in fiction should not be used to analyze characters in the Bible. In reply, this book introduces a comprehensive theory of character in New Testament narrative in four steps. In Chapter 1, I will identify a dominant pattern or paradigm of character reconstruction in the New Testament. In Chapter 2, I will deconstruct this pattern/paradigm, showing that characters in antiquity and modernity are more alike than different and that using modern methods to analyze characters in antiquity is both inevitable and legitimate. Then, in Chapter 3, I will propose a new paradigm for character reconstruction, which consists of three aspects: (i) character study in text and context; (ii) character analysis and classification; (iii) character evaluation and significance. Finally, in Chapter 4, I will validate the new paradigm by applying the theory to select characters in the Gospel of Mark, the Gospel of John, and the Acts of the Apostles.

This book builds on my earlier work on character reconstruction. In 2009, I wrote a twofold work on Johannine characters where I aimed at reversing the consensus view that Johannine characters are types, have little complexity, and show little or no development.[1] Arguing that the differences

---

1. Cornelis Bennema, "A Theory of Character in the Fourth Gospel with Reference to Ancient and Modern Literature," *BibInt* 17 (2009): 375–421; Cornelis Bennema, *Encountering Jesus: Character Studies in the Gospel of John* (Milton Keynes, UK: Paternoster, 2009).

in characterization in the Hebrew Bible, ancient Greek literature, and modern fiction are differences in emphases rather than kind, I suggested that it was better to speak of degrees of characterization along a continuum.[2] I then outlined a comprehensive theory of character that comprises three aspects: (i) the study of character in text and context, using information from the text and other sources; (ii) the analysis and classification of characters along Yosef Ewen's three dimensions (complexity, development, inner life), and plotting the resulting character on a continuum of degree of characterization (from agent to type to personality to individuality); (iii) the evaluation of characters in relation to John's point of view, purpose, and dualistic worldview. I then applied this theory to John's Gospel, showing that only eight out of twenty-three characters are "types." Since then I have contributed further essays on the subject.[3]

Here I seek to sharpen and develop my earlier theory of character in two ways. First, I engage with Christopher Skinner and Susan Hylen, whose books on Johannine character were published simultaneous with my 2009 work. Reading their work, I raised the question of whether I could (or should) enhance my theory by adding further continua of misunderstanding and ambiguity (see section 3.2). I also respond to various scholars who have critically interacted with my 2009 work, such as Richard Rohrbaugh, who reviewed my *Encountering Jesus* in 2011, Ruth Sheridan, Alicia Myers, Judith Christine Single Redman, and John Lyons. This kind of interaction is all a scholar hopes for, and their critique has stimulated my thinking and (hopefully) advanced the discourse on character reconstruction presented in this book. Second, this

---

2. I was especially indebted to Fred W. Burnett, who has excellently argued this case in "Characterization and Reader Construction of Characters in the Gospels," *Semeia* 63 (1993): 3–28.

3. Cornelis Bennema, "A Comprehensive Approach to Understanding Character in the Gospel of John," in *Characters and Characterization in the Gospel of John*, ed. Christopher W. Skinner (LNTS 461; New York: T. & T. Clark, 2013), 36–58; idem, "The Character of Pilate in the Gospel of John," in *Characters and Characterization in the Gospel of John*, ed. Christopher W. Skinner (LNTS 461; New York: T. & T. Clark, 2013), 240–53; essays on the crowd, Judas, and the chief priests in *Character Studies in the Fourth Gospel: Narrative Approaches to Seventy Figures in John*, ed. Steven A. Hunt, D. Francois Tolmie, and Ruben Zimmermann (WUNT 314; Tübingen: Mohr Siebeck, 2013), 347–55, 360–72, 383–87; idem, "Virtue Ethics in the Gospel of John: The Johannine Characters as Moral Agents," in *Rediscovering John: Essays on the Fourth Gospel in Honour of Frédéric Manns*, ed. L. Daniel Chrupcała (SBF 80; Milan: Edizioni Terra Santa, 2013), 167–81; idem, "Figurenanalyse und Wundererzählungen im Markusevangelium," in *Hermeneutik der frühchristlichen Wundererzählungen*, ed. Bernd Kollmann and Ruben Zimmermann (WUNT; Tübingen: Mohr Siebeck, forthcoming 2014); idem, "Gentile Characters and the Motif of Proclamation in the Gospel of Mark," in *Character Studies and the Gospel of Mark*, ed. Christopher W. Skinner and Matthew Ryan Hauge (LNTS; New York: T. & T. Clark, forthcoming 2014).

book broadens the scope of my earlier work. While my 2009 work on character was limited to the Gospel of John, this book aims to show that my theory works equally well in the Gospel of Mark and the Acts of the Apostles, and by extension to other New Testament narratives. Although I have retained many Johannine examples, I have tried to ensure that they do not take up a disproportionate amount of space. Having said that, I must highlight that the majority of work on characters in the New Testament has been done on the Gospel of John.

I must thank various people who have been instrumental in the completion of this book. I am grateful to Professor Emeritus Max Turner, my former doctoral supervisor and longstanding friend, who prompted me to challenge an existing paradigm. As I seek to do exactly that in this book, I have dedicated it to him. I thank my wife Susan for patiently weeding out, once again, all the clutter and odd expressions a non-native writer in English is prone to. I am grateful to publisher Brill in The Netherlands for granting me permission to reuse the material from an earlier article in their journal *Biblical Interpretation* (see n. 1, above, for details). I must especially thank Dr. Neil Elliott and the entire team at Fortress Press for believing in this project and their help in realizing this book. Fortress Press is also publishing the second edition of my *Encountering Jesus: Character Studies in the Gospel of John* (forthcoming 2014), so that, just as in 2009, we have a twofold work on characters in the New Testament. *Ad Dei gloriam.*

Cornelis Bennema
Wales Evangelical School of Theology, United Kingdom
Extraordinary Associate Professor, Unit for Reformed Theology and the
Development of the South African Society, Faculty of Theology,
North-West University, South Africa

Abbreviations

AB/AYB	Anchor Bible/Anchor Yale Bible
ANTC	Abingdon New Testament Commentaries
BCE	Before Common Era
BDAG	Bauer, W., F. W. Danker, W. F. Arndt, and F. W. Gingrich. *A Greek-English Lexicon of the New Testament and Other Early Christian Literature*. 3rd ed. Chicago: University of Chicago Press, 1999.
BECNT	Baker Exegetical Commentary on the New Testament
BETL	Bibliotheca Ephemeridum Theologicarum Lovaniensium
BibInt	*Biblical Interpretation*
BIS	Biblical Interpretation Series
BNTC	Black's New Testament Commentaries
BR	*Biblical Research*
BSac	*Bibliotheca Sacra*
BTB	*Biblical Theology Bulletin*
BZ	*Biblische Zeitschrift*
CBNTS	Coniectanea Biblica New Testament Series
CBQ	*Catholic Biblical Quarterly*
CE	Common Era
CQ	*Classical Quarterly*
DNTB	*Dictionary of New Testament Background*. Edited by Stanley E. Porter and Craig A. Evans. Downers Grove, IL: InterVarsity, 2000.
ESEC	Emory Studies in Early Christianity
EvT	*Evangelische Theologie*
ExAud	*Ex Auditu*
ExpTim	*Expository Times*
GR	*Greece and Rome*
HBM	Hebrew Bible Monographs
Int	*Interpretation*
ISPCK	Indian Society for Promoting Christian Knowledge
JBL	*Journal of Biblical Literature*
JETS	*Journal of the Evangelical Theological Society*
JHS	*Journal of Hellenic Studies*
JITC	*Journal of the Interdenominational Theological Center*
JR	*Journal of Religion*

JSNT	*Journal for the Study of the New Testament*
JSNTS	Journal for the Study of the New Testament Supplement Series
JSOT	*Journal for the Study of the Old Testament*
JSOTS	Journal for the Study of the Old Testament Supplement Series
JTS	*Journal of Theological Studies*
LCL	Loeb Classical Library
LNTS	Library of New Testament Studies (formerly JSNTS)
LTPM	Louvain Theological & Pastoral Monographs
NBD	*New Bible Dictionary*. Edited by D. R. W. Wood. 3rd ed. Leicester, UK: InterVarsity, 1996.
NCB	New Century Bible
NCBC	New Cambridge Bible Commentary
NIB	New Interpreter's Bible
NIBC	New International Biblical Commentary
NIGTC	New International Greek Testament Commentary
NIV	New International Version
NovT	*Novum Testamentum*
NovTSup	Novum Testamentum Supplement Series
NRSV	New Revised Standard Version
NTC	New Testament Commentary
NTM	New Testament Monographs
NTS	*New Testament Studies*
PBM	Paternoster Biblical Monographs
PNTC	Pillar New Testament Commentary
PRSt	*Perspectives in Religious Studies*
PTMS	Princeton Theological Monograph Series
SBB	Stuttgarter Biblische Beiträge
SBEC	Studies in Bible and Early Christianity
SBF	Studium Biblicum Franciscanum
SBLAB	Society of Biblical Literature Academia Biblica
SBLDS	Society of Biblical Literature Dissertation Series
SBLRBS	Society of Biblical Literature Resources for Biblical Study
SBLSBS	Society of Biblical Literature Sources for Biblical Study
SNTSMS	Society for New Testament Studies Monograph Series
SP	Sacra Pagina
SPCK	Society for Promoting Christian Knowledge
ThKNT	Theologischer Kommentar zum Neuen Testament
ThTo	*Theology Today*
TS	*Theological Studies*
TynBul	*Tyndale Bulletin*

WBC	Word Biblical Commentary
WUNT	Wissenschaftliche Untersuchungen zum Neuen Testament
WW	*Word and World*
ZNW	*Zeitschrift für die Neutestamentliche Wissenschaft*

1

Introduction

Identifying a Dominant Pattern/Paradigm

People are interested in people and like to hear their stories. The appeal of a good novel, movie, or biography is that it draws people into the story such that they identify with one or more of the characters. Some authors write simply to entertain readers, while others write in order to persuade their readers of a particular viewpoint. The biblical authors fall in the latter category. The author of the Gospel of John, for example, explicitly states that the purpose for his writing is that his audience may come and continue to believe that Jesus is the Messiah, the Son of God, in order to partake in the divine life (John 20:30-31). In order to accomplish this purpose John deliberately puts on the stage various characters that interact with Jesus, producing an array of belief-responses in order to challenge his readers to evaluate their stance regarding Jesus. Other biblical narratives also have an inbuilt perspective through which the authors seek to shape their audiences. The notion that various biblical authors use the characters in the story to communicate their point of view to the readers, and in so doing recommend some characters to be emulated and others to be avoided, is an important reason to study character.[1]

---

1. The same holds true for the Bible as a whole. While the Bible, at one level, is an anthology of individual stories, it arguably also contains the grand story of God's dealings with humanity and the world, with the purpose that people recognize God's desire to have a relationship with them and respond to him. Thus, analyzing the characters in the individual stories in the Bible also assists in understanding the protagonist of the meta-story and his program for this world. While postmodernists are critical of (even deny) metanarratives, others provide a good case for the Bible telling a single story with a single and integrated meaning (Kevin J. Vanhoozer, *Is There a Meaning in This Text?: The Bible, the Reader, and the Morality of Literary Knowledge* [Grand Rapids: Zondervan, 1998]; Richard Bauckham, *Bible and Mission: Christian Witness in a Postmodern World* [Grand Rapids: Baker Academic, 2003], ch. 4).

This leads us to another important rationale for this book. A story has two main elements: events and characters.[2] While much has been written on events and on the logical or causal sequence of events called "plot," character appears to be the neglected child of literary theory. According to Seymour Chatman, "It is remarkable how little has been said about the theory of character in literary history and criticism."[3] Similarly, Shlomith Rimmon-Kenan remarks, "The elaboration of a systematic, non-reductive but also non-impressionistic theory of character remains one of the challenges poetics has not yet met."[4] With few exceptions, literary criticism has not advanced beyond the well-known categories of "flat" and "round" coined by E. M. Forster in 1927 to classify characters. The absence of an articulate and comprehensive theory of character is partly due to the Aristotelian idea that character is fixed and secondary to plot, on which twentieth-century Russian Formalism and French Structuralism have capitalized.[5] Another reason is the complexity of the concept of character (characters resemble people but are not real) and the difficulty of analyzing character (something one can rarely read from the surface of the text).[6]

These observations also (or especially) hold true for narrative criticism, which applies literary theory to biblical narratives. In the last thirty-odd years, there has been an increased interest in the Bible as literature and story. Literary methods, when applied particularly to the Gospels, have proven fruitful. Nevertheless, biblical scholars rarely discuss how to study character. Fred Burnett, for example, points out that "[r]ecent work on narrative criticism of the Gospels has emphasized plot and story, but very little has been done with characterization. This is due mostly to the disarray of the theoretical discussion about characterization in current literary criticism."[7] Francois Tolmie comments that the lack of a uniform approach to characterization in biblical narratives is understandable because "contemporary literary criticism has not yet provided a systematic and comprehensive theory for the analysis of character."[8]

2. Seymour Chatman, *Story and Discourse: Narrative Structure in Fiction and Film* (Ithaca, NY/London: Cornell University Press, 1978), 19; Shlomith Rimmon-Kenan, *Narrative Fiction: Contemporary Poetics*, 2nd ed. (London/New York: Routledge, 2002 [1983]), 3, 6.

3. Chatman, *Story and Discourse*, 107.

4. Rimmon-Kenan, *Narrative Fiction*, 29.

5. Many modern writers have even pronounced the death of character (see Rimmon-Kenan, *Narrative Fiction*, 29–31). For them there is obviously no incentive to develop a theory of character.

6. Cf. Mieke Bal, *Narratology: Introduction to the Theory of Narrative*, trans. C. van Boheemen (Toronto: University of Toronto Press, 1985), 80.

7. Burnett, "Characterization," 3.

8. D. Francois Tolmie, *Jesus' Farewell to the Disciples: John 13:1–17:26 in Narratological Perspective* (BIS 12; Leiden: Brill, 1995), 117–18 (quotation from p. 118).

Elizabeth Struthers Malbon observes that "[w]ays of analyzing characterization in the Gospels are still being developed" but "[m]ore research remains to be done in this area."[9] At the outset of his monograph, Kelly Iverson points out that "a theory of character is a complex and by no means settled issue among literary critics."[10] More recently, Nicolas Farelly remarks that as "[c]haracterisation is arguably the most interesting element of the story . . . [i]t is all the more surprising that this area of narrative analysis has not produced a larger array of studies on the Fourth Gospel's characters."[11] As recently as 2013, two very different volumes on Johannine characterization appeared: one volume contains seven essays on the theory of character study, with each of them stressing different aspects;[12] the other volume analyzes seventy Johannine characters where contributors are free to choose their own approach, resulting in a wide variety of approaches.[13] In New Testament criticism, character study is thus still in its infancy.

We will see that many biblical critics assume that the Aristotelian view of character was dominant in all of ancient Greek literature and also influenced the Gospel narratives. Too often scholars perceive character in the Hebrew Bible (where characters can develop) to be radically different from that in ancient Greek literature (where characters are supposedly consistent ethical types). Many also sharply distinguish between modern fiction, with its psychological, individualistic approach to character, and ancient characterization where characters lack personality or individuality. Even though the last five years have seen an increased interest in methods and models for studying character in the Gospels, scholars often promulgate an approach that focuses on a particular aspect of character.[14] There is, as yet, no comprehensive

---

9. Elizabeth Struthers Malbon, *In the Company of Jesus: Characters in Mark's Gospel* (Louisville: Westminster John Knox, 2000), 11–12.

10. Kelly R. Iverson, *Gentiles in the Gospel of Mark: "Even the Dogs Under the Table Eat the Children's Crumbs"* (LNTS 339; London: T. & T. Clark, 2007), 1 n. 1.

11. Nicolas Farelly, *The Disciples in the Fourth Gospel: A Narrative Analysis of Their Faith and Understanding* (WUNT II/290; Tübingen: Mohr Siebeck, 2010), 7.

12. Christopher W. Skinner, ed., *Characters and Characterization in the Gospel of John* (LNTS 461; New York: T. & T. Clark, 2013), 1–127. In fact, my essay in this volume is the only one aiming at a comprehensive approach to character study.

13. Steven A. Hunt, D. Francois Tolmie, and Ruben Zimmermann, eds., *Character Studies in the Fourth Gospel: Narrative Approaches to Seventy Figures in John* (WUNT 314; Tübingen: Mohr Siebeck, 2013). The editors explain their decision for openness with respect to methodology on pp. xi–xii.

14. Besides my own 2009 work (for details, see Preface, n. 1), we can include Christopher W. Skinner, *John and Thomas—Gospels in Conflict? Johannine Characterization and the Thomas Question* (PTMS 115; Eugene, OR: Wipf & Stock, 2009) (he focuses on misunderstanding); Susan E. Hylen, *Imperfect Believers:*

theory of character in either literary theory or biblical criticism, and no consensus among scholars on how to analyze and classify characters. We are still faced with John Darr's challenge from 1992, that "it is important to 'do something about' the theoretical issues involved in characterization, rather than just 'talking about' characters."[15] The task of this book, then, is to develop a robust and extensive model for studying character in New Testament narrative. Before taking on such a daunting task, we must familiarize ourselves with the contributions of scholars on the subject.

1.1. The Current State of Affairs

The earliest studies that employ a narrative approach to the Gospels and Acts are those from the 1980s by David Rhoads and Donald Michie (on Mark), Alan Culpepper (on John), Robert Tannehill (on Luke–Acts), and Jack Dean Kingsbury (on Matthew), and except for Tannehill, each of them also looked at the approach to character.[16] Since then, numerous studies on character have appeared, but many do not use, mention, or show awareness of a theory for doing character analysis. In the literature review that follows, I will not simply rehearse the array of character studies in the New Testament, but focus on those that have either referred or contributed to the *theoretical* aspect of character studies. In order to provide an accurate sketch of the current state of affairs in New Testament character studies, I have selected the Gospel of Mark, the

---

Ambiguous Characters in the Gospel of John (Louisville: Westminster John Knox, 2009) (she focuses on ambiguity); Sönke Finnern, *Narratologie und biblische Exegese: Eine integrative Methode der Erzählanalyse und ihr Ertrag am Beispiel von Matthäus 28* (WUNT II/285; Tübingen: Mohr Siebeck, 2010), 125–64 (he relies on Jens Eder's work on character in film); Alicia D. Myers, *Characterizing Jesus: A Rhetorical Analysis on the Fourth Gospel's Use of Scripture in Its Presentation of Jesus* (LNTS 458; New York: T. & T. Clark, 2012) (she turns to ancient Greco-Roman characterization techniques); Skinner, ed., *Characters and Characterization* (various scholars focus on particular aspects of character). For the study of character in literary and media theory, see Jens Eder, Fotis Jannidis, and Ralf Schneider, eds., *Characters in Fictional Worlds: Understanding Imaginary Beings in Literature, Film, and Other Media* (Revisionen 3; Berlin/New York: De Gruyter, 2010).

15. John A. Darr, *On Character Building: The Reader and the Rhetoric of Characterization in Luke–Acts* (Louisville: Westminster John Knox, 1992), 37.

16. David Rhoads and Donald Michie, *Mark as Story: An Introduction to the Narrative of a Gospel* (Philadelphia: Fortress Press, 1982), chs. 5–6; R. Alan Culpepper, *Anatomy of the Fourth Gospel: A Study in Literary Design* (Philadelphia: Fortress Press, 1983), ch. 5; Robert C. Tannehill, *The Narrative Unity of Luke–Acts: A Literary Interpretation*, 2 vols. (Minneapolis: Fortress Press, 1986, 1989); Jack Dean Kingsbury, *Matthew as Story* (Minneapolis: Augsburg Fortress Press, 1988), 9–27. Tannehill's work is a narratological commentary on Luke–Acts and does not deal with the theoretical aspects of narrative criticism.

Gospel of John, and the Acts of the Apostles as a fair representation of the narrative material in the New Testament. The length of the literature review for each selected New Testament book is in proportion to the amount of work done on the subject.

THE GOSPEL OF MARK

Many scholars have examined various Markan characters, but all too often without a clear approach to character.[17] I will present some who do use or refer to an explicit method and draw out their contributions to the theory of character. Before Rhoads and Michie's landmark narratological study on Mark, *Robert Tannehill* and *Norman Petersen* had already advocated reading Mark's Gospel as a narrative rather than a redaction. Drawing on the work of literary critics, they focus on the narrator's or implied author's evaluative point of view and how this is recommended to the reader.[18] They realize that the role of the characters in a narrative is shaped by the composition of the author and reflects his concerns. According to Tannehill, the author assumes that there are essential similarities between the characters in the narrative world and the readers in the real world, so that what the author reveals about the characters may become a revelation about the readers and so enable them to change.[19]

David Rhoads, Joanna Dewey, and Donald Michie outline different approaches to characterization.[20] On the one hand, they contend that Mark's characterization conforms to ancient Greco-Roman characterization where characters are unchanging, consistent, and predictable. Thus most Markan characters are types or agents—they are consistent throughout the narrative, show little development, and represent typical responses. On the other hand, they consider that Mark's characterization is influenced by characterization in

17. E.g., Ernest Best, *Mark: The Gospel as Story* (Edinburgh: T. & T. Clark, 1983); Jack Dean Kingsbury, *Conflict in Mark: Jesus, Authorities, Disciples* (Minneapolis: Augsburg Fortress Press, 1989), 4–27; Susan Lochrie Graham, "Silent Voices: Women in the Gospel of Mark," *Semeia* 54 (1991): 145–58; Susan Miller, *Women in Mark's Gospel* (LNTS 259; London: T. & T. Clark, 2004). For the most recent and detailed review of character studies in the Gospel of Mark, see the opening essay in Christopher W. Skinner and Matthew Ryan Hauge, eds., *Character Studies and the Gospel of Mark* (LNTS; New York: T. & T. Clark, forthcoming 2014).

18. Robert C. Tannehill, "The Disciples in Mark: The Function of a Narrative Role," *JR* 57 (1977): 386–405; Norman R. Petersen, "'Point of View' in Mark's Narrative," *Semeia* 12 (1978): 97–121.

19. Tannehill, "Disciples in Mark," 405.

20. David M. Rhoads, Joanna Dewey, and Donald Michie, *Mark as Story: An Introduction to the Narrative of a Gospel*, 3rd ed. (Philadelphia: Fortress Press, 2012 [1999, 1982]), 100–104. Joanna Dewey became a co-author in the second edition. I refer to the third edition since this reflects their most recent understanding of character.

the Hebrew Bible where characters can change and be diverse. Considering Mark's "standards of judgment" (the values and beliefs embedded in the narrative) and its resulting moral dualism (a life on God's terms versus a life on human terms), Rhoads, Dewey, and Michie contend that even though the Markan characters consistently typify these standards and embody either of these two ways of life, they are not simply moral exemplars or stock characters.[21] In fact, they observe that Mark "uses many methods in characterization and, for an ancient narrative, offers some surprisingly complex characters."[22] For the final reconstruction of character, they use some of Baruch Hochman's categories (see our section 2.3) to "assess whether a character is complex (with many traits) or simple (having few traits), open to change or fixed, difficult to figure out or transparent, consistent or inconsistent."[23] Because of these features, they classify a character as "round" (having changing and conflicting traits, is complex and unpredictable, and is intriguing and mysterious), "flat" (less complex, fewer traits, predictable), or "stock" (plot functionary, few traits).[24]

　　Elizabeth Struthers Malbon's work on Markan characters and characterization is extensive and spans several decades.[25] She claims that while New Testament narrative critics are generally aware of the differences in characterization between modern novels and the Gospels, "[t]he secular literary theory on which biblical narrative critics so often lean is not particularly supportive at this point."[26] Nevertheless, in her particular view of ancient

---

21. Cf. Theodore J. Weeden, *Mark—Traditions in Conflict* (Philadelphia: Fortress Press, 1971). While this is a redaction-critical work rather than a narratological one, Weeden stresses the importance of characterization, arguing that the Markan characters exemplify moral principles and urge the reader to make moral judgments.

22. Rhoads, Dewey, and Michie, *Mark as Story*, 100. Cf. David Rhoads, "Losing Life for Others in the Face of Death: Mark's Standards of Judgment," *Int* 47 (1993): 358–69.

23. Rhoads, Dewey, and Michie, *Mark as Story*, 103.

24. While the second edition still uses the terms *round, flat,* and *stock* (pp. 102–3), the third edition has dropped these, although the descriptions are similar (p. 103). Cf. David Rhoads, *Reading Mark, Engaging the Gospel* (Minneapolis: Fortress Press, 2004), 11–13.

25. Elizabeth Struthers Malbon, "Fallible Followers: Women and Men in the Gospel of Mark," *Semeia* 28 (1983): 29–48; idem, "The Jewish Leaders in the Gospel of Mark: A Literary Study of Markan Characterization," *JBL* 108 (1989): 259–81; idem, "The Major Importance of the Minor Characters in Mark," in *The New Literary Criticism and the New Testament,* ed. Elizabeth Struthers Malbon and Edgar V. McKnight (JSNTS 109; Sheffield: Sheffield Academic Press, 1994), 58–86; idem, *In the Company of Jesus;* idem, *Mark's Jesus: Characterization as Narrative Christology* (Waco, TX: Baylor University Press, 2009); idem, "Characters in Mark's Story: Changing Perspectives on the Narrative Process," in *Mark as Story: Retrospect and Prospect,* ed. Kelly R. Iverson and Christopher W. Skinner (SBLRBS 65; Atlanta: Society of Biblical Literature, 2011), 45–69.

26. Malbon, *In the Company of Jesus,* 11.

characterization, she also uses Forster's modern categories of "flat" and "round" characters. While Malbon points out that characterization by "types" was conventional in ancient literature and that Mark seems to continue this convention, she admits that perhaps Mark also challenges this convention in that his "flat" characters are either good types to emulate *or* bad types to avoid, and his "round" characters are both good *and* bad types.[27] Finally, she asserts that the Markan characters must be evaluated according to their response to Jesus.[28] The dominant undercurrent in Malbon's work is that characters cannot be understood on their own but only in relation to other characters.[29]

Mary Ann Tolbert observes that despite the large number of studies on the Markan disciples, "little consensus exists about how these Markan characters are to be understood or their role and fate evaluated."[30] She contends that the source of the problem is that many scholars do not know how to read ancient stories. Tolbert then briefly outlines ancient character building: (i) ancient Greek drama and biography stress the typological nature of its characters, that is, they are portrayed as exemplars of general, ethical qualities; (ii) ancient characters are subordinate to the overall plot or action; (iii) all characters are fashioned to promote the author's rhetorical goal to persuade or move the readers to action.[31] Tolbert contends that such understanding of character reconstruction also applies to Mark's Gospel and she consequently criticizes biblical scholars who use modern character classifications (such as E. M. Forster's "flat" and "round" categories) to analyze ancient characters, because the blending of the typical/general with the individual in ancient characterization does not fit modern psychologized approaches to character.[32]

Joel Williams presents the most extensive discussion on character in Mark's Gospel to date.[33] In a study on the Markan characterization of the minor characters, Williams follows Seymour Chatman's so-called open theory of

---

27. Malbon, "Jewish Leaders," 278–80; idem, *In the Company of Jesus*, 12.

28. Malbon, "Major Importance," 81; idem, "Characters in Mark's Story," 61.

29. Malbon, "Characters in Mark's Story," 61.

30. Mary Ann Tolbert, "How the Gospel of Mark Builds Character," *Int* 47 (1993): 347.

31. Tolbert, "Character," 348–49. Cf. Mary Ann Tolbert, *Sowing the Gospel: Mark's World in Literary-Historical Perspective* (Minneapolis: Fortress Press, 1989), 76–77. In this earlier work, Tolbert understands the Markan characters as illustrative of the four types of hearing or responses to Jesus presented in the parable of the sower in Mark 4: Jesus' opponents are the soil along the path, the disciples are the rocky soil, some characters symbolize the thorny soil (Herod, the rich young ruler), and many minor characters represent the good soil (*Sowing the Gospel*, 148–64).

32. Tolbert, "Character," 349, 357 n. 9.

33. Joel F. Williams, *Other Followers of Jesus: Minor Characters as Major Figures in Mark's Gospel* (JSNTS 102; Sheffield: JSOT Press, 1994).

character (see our section 2.3). In reaction to a structuralist approach that views characters as subordinated to the plot and hence focuses on what characters *do* in a story, Chatman contends that characters are autonomous beings, and hence also reconstructs who the characters *are* in terms of their traits or qualities.[34] Williams also adheres to Shlomith Rimmon-Kenan's understanding of characterization, referring to the textual indicators that the author uses to state or present the traits of a particular character.[35] Drawing on the work of various literary and narrative critics, Williams produces an extensive list of literary devices that Mark uses to characterize the people in his Gospel.[36] Finally, in conversation with scholars such as Wolfgang Iser, Stanley Fish, Stephen Moore, and Robert Tannehill, Williams provides a detailed discussion about the role of the reader in relation to characterization.[37] While Williams's theoretical discussion is extensive, it focuses on characterization, that is, on the various techniques the author uses to disperse information about the character in the text, and he does not indicate how the reader should reconstruct character from the text.

In his monograph on Markan discipleship, *Whitney Taylor Shiner* uses W. J. Harvey's character categories (protagonists, cards, ficelles; see our section 2.3) and contends that Alan Culpepper's observation about characters in the Gospel of John also holds true for the Gospel of Mark: Jesus is the protagonist and most of the other characters are ficelles, who serve primarily to further the portrayal of Jesus.[38] Shiner also contends that the Markan characters show little or no inner life, and where inner life is revealed, it merely serves "to develop the plot or to define a narrative or rhetorical role rather than to develop the characters as characters."[39] The lack of characterization in Mark, Shiner argues, is because most characters are groups—the religious authorities, the disciples, the minor characters—rather than individuals.[40]

Modeled on Culpepper's *Anatomy of the Fourth Gospel*, Stephen Smith deals with the chief aspects of narrative criticism in Mark's Gospel.[41] Regarding

---

34. Williams, *Other Followers*, 57–58.

35. Williams, *Other Followers*, 60.

36. Williams, *Other Followers*, 60–67.

37. Williams, *Other Followers*, 67–88.

38. Whitney Taylor Shiner, *Follow Me! Disciples in Markan Rhetoric* (SBLDS 145; Atlanta: Scholars, 1995), 8–9.

39. Shiner, *Follow Me*, 10–11 (quotation from p. 11).

40. Shiner, *Follow Me*, 10.

41. Stephen H. Smith, *A Lion with Wings: A Narrative-Critical Approach to Mark's Gospel* (The Biblical Seminar 38; Sheffield: Sheffield Academic Press, 1996).

Markan characterization, Smith discusses various methods the author has at his disposal to reveal a character's traits (referring to Rimmon-Kenan), and how we can classify a character based on the number and diversity of traits (he uses Forster's "flat" and "round" categories).[42] Other features of characterization Smith refers to are the concept of "distance"—the way the author leads a reader to sympathize with or avoid a character, which relates to "point of view"—and the relationship between characters and plot (according to Smith, the Markan characters are subservient to the plot).[43]

In his analysis of the Markan Herod Antipas, *Abraham Smith* also examines Greco-Roman literature and claims that characterization was largely typical. For Aristotle, who wrote extensively about drama, character is subordinated to plot and illustrates general truths by showing action appropriate for their character type. Smith argues that typological characterization was also dominant in other Greco-Roman genres, such as biographies, novels, and histories.[44] Mark likewise uses typological characterization and Smith argues that Mark repeatedly drew on stock features about a "tyrant" to portray Herod Antipas.[45]

In his treatment of the Gentiles in Mark's Gospel, *Kelly Iverson*'s methodological considerations include that of character. While Iverson contends that "the application of contemporary literary theories to the biblical text is potentially anachronistic," he nevertheless decides that the potential benefit of better understanding biblical characters using modern literary theories outweighs the risk.[46] What then follows is a brief discussion of the contributions of various contemporary literary critics regarding the nature of character resulting in the decision to adopt Chatman's "open theory of character" (see our section 2.3).[47]

The work of *Geoff Webb* is very different in that he relates Bakhtinian categories (dialogue, genre-memory, chronotope, carnival) to Markan characterization.[48] For example, using Bakhtin's dialogical approach, Webb

---

42. Smith, *Lion with Wings*, 53–57.

43. Smith, *Lion with Wings*, 57–59. Smith explains the relationship between character and plot in ch. 3, and between character and point of view in ch. 5.

44. Abraham Smith, "Tyranny Exposed: Mark's Typological Characterization of Herod Antipas (Mark 6:14-29)," *BibInt* 14 (2006): 263–66.

45. Smith, "Tyranny," 266–87.

46. Iverson, *Gentiles*, 5 n. 23.

47. Iverson, *Gentiles*, 6–9.

48. Geoff R. Webb, *Mark at the Threshold: Applying Bakhtinian Categories to Markan Characterisation* (BIS 95; Leiden: Brill, 2008).

states that characters are shaped in the dialogue between author, reader, and text, although characters are never finalized since each rereading of the text will shape them in new and unforeseen ways.[49] Over against an anachronistic psychological approach to character (such as Forster's "flat"/"round" distinction) or structuralist approaches that subordinate character to the plot, Webb claims that dialogic criticism, which sees characters as voice sources in the text, is particularly appropriate for the study of character in ancient writings such as the Gospels.[50] Webb perceives a distinction between characterization in the Old Testament and ancient Greek literature. While characterization in Greek antiquity is generally uncomplicated (characters are static, opaque, unchanging), Old Testament heroes were in a process of learning.[51] Webb contends that Markan characterization follows the pattern of Old Testament narrators.[52]

Summary. Many scholars contend that Markan characterization resembles (either in part or in whole) the typical characterization in Greco-Roman literature where characters are consistent, unchanging, and represent typical responses (Rhoads, Dewey, and Michie, Malbon, Tolbert, Abraham Smith). Tolbert's Aristotelian approach to character (characters are types/flat and plot functionaries) is typical of the kind of character reconstruction that was established in the 1980s and remains a dominant model to date. Those who acknowledge the influence of the Old Testament on Markan characterization often see a contrast between Hebraic characterization (characters can change) and Hellenic characterization (static, unchanging characters) (Rhoads, Dewey, and Michie, Webb). While some of these scholars seemingly have no problem using aspects of modern literary methods in the study of ancient narratives (Rhoads, Dewey, and Michie, Malbon), Tolbert objects to this practice. Others exclusively/mainly depend on modern literary criticism to understand Markan characterization (Williams, Shiner, Stephen Smith, Iverson, Webb), but do not always discuss the legitimacy of applying modern methods to ancient narratives. Whether resorting to Greco-Roman or modern approaches to characterization, many scholars view the majority of Markan characters as flat (Tolbert, A. Smith, S. Smith, Shiner; cf. Rhoads, Dewey, and Richie, and Malbon). Some scholars classify the Markan characters, but there is no consensus on a system of classification (Rhoads, Dewey, and Richie use Hochman; Malbon and S. Smith use Forster; Shiner uses Harvey). Only a few scholars seek to evaluate the

49. Webb, *Mark at the Threshold*, 9–10.
50. Webb, *Mark at the Threshold*, 10–11.
51. Webb, *Mark at the Threshold*, 11–12.
52. Webb, *Mark at the Threshold*, 13.

characters, but they differ in the criterion for character evaluation (for Rhoads, Dewey, and Richie it is the narrative's norms; for Malbon it is the character's response to Jesus).

THE GOSPEL OF JOHN

Most character studies in the New Testament have been done in the Gospel of John, but many more scholars than is the case in Markan studies do not discuss or use any theory of character.[53] Once again, I will focus on those who do.

In what I still consider the most significant narratological work on the Gospel of John, *Alan Culpepper* devotes a chapter to Johannine characters.[54]

---

53. Eva Krafft, "Die Personen des Johannesevangeliums," *EvT* 16 (1956): 18–32; Raymond E. Brown, "Roles of Women in the Fourth Gospel," *TS* 36 (1975): 688–99; Raymond F. Collins, "Representative Figures," in *These Things Have Been Written: Studies on the Fourth Gospel* (LTPM 2; Louvain/Grand Rapids: Peeters/Eerdmans, 1990), 1–45 (originally in *Downside Review* 94 [1976]: 26–46; 95 [1976]: 118–32); idem, "From John to the Beloved Disciple: An Essay on Johannine Characters," *Int* 49 (1995): 359–69; Sandra M. Schneiders, "Women in the Fourth Gospel and the Role of Women in the Contemporary Church," *BTB* 12 (1982): 35–45; Elisabeth Schüssler Fiorenza, *In Memory of Her: A Feminist Theological Reconstruction of Christian Origins* (London: SCM, 1983), 323–33; Turid Karlsen Seim, "Roles of Women in the Gospel of John," in *Aspects on the Johannine Literature*, ed. Lars Hartman and Birger Olsson (CBNTS 18; Uppsala: Uppsala University Press, 1987), 56–73; Margaret Davies, *Rhetoric and Reference in the Fourth Gospel* (JSNTS 69; Sheffield: JSOT Press, 1992), 154–58, 313–49; Sjef van Tilborg, *Imaginative Love in John* (BIS 2; Leiden: Brill, 1993), ch. 1.1 and ch. 4; Robert G. Maccini, *Her Testimony Is True: Women as Witnesses according to John* (JSNTS 125; Sheffield: Sheffield Academic Press, 1996); Adeline Fehribach, *The Women in the Life of the Bridegroom: A Feminist Historical-Literary Analysis of the Female Characters in the Fourth Gospel* (Collegeville, MN: Liturgical, 1998); Ruth Edwards, *Discovering John* (London: SPCK, 2003), ch. 10; Margaret M. Beirne, *Women and Men in the Fourth Gospel: A Genuine Discipleship of Equals* (JSNTS 242; London: Sheffield Academic Press, 2003); Jean K. Kim, *Woman and Nation: An Intercontextual Reading of the Gospel of John from a Postcolonial Feminist Perspective* (BIS 69; Leiden: Brill, 2004); James M. Howard, "The Significance of Minor Characters in the Gospel of John," *BSac* 163 (2006): 63–78; Frances Taylor Gench, *Encounters with Jesus: Studies in the Gospel of John* (Louisville: Westminster John Knox, 2007). For detailed reviews of these character studies, see Bennema, *Encountering Jesus*, 2–10; Christopher W. Skinner, "Characters and Characterization in the Gospel of John: Reflections on the *Status Questionis*," in *Characters and Characterization in the Gospel of John*, ed. Christopher W. Skinner (LNTS 461; New York: T. & T. Clark, 2013), xvii–xxxii; Steven A. Hunt, D. Francois Tolmie, and Ruben Zimmermann, "An Introduction to Character and Characterization in John and Related New Testament Literature," in *Character Studies in the Fourth Gospel: Narrative Approaches to Seventy Figures in John*, ed. Steven A. Hunt, D. Francois Tolmie, and Ruben Zimmermann (WUNT 314; Tübingen: Mohr Siebeck, 2013), 1–33. Stan Harstine only has a minimal discussion of character, observing the difficulty of applying modern narrative categories to ancient narratives and then referring to Scholes and Kellogg, and Harvey to provide some theoretical guidelines (*Moses as a Character in the Fourth Gospel: A Study of Ancient Reading Techniques* [JSNTS 229; London: Sheffield Academic Press, 2002], 19–22).

He provides a brief theoretical discussion on characterization, arguing that John draws from both Greek and Hebrew models of character, although most Johannine characters represent particular ethical types (as in Greek literature). Using the modern character classifications of literary critics E. M. Forster and W. J. Harvey (see our section 2.3), Culpepper argues that most of John's minor characters are types that the reader can recognize easily.[55] According to Culpepper, the Johannine characters are particular kinds of choosers: "Given the pervasive dualism of the Fourth Gospel, the choice is either/or. *All* situations are reduced to two clear-cut alternatives, and *all* the characters eventually make their choice."[56] He then produces, in relation to John's ideological point of view, an extensive taxonomy of belief-responses in which a character can progress or regress from one response to another.[57]

Mark Stibbe's important work on characterization in John 8, 11, and 18–19 shows how narrative criticism can be applied to John's Gospel, and he was the first to present a number of characters, like Pilate and Peter, as more complicated than had been previously thought.[58] Stibbe provides brief theoretical considerations on characterization, stressing that readers must (i) construct character by inference from fragmentary information in the text (as in ancient Hebrew narratives); (ii) analyze characters with reference to history rather than according to the laws of fiction; and (iii) consider the Gospel's ideological point of view, expressed in 20:31.[59]

In his narratological analysis of John 13–17, *Francois Tolmie* also examines the characters that appear in this text.[60] He undergirds his study with an extensive theoretical discussion. He follows the narratological model of Shlomith Rimmon-Kenan (who in turn draws on Seymour Chatman), and

54. Culpepper, *Anatomy of the Fourth Gospel*, 99–148.

55. Culpepper, *Anatomy of the Fourth Gospel*, 102–4. I explain Forster and Harvey's character classifications in section 2.3.

56. Culpepper, *Anatomy of the Fourth Gospel*, 104 (emphasis added).

57. Culpepper, *Anatomy of the Fourth Gospel*, 145–48. In a recent essay, R. Alan Culpepper acknowledges that the Johannine characters are more than their responses ("The Weave of the Tapestry: Character and Theme in John," in *Characters and Characterization in the Gospel of John*, ed. Christopher W. Skinner [LNTS 461; New York: T. & T. Clark, 2013], 18–35).

58. Mark W. G. Stibbe, *John as Storyteller: Narrative Criticism and the Fourth Gospel* (SNTSMS 73; Cambridge: Cambridge University Press, 1992), 97–99, 106–13, 119; idem, *John's Gospel* (London: Routledge, 1994), 90–96, 121–25. In addition, Stibbe produced a narratological commentary on John's Gospel, highlighting how John portrays the various characters in his Gospel (*John* [Sheffield: JSOT Press, 1993]).

59. Stibbe, *John as Storyteller*, 24–25, 28; idem, *John's Gospel*, 10–11.

60. Tolmie, *Jesus' Farewell*, 117–44.

utilizes the actantial model of A. J. Greimas and the character classification of Yosef Ewen (but also refers to E. M. Forster and W. J. Harvey; see our section 2.3). Tolmie only discusses contemporary fiction and disregards character in ancient Hebrew and Greek literature. With the exception of God, Jesus, and the Spirit, Tolmie concludes that all characters in John 13–17 are flat—they have a single trait or are not complex, show no development, and reveal no inner life.

David Beck explores the concept of anonymity in relation to discipleship, arguing that only the unnamed characters serve as models of appropriate responses to Jesus.[61] He also provides a brief theoretical discussion on character. Rejecting three methods of character analysis (Forster's psychological model, Greimas's structuralist approach, and Fokkema's semiotic approach), he adopts John Darr's model, which is influenced by the reader-oriented theory of Wolfgang Iser and which considers how characterization entices readers into fuller participation in the narrative.[62]

Colleen Conway looks at Johannine characterization from the perspective of gender, asking whether men and women are presented differently.[63] She also provides an informed theoretical discussion of character in which she leans toward the contemporary theories of Seymour Chatman and Baruch Hochman (although she does not use the latter's classification), and includes Hebrew techniques of characterization (but leaves out character in ancient Greek literature).[64] In a subsequent article, Conway challenges the consensus view that Johannine characters represent particular belief-responses.[65] She criticizes the "flattening" of characters and argues that Johannine characters show varying degrees of ambiguity and do more to complicate the clear choice between belief and unbelief than to illustrate it. Instead of positioning the minor characters on a spectrum of negative to positive faith-responses, she claims that they appear unstable in relation to Jesus as if shifting up and down such a spectrum. In doing so, the characters challenge, undercut, and subvert the

61. David R. Beck, *The Discipleship Paradigm: Readers and Anonymous Characters in the Fourth Gospel* (BIS 27; Leiden: Brill, 1997). Beck's monograph builds on his earlier essay, "The Narrative Function of Anonymity in Fourth Gospel Characterization," *Semeia* 63 (1993): 143–58. Beck recently revisits the subject ("'Whom Jesus Loved': Anonymity and Identity. Belief and Witness in the Fourth Gospel," in *Characters and Characterization in the Gospel of John*, ed. Christopher W. Skinner [LNTS 461; New York: T. & T. Clark, 2013], 221–39).

62. Beck, *Discipleship Paradigm*, 6–8.

63. Colleen M. Conway, *Men and Women in the Fourth Gospel: Gender and Johannine Characterization* (SBLDS 167; Atlanta: Society of Biblical Literature, 1999).

64. Conway, *Men and Women*, 50–63.

65. Colleen M. Conway, "Speaking through Ambiguity: Minor Characters in the Fourth Gospel," *BibInt* 10 (2002): 324–41.

dualistic world of the Gospel because they do not line up on either side of the belief/unbelief divide.

Ingrid Kitzberger traces the female characters from the Synoptics that appear in John's Gospel but are not visible at first sight.[66] For her analysis, she combines Seymour Chatman's view of character, Wolfgang Müller's "interfigural" view of character (i.e., interrelations that exist between characters of different texts), and a reader-response approach. She concludes that "interfigural encounters create a network of relationships, between characters in different texts, and between characters and readers reading characters."[67]

In his monograph on point of view in John's Gospel, *James Resseguie* explores various Johannine characters from a material point of view and classifies them according to their dominance or status in society rather than, for example, their faith-response.[68] He claims that the characters' material points of view contribute or relate to the Gospel's overall ideology. Subsequently, in an introductory book on narrative criticism, Resseguie devotes one chapter to character.[69] After explaining some theoretical aspects of character, Resseguie, once again, analyzes a few characters according to their position in society. There are two surprising issues in Resseguie's approach. First, there is a logical discontinuity between his theory of character and his analysis of character; nothing in the first part[70] prepares for classifying characters according to their social standing. Second, he does not explain why he contends John's overall ideology is sociological in nature rather than soteriological (as John 20:30-31 seems to indicate).

In his book, *Craig Koester* has a chapter on characterization, supporting the idea that each of John's characters represents a particular faith-response.[71] Koester's strength lies in interpreting the Johannine characters on the basis of the text and its historical context. He sees parallels between John's story and ancient Greek drama or tragedy, where characters are types who convey general truths by representing a moral choice.

---

66. Ingrid Rosa Kitzberger, "Synoptic Women in John: Interfigural Readings," in *Transformative Encounters: Jesus and Women Re-viewed*, ed. Ingrid Rosa Kitzberger (BIS 43; Leiden: Brill, 2000), 77–111.

67. Kitzberger, "Synoptic Women," 108–9.

68. James L. Resseguie, *The Strange Gospel: Narrative Design and Point of View in John* (BIS 56; Leiden: Brill, 2001), 109–68.

69. James L. Resseguie, *Narrative Criticism of the New Testament: An Introduction* (Grand Rapids: Baker Academic, 2005), 121–65.

70. Resseguie, *Narrative Criticism*, 121–32.

71. Craig R. Koester, *Symbolism in the Fourth Gospel: Meaning, Mystery, Community*, 2nd ed. (Minneapolis: Fortress Press, 2003), 33–77.

Exploring the relationship between John's Gospel and ancient Greek tragedy, *Jo-Ann Brant* examines the Johannine characters against the backdrop of Greek drama.[72] For example, "the Jews" are not actors in the Johannine drama but function as the deliberating chorus in a Greek drama—a corporate voice at the sidelines, witnesses to the action. As such, by watching "the Jews" and their response of unbelief, the believing audience has an opportunity to look into the mind of the other, whose perspective it does not share. Brant deliberately refrains from evaluating the Johannine characters. Drawing parallels with ancient Greek tragedy, she argues that readers are not members of a jury, evaluating characters as right or wrong, innocent or guilty, or answering christological questions about Jesus' identity, but are called to join the Johannine author in commemorating Jesus' life.

For my own part, in 2009 I produced a twofold work on Johannine characters where I seek to reverse the consensus view that Johannine characters are types, have little complexity, and show little or no development. Arguing that the differences in characterization in the Hebrew Bible, ancient Greek literature, and modern fiction are differences in emphases rather than kind, I suggest that it is better to speak of degrees of characterization along a continuum.[73] I then outline a comprehensive theory of character that comprises three aspects: (i) the study of character in text and context, using information from the text and other sources; (ii) the analysis and classification of characters along Yosef Ewen's three dimensions (complexity, development, inner life), and plotting the resulting character on a continuum of degree of characterization (from agent to type to personality to individuality); (iii) the evaluation of characters in relation to John's point of view, purpose, and dualistic worldview.[74] After that, I apply my theory to John's Gospel, showing that only eight out of twenty-three characters are "types."[75]

Susan Hylen identifies the following problem in Johannine character studies: while the majority of interpreters read most Johannine characters as "flat"—embodying a single trait and representing a type of believer—the sheer variety of interpretations proves that it is difficult to evaluate John's characters.[76] She presents an alternative strategy for reading them, arguing that John's

---

72. Jo-Ann A. Brant, *Dialogue and Drama: Elements of Greek Tragedy in the Fourth Gospel* (Peabody, MA: Hendrickson, 2004), 159–232.

73. I am indebted to Burnett, who has excellently argued this case in "Characterization," 3–28.

74. Bennema, "Theory of Character," 375–421. I sharpened my theory further in another article ("Comprehensive Approach," 34–56).

75. Bennema, *Encountering Jesus.*

76. Hylen, *Imperfect Believers.*

characters display various kinds of ambiguity. For example, Nicodemus's ambiguity lies in the uncertainty of what he understands or believes. The Samaritan woman, the disciples, Martha, the beloved disciple, and "the Jews" display a more prominent ambiguity, namely that of belief in Jesus mixed with disbelief and misunderstanding. Finally, although Jesus' character is unambiguously positive, it is also ambiguous in the many metaphors John uses to characterize Jesus.

Christopher Skinner uses misunderstanding as a lens through which to view the Johannine characters.[77] On the basis that the Prologue is the greatest source of information about Jesus, Skinner contends that "[e]ach character in the narrative approaches Jesus with varying levels of understanding but no one approaches him fully comprehending the truths that have been revealed to the reader in the prologue. Thus, it is possible for the reader to evaluate the correctness of every character's interaction with Jesus on the basis of what has been revealed in the prologue."[78] Examining six male characters (Thomas, Peter, Andrew, Philip, Judas [not Iscariot], and Nicodemus), three female characters (the Samaritan woman, Martha, and Mary), and one male character group (the twelve disciples), Skinner shows that all Johannine characters are uncomprehending to a degree.

Nicolas Farelly undertakes a narratological analysis of the disciples in John's Gospel. Much of his study is dominated by the question of how the reader is expected to respond to the characterization of the disciples, and Farelly contends that implied readers learn about characters primarily through discovering their role in the plot.[79] Consequently, Farelly explores the relationship between plot and character, concluding that characters are more than mere plot functionaries: "[C]haracters do 'exist' to serve specific plot functions . . . but they do not lose their impact as constructed persons."[80] Finally, Farelly discusses the readers' participation in the narrative through identification with the characters, which includes both involvement and distancing because the world of the narrative is like and unlike the world of the readers.[81]

In her study of the character of Peter in John's Gospel, *Tanja Schultheiss* discusses various aspects of characterization and is against applying modern ("anachronistic") approaches to ancient narratives.[82] Besides, she addresses issues such as the relation between character and plot, and the presentation and

---

77. Skinner, *John and Thomas*.

78. Skinner, *John and Thomas*, 37.

79. Farelly, *Disciples in the Fourth Gospel*, 7–8.

80. Farelly, *Disciples in the Fourth Gospel*, 164–67 (quotation from p. 167).

81. Farelly, *Disciples in the Fourth Gospel*, 184–95.

classification of character.[83] Challenging my historical-narratological approach (i.e., a literary approach that considers the socio-historical context),[84] Schultheiss suggests the examination of each relevant text using a synchronic approach (restricted to the Johannine text) followed by a diachronic approach (analyzing the corresponding Synoptic texts).[85]

Ruth Sheridan provides a critical appraisal of various literary theories of characterization in her character analysis of "the Jews" in John 1–12.[86] She begins with the contributions of E. M. Forster, Seymour Chatman, Yosef Ewen, and Shlomith Rimmon-Kenan, and then turns to the Johannine scholars Craig Koester, Alan Culpepper, Francois Tolmie, and myself, who have applied the methods of character analysis of these literary critics to John's Gospel. Disregarding these Johannine scholars for the rest of her study, Sheridan decides to adopt aspects of narratological and intertextual theory, and to apply Rimmon-Kenan's method of character reconstruction to her reading of "the Jews."[87]

In a monograph on the characterization of the Johannine Jesus, *Alicia Myers* uses categories of ancient rhetorical practices of characterization, as found in Greco-Roman rhetorical handbooks (those of Aristotle, Cicero, and Quintilian) and various *progymnasmata*. Her approach consists of three elements: (i) rhetorical *topoi* of characterization (the presentation of a character through a list of aspects or "topics"); (ii) rhetorical techniques of characterization (*ekphrasis, synkrisis, prosopopoiia*); (iii) rhetorical expectations of characterization.[88] Myers argues that ancient authors used common *topoi* and rhetorical techniques to construct "typical" characters in order to persuade their audiences to either imitate a character's virtues or avoid his vices. She stresses that in Greco-Roman antiquity, characters were consistent or predictable in order to be credible.[89] With this theoretical grounding, she explores how John's use of Scripture contributes to the characterization of Jesus.

---

82. Tanja Schultheiss, *Das Petrusbild im Johannesevangelium* (WUNT II/329; Tübingen: Mohr Siebeck, 2012), 53–60.

83. Schultheiss, *Petrusbild*, 69–72.

84. Schultheiss, *Petrusbild*, 40 n. 232, 59 n. 61.

85. Schultheiss, *Petrusbild*, 72–79.

86. Ruth Sheridan, *Retelling Scripture: "The Jews" and the Scriptural Citations in John 1:19–12:15* (BIS 110; Leiden: Brill, 2012), 68–90.

87. Sheridan, *Retelling Scripture*, 97.

88. Myers, *Characterizing Jesus*, 42–61. William M. Wright uses a similar approach ("Greco-Roman Character Typing and the Presentation of Judas in the Fourth Gospel," *CBQ* 71 [2009]: 545–50).

89. Myers, *Characterizing Jesus*, 55–61.

The most recent work on Johannine characters is two collections of essays that appeared in 2013. The volume edited by Christopher Skinner features seven essays on methods or models for reading Johannine characters, but only two essays break significantly new ground.[90] *Alan Culpepper* explores a neglected aspect in character studies, namely how the Johannine characters relate to the development of the narrative's major themes.[91] *Judith Christine Single Redman* "examines the contributions made by theories of character and characterization, and the work of psychologists on eyewitness testimony and human memory to our understanding of where along this continuum [of actual representations of reality] the characters in the Gospel according to John might fall."[92] The significance of her essay for our study lies in her critique of those who think that the Johannine characters have a representative value. Supporting Conway's argument that the Johannine characters cannot be contained in binary categories and hence there is no clarity about what they represent, Redman asserts that John never intended his characters to be evaluated (contra Culpepper and myself), and consequently the Johannine characters cannot be used as yardsticks against which to evaluate people's belief.[93] Instead, she contends that the Johannine characters are intended to "provide examples for the reader of what a belief in Jesus that brings life might look like in real life."[94]

The other volume, edited by Steven Hunt, Francois Tolmie, and Ruben Zimmermann, contains no overarching theoretical framework, and although many authors clarify their approach, most draw on existing aspects of character theory rather than contributing to it.[95] A significant exception, however, is *William John Lyons*'s essay on the Johannine character of Joseph of Arimathea, where he takes issue with the sources I use (mainly the Synoptics and John)

90. See n. 12, above, for bibliographical details. Of the five other essays, James Resseguie does not go beyond his earlier work; Raymond Collins explores the comparative-contrast dynamic in some Johannine character pairs, but his essay does not explicitly contribute to the theory of character; Susan Hylen, Christopher Skinner, and I all sharpen and extend our 2009 work, and while this is significant, we do not propose a radically different theory. The present book includes the material I contributed to Skinner's volume.

91. Culpepper, "Weave of the Tapestry," 18–35.

92. Judith Christine Single Redman, "Eyewitness Testimony and the Characters in the Fourth Gospel," in *Characters and Characterization in the Gospel of John*, ed. Christopher W. Skinner (LNTS 461; New York: T. & T. Clark, 2013), 59–78 (quotation from p. 59).

93. Redman, "Eyewitness Testimony," 63–67.

94. Redman, "Eyewitness Testimony," 76.

95. See n. 13, above, for bibliographical details. The uniqueness of this 700-page volume lies in its exhaustive treatment of *all* (seventy) characters in the Johannine narrative (the character of God, Jesus, the Spirit, and the narrator have not been considered).

to reconstruct the identity of Joseph of Arimathea.[96] Instead, he presents two possible readings—one where the implied reader only has access to John's Gospel and another where the reader also knows Mark's Gospel. I will return to the issue of possible readers and the sources they might have had access to for character reconstruction in section 3.1.

Summary. Johannine scholars present a broad variety of approaches to study character. Some draw on ancient methods of characterization, whether Hebrew, Greek, or both (Stibbe, Koester, Brant, Myers), others employ modern literary methods (Tolmie, Beck, Sheridan), and still others use both (Culpepper, Conway, myself). Regarding character analysis, scholars use a variety of lenses through which to examine the Johannine characters: gender (Conway), anonymity (Beck), social status (Resseguie), ambiguity (Hylen), misunderstanding (Skinner), complexity, development, and inner life (myself), common ancient *topoi* (Myers). As for character classification, many scholars categorize most Johannine characters as types or ficelles (Culpepper, Koester, many scholars mentioned in n. 53, above; cf. Myers). Only Tolmie and I use a more complex, nonreductionist classification, but while Tolmie, ironically, reduces the characters to being flat, I see a broad spectrum of characters. While some scholars question or object to the evaluation of characters (Conway, Brant, Hylen, Redman), Culpepper and I both use the criterion of the character's response to Jesus, but where Culpepper creates an entire hierarchy of responses, I only use the qualifiers "adequate" and "inadequate." Finally, Conway points out a glaring discrepancy: while many scholars argue that most of John's minor characters personify one single trait or belief-response to Jesus, there is surprisingly little agreement on what each character typifies or represents. A response to Conway's challenge would require a fresh analysis of Johannine characters.

THE ACTS OF THE APOSTLES

As in the case of the Gospels, few studies on character in the Acts of the Apostles refer to a theory of character.[97] In the early 1990s, *David Gowler* produced a

---

96. William John Lyons, "Joseph of Arimathea: One of 'the Jews,' But with a Fearful Secret!," in *Character Studies in the Fourth Gospel: Narrative Approaches to Seventy Figures in John*, ed. Steven A. Hunt, D. Francois Tolmie and Ruben Zimmermann (WUNT 314; Tübingen: Mohr Siebeck, 2013), 646–57. While I use information from the Synoptics to reconstruct the identity of Joseph in John's Gospel, for his role or *function* I rely solely on information in the Johannine narrative (Bennema, *Encountering Jesus*, 191–94).

97. The following studies, for example, do not resort to a theory of character: Tannehill, *Narrative Unity* (Vol. 2); C. Clifton Black, "The Presentation of John Mark in the Acts of the Apostles," *PRSt* 20

pioneering work on character in Luke–Acts, half of which was given over to a discussion on character in both modern literary theory and ancient narratives.[98] Regarding characterization in modern literary theory, Gowler describes the rise of the novel and the corresponding importance of characters and the role of the reader, because a character does not exist until the reader retrieves it from the text. In dialogue with Seymour Chatman, Shlomith Rimmon-Kenan, W. J. Harvey, and Baruch Hochman, Gowler agrees that characters are both persons and words—characters are generated by the text but cannot be merely dissolved into the text. Contra the structuralists and supporting Chatman and Rimmon-Kenan, Gowler affirms that character and plot are interdependent.[99] Gowler then turns to the important issue of how character should be studied. Evaluating the strengths and weaknesses of the character classifications proposed by E. M. Forster, W. J. Harvey, Yosef Ewen, and Baruch Hochman (see our section 2.3), he decides to apply Hochman's model to his study of the Pharisees.[100] However, he provides no rationale for his choice, apart from stating that Hochman's model is the most comprehensive one. Lastly, Gowler turns to the (direct and indirect) presentation of character in the text.[101]

The second part of Gowler's theoretical discussion pertains to characterization in ancient narratives. Besides looking at the Hebrew Bible, Gowler examines in detail select writings from the vast corpus of ancient Greek literature: three tragedies (Aeschylus' *Agamemnon*, Sophocles' *Antigone*, and Euripides' *Medea*), two ancient biographies (Plutarch's *Parallel Lives* and Suetonius' *Lives of the Caesars*), three ancient histories (Tacitus' *Annals*, Josephus' *Jewish War*, and 1 Maccabees), and two ancient novels (Chariton's *Chaereas and Callirhoe* and Apuleius' *The Golden Ass*).[102] Gowler concludes that

---

(1993): 235–54; Pheme Perkins, *Peter: Apostle for the Whole Church* (Columbia: University of South Carolina Press, 1994); Philip H. Kern, "Paul's Conversion and Luke's Portrayal of Character in Acts 8–10," *TynBul* 54 (2003): 63–80; Scott Shauf, "Locating the Eunuch: Characterization and Narrative Context in Acts 8:26–40," *CBQ* 71 (2009): 762–75; S. Jonathan Murphy, "The Role of Barnabas in the Book of Acts," *BSac* 167 (2010): 319–41. Providing a minimal theoretical discussion, Abraham Smith sees many affinities between Luke–Acts and the ancient Greek novel, including that the Lukan characters are plot functionaries and typological ("'Do You Understand What You Are Reading?': A Literary Critical Reading of the Ethiopian (Kushite) Episode (Acts 8:26–40)," *JITC* 22 [1994]: 48–70).

98. David B. Gowler, *Host, Guest, Enemy and Friend: Portraits of the Pharisees in Luke and Acts* (ESEC 2; New York: Peter Lang, 1991), 29–176. He adds another fifty-odd pages in appendixes.

99. Gowler, *Host, Guest, Enemy and Friend*, 31–49.

100. Gowler, *Host, Guest, Enemy and Friend*, 50–54, 306–17. He also provides a detailed explanation of Hochman's eight continua and how they can be adapted for ancient narratives (*Host, Guest, Enemy and Friend*, 321–32).

101. Gowler, *Host, Guest, Enemy and Friend*, 55–70.

both Greek and Hebraic literature present characters in a "variety of ways, as simple or complex, and as developing or static."[103]

Shortly after Gowler, *John Darr*'s work on Lukan characters appeared, highlighting various aspects of character in modern literary methods, such as: (i) character and plot are interdependent; (ii) characters are delineated largely in relation to each other; (iii) character is cumulative as readers proceed along the text continuum; (iv) character is revealed through "showing" or "telling"; (v) characters are not just words or textual functions, but neither are they people; (vi) the reader reconstructs character with the help of extratextual information.[104] With regard to Luke–Acts, Darr contends that characterization occurs more through showing than telling, that its characters are largely typed, and that we can divide the characters into three groups, according to Harvey's taxonomy (see our section 2.3).[105] Darr also contends that the rhetoric of Luke–Acts compels the involvement of the reader in that the reader witnesses what the characters witness and is forced to reflect on his own response. Thus the reader is shaped in the very process of character construction.[106]

In a 1993 article on the characterization of the Lukan narrator, Darr expands on his theory that readers build characters. First, he recognizes that the reader one postulates at least partially determines how characters are reconstructed. On the one hand, Darr admits that literary critics create readers in their own image; that is, to a certain extent, the reader is always a heuristic construct of the literary critic. On the other hand, he also values the reconstruction of a text-specific reader, that is, an approximation of the intended reader with a degree of knowledge of the socio-cultural conventions assumed by the original author. Darr's reader, then, is *a heuristic hybrid*, a fusion of ancient and modern cultural horizons.[107] Second, Darr asserts that a text is not seamless but "full of gaps, indeterminacies, tensions, inconsistencies, and ambiguities" and it is the reader who seeks to "build a consistent, coherent narrative world" by piecing together textual and extratextual information.[108] Third, "all of the information (shown and told) that the reader receives is filtered through the narrator's particular point of view."[109]

102. Gowler, *Host, Guest, Enemy and Friend*, 88–169.

103. Gowler, *Host, Guest, Enemy and Friend*, 173.

104. Darr, *On Character Building*, 38–49.

105. Darr, *On Character Building*, 38, 44, 48.

106. Darr, *On Character Building*, 56–59.

107. John A. Darr, "Narrator as Character: Mapping a Reader-Oriented Approach to Narration in Luke–Acts," *Semeia* 65 (1993): 47–48.

108. Darr, "Narrator as Character," 50–51.

Before examining the character of the Holy Spirit in Luke–Acts, *William Shepherd* provides a comprehensive overview of theories on character and characterization.[110] Based on the work of, *inter alios*, literary critic Northrop Frye, structuralist Claude Lévi-Strauss, and historian Hayden White, Shepherd argues that the application of modern literary methods to ancient biblical texts is entirely appropriate because the modern use of "narrative" now encompasses fiction and nonfiction, ancient and modern texts.[111] Shepherd then discusses the nature of character, preferring a "mimetic" view of character (characters are like people) to a "semiotic" view of character advocated by structuralism.[112] For him, character can neither be reduced to the plot (as in structuralism) nor be independent of it.[113] Shepherd then turns to the classification of characters. Surveying the classifications of E. M. Forster, W. J. Harvey, and Yosef Ewen, Shepherd settles for Baruch Hochman's classification of eight categories (see our section 2.3).[114] Based on the work of reader-response critics, Shepherd acknowledges that character is both "in" the text and "in front of" the text; character is both generated by the text and constructed by the reader through "filling the gaps" (to use Wolfgang Iser's term). At the same time, Shepherd agrees with Stanley Fish that "gap-filling" is learned behavior for the reader, that is, part of the reading conventions practiced by the reader's interpretive community.[115]

John Roth uses an audience-oriented literary approach to analyze the character types of the blind, the lame, and the poor in Luke–Acts.[116] He grounds his approach in speech act theory, developed by critics such as J. L. Austin, J. Searle, R. Jakobson, and S. Lanser. Roth's interest is in the reader's role in producing a text's meaning and the text's effect on the reader. He decides to adopt Wolfgang Iser's model of reading, where the reader examines the text as a coherent whole to fill the gaps.[117] After discussing the reading process and the construction of an authorial audience, Roth turns to the subject of character.

---

109. Darr, "Narrator as Character," 54.

110. William H. Shepherd, *The Narrative Function of the Holy Spirit as a Character in Luke–Acts* (SBLDS 147; Atlanta: Scholars, 1994), 43–90.

111. Shepherd, *Narrative Function*, 44–51.

112. Shepherd, *Narrative Function*, 51–65.

113. Shepherd, *Narrative Function*, 65–66.

114. Shepherd, *Narrative Function*, 67–78.

115. Shepherd, *Narrative Function*, 80–84.

116. S. John Roth, *The Blind, the Lame, and the Poor: Character Types in Luke–Acts* (JSNTS 144; Sheffield: Sheffield Academic Press, 1997).

117. Roth, *Blind*, 58–63.

Taking Forster's "flat" and "round" categories as the basis, he looks at character traits and point of view (using Boris Uspensky's model) to explain a character's flatness or roundness.[118] Roth concludes that we must distinguish between characterization in ancient literature, where characters are mostly types and "flat" (following Scholes and Kellogg, Darr, and Tolbert), and characterization in modern literature where characters possess individuality and psychological depth.[119]

Richard Thompson's theoretical foundation for his study on the church as a narrative character in Acts deals with two aspects.[120] First, he concentrates on the reader and the reading process, explaining that the focus of ancient narratives, including Acts, is not the events per se but the relationship or connection between those events. In doing so, the author guides the reader through the narrative toward a judgment and response. Thompson also contends that the reader, not the text alone, realizes meaning. However, "[s]ince no text provides the reader with all the information or connections necessary for its realization, these textual indeterminacies or 'gaps' stimulate the reader's imagination so that one fills in those gaps in ways that build a consistent reading."[121] Second, Thompson deals with characters in ancient narratives. He stresses that "the reader must actively make judgments and decisions about those characters from the information that the text provides."[122] Besides, based primarily on the work of Christopher Gill, Thompson highlights that ancient literature often contains two categories of character portrayal—characters as typical figures and characters as individual personalities. Thompson acknowledges, however, that characterization in ancient literature varies, and one may discover degrees of character depiction.[123]

For her study of the character of God in Acts, Ling Cheng seeks some theoretical grounding.[124] She finds Forster's dualistic categories of "flat" and "round" characters too simplistic for her study. She also dismisses Berlin's classification of characters because Berlin does not (in her view) distinguish sharply enough between her three character types. Cheng finally settles on

---

118. Roth, Blind, 74–75.

119. Roth, Blind, 76–78.

120. Richard P. Thompson, Keeping the Church in Its Place: The Church as Narrative Character in Acts (New York: T. & T. Clark, 2006), ch. 1.

121. Thompson, Keeping the Church in Its Place, 9–17 (quotation from p. 16).

122. Thompson, Keeping the Church in Its Place, 20.

123. Thompson, Keeping the Church in Its Place, 22–25.

124. Ling Cheng, The Characterisation of God in Acts: The Indirect Portrayal of an Invisible Character (PBM; Milton Keynes, UK: Paternoster, 2011), 2–12.

Harvey's threefold character classification of protagonist, intermediate figures (cards and ficelles), and background characters. She decides that Harvey's classification is most suited for her study of Acts, where characters function as a plot device.[125] Cheng's conclusions are somewhat puzzling, because I view Berlin's proposal to place characters on a continuum rather than mutually exclusive categories as a major step forward in the whole character debate (see our section 2.3). Finally, Cheng deals briefly with characterization (the literary technique of presenting characters) and argues that in Acts, characterization is inclined more toward showing than telling.[126] Cheng's theoretical foundation would have been strengthened significantly had she interacted with the work of David Gowler and William Shepherd.

Summary. While all the scholars, whose work we examined, use modern literary methods to analyze characters in ancient narratives, only some discuss whether this is legitimate (Gowler, Shepherd, Roth). While Gowler, Shepherd, and Thompson argue for continuity between ancient and modern characterization (and that, therefore, ancient characters can be complex), Roth sees a sharp contrast (ancient characters are flat; modern characters can be round; cf. Darr).

1.2. Identifying a Pattern or Paradigm of Character Reconstruction

Based on this extensive literature review, I conclude that it is possible to detect a pattern or even a paradigm in the study of character in New Testament narrative. While *pattern* refers to a "discernible regularity" or "perceptible structure," *paradigm* is a narrower category, denoting a "normative pattern" or "generally accepted perspective." Looking at what we have summarized regarding each of the three New Testament books, it would be legitimate to ask whether we can even speak of a pattern, not to mention a paradigm. Perhaps pandemonium is a better term to describe what has been happening in the study of New Testament character over the last thirty-odd years. Nevertheless, I will seek to uncover some trends and establish a minimum pattern.

Among the numerous issues in the study of character in New Testament narrative, it appears that three assumptions, beliefs, or practices are prominent—albeit not always in agreement. First, there is a contrast between Hebraic and Hellenic characterization. Many scholars hold that characters in the

---

125. Cheng, *Characterisation of God*, 5–6. However, on p. 14 she claims that character and plot are interdependent.

126. Cheng, *Characterisation of God*, 10–11.

Hebrew Bible can be complex, dynamic, and show change, whereas Greco-Roman characters are typical—uncomplicated, static, and unchanging. Second, there is a contrast between ancient and modern characterization. The majority view is that characters in ancient narratives are radically different from the psychologized, developed, and individualized characters in the modern novel. Third, there is the prevalent practice of applying modern literary methods of fiction to ancient historical narratives such as those in the New Testament. A few scholars object to this practice (e.g., Tolbert and Myers), but the majority of biblical scholars use insights from modern literary methods to study characters in biblical narratives, even if it is as minimal as speaking of "round" and "flat" characters. I contend that these features constitute a minimum pattern in New Testament character studies.

Pressing further, it appears that several scholars operate with a paradigm that is based on three assumptions: (i) characters in Greco-Roman literature are "Aristotelian" (flat, types, plot functionaries); (ii) characters in the Gospels and Acts are not like characters in modern fiction (round, individualistic, psychologized) but resemble Greco-Roman characters and hence are mostly flat/types; (iii) (yet) modern literary methods can be used to analyze ancient characters. There is an inherent inconsistency here: if ancient characters are unlike modern characters, we should not use modern methods; for if we apply modern methods to ancient narratives, most characters will appear flat since they do not meet modern criteria for roundness. I am not suggesting that every scholar operates with this paradigm, but many do, whether explicitly, implicitly, or in part. Besides, while I maintain that there is at least a minimum pattern in New Testament character studies, I admit that it is perhaps not a *normative* pattern required for a paradigm. To rephrase it, even if there is not enough to speak of a (dominant) paradigm, there certainly is a dominant pattern within the haphazard array of approaches.[127]

We should also note that many scholars who reconstruct character without an apparent theoretical grounding or clarification on their approach to character often conform to the above-mentioned pattern or paradigm. Although I have only made cursory reference to this large number of character studies (see nn. 17, 53, and 97, above), I have dealt extensively with many of these regarding the Gospel of John, showing that such pattern or paradigm indeed exists.[128] Besides, we can often infer from the studies themselves the kind of method

127. This pattern or paradigm is more discernible in character studies on the Gospels than on Acts, but this may simply be because of the much larger number of character studies on the Gospels.

128. Bennema, *Encountering Jesus*, 2–10. Such an exercise here would divert from the book's focus and overburden the reader.

scholars use or the assumptions underlying their work. For example, studies that view all characters as types would suggest an Aristotelian approach; studies that distinguish sharply between characterization in the Old Testament and New Testament probably assume that the New Testament characters are typical; studies that mostly speak of "round" and "flat" characters probably use reductionist classifications; while studies that only use modern literary categories may not have considered the temporal, cultural, and conceptual distance that exists between modern fiction and biblical narratives.

Admittedly, there have been voices that spoke out against this pattern/paradigm or aspects of it. Some have argued that modern methods of character in fiction cannot be used to analyze characters in the Bible (e.g., Tolbert and Myers). Others see more continuity between Hebraic and Hellenic characterization, and between ancient and modern characterization (e.g., Gowler, Shepherd, myself). Besides, an increasing number of scholars now see greater complexity in the New Testament characters.[129] Nevertheless, much of the stereotypical thinking remains. The current interest in New Testament characters has, regrettably, not led to a consensus on how to study character in biblical narrative. Nor has a comprehensive, nonreductionist theory of character been proposed and shown to work. At best, a plethora of approaches provides liberty, eclecticism, and choice, and has led to a wide array of results;[130] at worst, the approaches are simplistic and reductionist, and lead to a one-sided or distorted view that most New Testament characters are flat and types. Irrespective of how one looks at it, it is fair to conclude that regarding the study of character in New Testament narrative, there is no consensus and no comprehensive theory.

In the end, whether one sees a pattern, a paradigm, or just an array of haphazard approaches, the most significant conclusion is that *there is no robust, comprehensive theory of character in New Testament narrative.* While some/many scholars do not clarify their approach to studying character or discuss any theory of character, others provide a range of theoretical considerations. There is no consensus on how to analyze, classify, and evaluate characters. As for character analysis, while some draw on ancient methods of characterization (whether Hebrew, Greek, or both), virtually all scholars employ modern literary methods. Others use a specific focus, such as misunderstanding, ambiguity, anonymity, gender, or social status. Besides, many scholars tend to oversimplify

---

129. See, for example, the observations by Alan Culpepper, Judith Redman, and Susan Hylen regarding John's Gospel in Skinner, ed., *Characters in Characterization,* 22–23, 61–63, 96.

130. A good example is the recent volume with essays on seventy Johannine characters (Hunt, Tolmie, and Zimmermann, eds., *Character Studies in the Fourth Gospel*).

most New Testament characters, viewing them as flat—opaque, unchanging, and uncomplicated. Nevertheless, as Conway has astutely pointed out, there is surprisingly little agreement on what each character typifies or represents. As for character classification, while many scholars still use fixed, reductionist categories (e.g., flat and round), others have proposed positioning characters on a continuum, but again, there is no consensus on how this should look. As for character evaluation, most scholars avoid doing so or even object to it, and among those who do, there are no agreed criteria for evaluation. But how can we compare characters except in relation to one another? Finally, there is no consensus on whether New Testament characters have any representative value or ongoing significance, and if so, what this is. All this leads us to the conclusion that we need a comprehensive, nonreductionist theoretical framework in which we can analyze, classify, and evaluate the New Testament characters and determine their possible significance. This takes us to the next section.

1.3. The Plan and Approach of the Book

The study of New Testament character has burgeoned in the last thirty-odd years, with different approaches, findings, and conclusions coming at a remarkable pace. Instead of adding to this expanding and diverging corpus, this study attempts to regulate and consolidate extant data by proposing a paradigm for character reconstruction in New Testament narrative. The aim of this study is to formulate a robust, comprehensive theory of character for New Testament studies—a theoretical framework that will enable and validate a sound, nonreductive interpretation of New Testament characters.

Our review of literature shows that many scholars seemingly follow a pattern or paradigm of character reconstruction in the New Testament. In Chapter 2, I will attempt a comprehensive critique of and challenge to this pattern/paradigm. I will argue that the differences in characterization in the Hebrew Bible, ancient Greek literature, and modern narrative are differences in emphases rather than kind. It is therefore better to speak of degrees of characterization along a continuum. Following this deconstruction phase, Chapter 3 is devoted to the construction of a new paradigm to study character. This comprehensive theory of character for New Testament studies consists of three aspects. First, I study character in text and context, using information from the text and other sources. I also delineate the kind of reader I assume for this task. Second, I analyze and classify the Johannine characters along three dimensions (complexity, development, inner life), and plot the resulting character on a continuum of degree of characterization (from agent to type to personality to individuality). Third, I evaluate the characters in relation to the narrative's point of view and plot, and I seek to determine their representative value for today. Finally, in Chapter 4, I will seek to validate this new paradigm by applying the theory to select characters in the Gospel of Mark, the Gospel of John, and the Acts of the Apostles.

While the scope of the book's field of reference is literary narrative, both ancient and modern, the specific focus is character in New Testament narrative. Our study has two limitations. First, I will focus on character (the reader's reconstruction of character) rather than characterization (the author's construction of character). To rephrase, I seek to understand what character is and how the reader can reconstruct character from indicators in the text; not characterization, as far as it refers to the author's techniques of constructing character by placing various indicators along the text continuum. The second limitation is that I will only examine the Gospels and the Acts of the Apostles because these contain most narrative material in the New Testament and are, therefore, most suited for the analysis of characters. Among the Gospels, I concentrate on the "bi-optic Gospels" Mark (the earliest Gospel, on which Matthew and Luke show a literal dependency) and John (while John might have known Mark, he also wrote independently of Mark).[131] For the sake of convenience, I will use "Mark," "John," and "Luke" to refer to the authors of the works, which is not a claim about their historical identity. Our focus on the Gospels and Acts does not mean that our proposed theory is not applicable to other parts of the New Testament, but that building and demonstrating our theory using a narrower section of the New Testament is simply more feasible.

I must clarify some of the terminology in this book. First, when dealing with modern literary theory, I prefer the term *narrative* to fiction or novel since narrative is now generally understood to include both fiction and nonfiction. By "narrative," I mean those literary works that contain a story and a storyteller.[132] While fifty years ago the dominant object of literary narrative study was the novel, its scope has broadened significantly today.[133] In fact, "narrative has displaced the novel as the central concern of literary critics."[134]

---

131. The term *bi-optic Gospels* comes from Paul N. Anderson, *The Riddles of the Fourth Gospel: An Introduction to John* (Minneapolis: Fortress Press, 2011), 126.

132. Cf. Robert Scholes, James Phelan, and Robert Kellogg, *The Nature of Narrative*, 2nd ed. (Oxford: Oxford University Press, 2006 [1966]), 4. Except for minor stylistic adjustments, the second edition has kept the text of the 1966 edition by Robert Scholes and Robert Kellogg, but is supplemented with an extensive overview of narrative theory from 1966 to 2006 by James Phelan.

133. See especially James Phelan's above-mentioned overview in Scholes, Phelan, and Kellogg, *Nature of Narrative*, 283–336.

134. Shepherd, *Narrative Function*, 49.

Second, I will use the term *modern/ity* in the sense of "contemporary," over against "antiquity" rather than in contradistinction to "postmodern/ity." Third, I largely adopt Uri Margolin's definition of character: "'Character' designates any entity, individual or collective—normally human or human-like—introduced in a work of narrative fiction. Characters exist within storyworlds, play a role in the narrative, and can hence be defined as *storyworld participants*."[135] However, instead of Margolin's narrower term *narrative fiction*, I use *narrative* to refer to any literary work (fiction and nonfiction) in both ancient and modern times. In adapted form, then, the term *character* refers to "a human actor, individual or collective, imaginary or real, who plays a role in the story of a literary narrative." While characters may resemble people, they only exist within the story world of the text (even when they represent real people in the real world).

135. Uri Margolin, "Character," in *Cambridge Companion to Narrative*, ed. D. Herman (Cambridge: Cambridge University Press, 2007), 66–79.

2

Character in Antiquity and Modernity
Deconstructing the Dominant Pattern/Paradigm

In the previous chapter, I suggested that many scholars assume or work with a set of beliefs or a paradigm based on particular views regarding character in antiquity and modernity. The minimum pattern prevalent in New Testament character studies shares three assumptions: (i) Hebraic and Hellenic characterization is radically different; (ii) ancient and modern characterization is radically different; (iii) modern literary methods of fiction apply to biblical narratives. We observed that this pattern (or paradigm) is a fair sample or reflection of the kind of thinking and practice that is common in biblical scholarship regarding the study of character in New Testament narrative. While acknowledging there are different voices too (and some of these will be in agreement with the argument in this chapter), this has not resulted in a consensus on how to approach character in the New Testament. In this chapter, I wish to argue that the pattern or paradigm we identified is flawed and needs replacing with one that more accurately reflects the nature of character in antiquity and also justifies the incorporation of insights from modern literary theory. We must, therefore, reexamine character in *both* ancient Hebrew and Greco-Roman literature *and* modern literary narrative in order to develop a robust, comprehensive theory of character for New Testament studies. In this chapter, I seek to deconstruct the existing pattern or paradigm of character reconstruction, and in the next chapter, I will construct a new paradigm.

The rationale for looking at ancient Hebrew and Greco-Roman literature is easy to explain. First, the Jewish roots of early Christianity are obvious: (i) the Hebrew Bible (the source document of Judaism) was readily accepted by early Christians as part of their heritage, and (ii) the New Testament (the source document of early Christianity) builds on and reflects this Jewish heritage.

It would be safe, therefore, to assume that the New Testament authors were familiar with characterization in the Hebrew Bible. Second, early Christianity spread rapidly beyond Palestine into various parts of the Greco-Roman world, and most New Testament documents were composed in this environment. As such, the authors may also have had an understanding of characterization in Greco-Roman literature. Besides, all of first-century Judaism—both in Palestine and the Diaspora—had been permeated to various degrees by Hellenistic culture.[1] It is therefore not surprising that Gospel critics have almost reached a consensus that the Gospels, in terms of genre, belong or correspond to the Greco-Roman biography or βίος.[2] Fred Burnett goes so far as to say that, due to a lack of comparable presentation of character in Jewish literature, Gospel critics have been forced to turn to Greek classical literature for the study of character.[3] I will closely examine ancient Greco-Roman literature because many biblical scholars still view characters in this body of literature as types.

The rationale for looking at modern literary narrative is that narrative criticism of the Gospels is derived from contemporary literary theory. In addition, character and characterization are subjects of literary inquiry, so we assume that we can gain insights from the study of character in modern literary theory. There is the danger, however, that we may compare apples and oranges since critics contend that character and characterization in ancient and modern literature are very different. We have also seen that many scholars contend that within ancient literature, character in the Hebrew Bible differs greatly from that in Greek literature. Hence, we must examine whether it is legitimate to apply modern methods used in literary theory to ancient narratives *and* if we can compare Hebrew and Greek literature regarding character.

On this point, I draw attention to one challenge to my previous study of ancient character. Richard Rohrbaugh, an authority on the social and cultural

---

1. This has been forcefully argued by Martin Hengel, *Judaism and Hellenism: Studies in Their Encounter in Palestine during the Early Hellenistic Period*, 2 vols. (London: SCM, 1974).

2. The compelling case for this has been provided by Richard A. Burridge, *What Are the Gospels? A Comparison with Graeco-Roman Biography*, 2nd ed. (Grand Rapids: Eerdmans, 2004). Cf. David E. Aune, "Greco-Roman Biography," in *Greco-Roman Literature and the New Testament: Selected Forms and Genres*, ed. David E. Aune (SBLSBS 21; Atlanta: Scholars, 1988), 107–26; Graham Stanton, *The Gospels and Jesus*, 2nd ed. (Oxford: Oxford University Press, 2002), 14–18; James D. G. Dunn, *Jesus Remembered*, vol. 1 of *Christianity in the Making* (Grand Rapids: Eerdmans, 2003), 184–86; Richard Bauckham, *Jesus and the Eyewitnesses: The Gospels as Eyewitness Testimony* (Grand Rapids: Eerdmans, 2006), 276. Among those who are skeptical of viewing the Gospels as ancient βίοι is Peter Stuhlmacher, "The Genre(s) of the Gospels," in *The Interrelations of the Gospels*, ed. D. L. Dungan (BETL 95; Leuven: Leuven University Press, 1990), 484–94. Burridge responds to some critical reviews in his *What Are the Gospels?*, ch. 11.

3. Burnett, "Characterization," 7–8.

world of the New Testament, questions the legitimacy of applying modern literary methods to analyze characters in ancient texts. In a scathing review of my 2009 work, he alleges that I naïvely use modern trait-names for understanding ancient characters, and questions how I infer a character's traits from the text.[4] If Rohrbaugh is right, my efforts to deconstruct and reconstruct a paradigm to understand character in the New Testament will be largely in vain. I must therefore address two pertinent hermeneutical issues: (i) the legitimacy of applying modern literary methods to study ancient characters; and (ii) the suitability of the method of inference to reconstruct characters from a text. Is it hermeneutically viable and valid to compare ancient and modern characterization? I will seek to respond to Richard Rohrbaugh's criticism, arguing that it is not only legitimate but also necessary to draw on modern labels to infer a character's traits.

2.1. Character in Ancient Hebrew Literature

Looking at ancient narrative literature, Robert Scholes and Robert Kellogg comment that "[c]haracters in primitive stories are invariably 'flat,' 'static,' and quite 'opaque'" and "[t]he inward life is assumed but not presented in primitive narrative literature, whether Hebraic or Hellenic."[5] This view, however, has not won over critics of Hebrew narrative, due to the influential works of scholars such as Robert Alter, Adele Berlin, Meir Sternberg, and Shimon Bar-Efrat.[6] Alter argues that the Bible's sparse portrayal of character in fact creates scope for a variety of possible interpretations of human individuality because "[w]e are compelled to get at character and motive . . . through a process of inference from fragmentary data, often with crucial pieces of narrative exposition strategically withheld, and this leads to multiple or sometimes even wavering perspectives on the characters."[7] Both Alter and Sternberg have developed the idea that the author's reticence in characterization invites (even requires) the reader to reconstruct character through inference or "filling the gaps."[8] In addition, since information about a character is conveyed primarily

---

4. Richard L. Rohrbaugh, Review of Cornelis Bennema, *Encountering Jesus: Character Studies in the Gospel of John*, BTB 41 (2011): 110–11.

5. Scholes, Phelan, and Kellogg, *Nature of Narrative*, 164–67 (quotations from p. 164 and p. 166 respectively). This view has been maintained since the 1966 edition.

6. Robert Alter, *The Art of Biblical Narrative* (London: George Allen & Unwin, 1981); Adele Berlin, *Poetics and Interpretation of Biblical Narrative* (Sheffield: Almond Press, 1983); Meir Sternberg, *The Poetics of Biblical Narrative: Ideological Literature and the Drama of Reading* (Bloomington: Indiana University Press, 1985); Shimon Bar-Efrat, *Narrative Art in the Bible* (JSOTS 70; Sheffield: Almond Press, 1989).

7. Alter, *Art of Biblical Narrative*, 114–15, 126 (quotation taken from p. 126).

through indirect characterization, that is, through the subject's speech and actions rather than inward speech or statements by the narrator, we are essentially left in the realm of inference.[9] Sternberg emphasizes that the reader's task of gap-filling is legitimate and by no means an arbitrary process, since any hypothesis must be validated by the text.[10]

Alter adds that Hebrew characters who are dealt with at any length exhibit a capacity for change, and this developing and transforming nature of character is one reason biblical characters cannot be reduced to fixed Homeric types—Jacob is not simply "wily Jacob," Moses is not "sagacious Moses."[11] Sternberg agrees that biblical characters can display change, unpredictability, ambiguity, complexity, and surprise.[12] Indeed, characters such as Abraham, Jacob, Joseph, Saul, or David can hardly be labeled as "static," "type," or "flat." Sternberg goes on to say that "[c]onsidering the range of the Bible's portrait gallery, it is amazing how distinct and memorable its figures remain, without benefit of formal portrayal. And this is largely due to the surplus of inner life expressed in act and speech."[13] Gowler affirms that Scholes and Kellogg's claim that the inner life of characters is assumed rather than presented is easily disproved because the narrator does provide readers with the inner life of characters when necessary, as Gen. 27:41 and 2 Sam. 13:15, for example, indicate.[14] Alter aptly concludes that "the underlying biblical conception of character as often unpredictable, in some ways impenetrable, constantly emerging from and slipping back into a penumbra of ambiguity, in fact has greater affinity with dominant modern notions than do the habits of conceiving character typical of the Greek epics."[15]

On the relation between character and plot, Sternberg argues that character is not subordinated to plot (as in Aristotle's view and modern

8. Alter, *Art of Biblical Narrative*, ch. 6; Sternberg, *Poetics of Biblical Narrative*, ch. 6. Cf. Bar-Efrat, *Narrative Art*, ch. 2; Berlin, *Poetics and Interpretation*, 33–42.

9. Cf. Alter, *Art of Biblical Narrative*, 116–17. Bar-Efrat points out that in real life too we usually infer people's character from what they say and do (*Narrative Art*, 89).

10. Sternberg, *Poetics of Biblical Narrative*, 188–89.

11. Alter, *Art of Biblical Narrative*, 126.

12. Sternberg, *Poetics of Biblical Narrative*, 323–28. Cf. Bar-Efrat, *Narrative Art*, 86–92.

13. Sternberg, *Poetics of Biblical Narrative*, 329. For examples of characters' inner life, see Bar-Efrat, *Narrative Art*, 53–64. Cf. also Barbara M. Leung Lai, *Through the "I"-Window: The Inner Life of Characters in the Hebrew Bible* (HBM 34; Sheffield: Phoenix, 2011).

14. Gowler, *Host, Guest, Enemy and Friend*, 115.

15. Alter, *Narrative Art*, 129. Although Alter's conclusion holds true for Homeric characters, later Greek literature was capable of more complex portrayals of character with aspects of inner life and development (see section 2.2).

structuralism) but that there is a two-way traffic between them, an inferential movement from character to action to character.[16]

In sum, there appears to be a consensus among current scholarship about character in the Hebrew Bible, but the notion that Hebraic characters are very different from those in Greco-Roman literature persists, so we now turn to this body of literature to test this idea.

2.2. CHARACTER IN ANCIENT GRECO-ROMAN LITERATURE

Aristotle's view on character has been immensely influential on New Testament scholars and contributed to the existing pattern or paradigm to understand character. Let me mention an important passage from his *Poetics*:

> [7] And since tragedy represents action and is acted by living persons, who must of necessity have certain qualities of character and thought—for it is these which determine the quality of an action; indeed thought and character are the natural causes of any action and it is in virtue of these that all men succeed or fail—[8] it follows then that it is the plot which represents the action. By "plot" I mean here the arrangement of the incidents: "character" is that which determines the quality of the agents, and "thought" appears wherever in the dialogue they put forward an argument or deliver an opinion. [9] Necessarily then every tragedy has six constituent parts, and on these its quality depends. These are plot, character, diction, thought, spectacle, and song. . . . [12] The most important of these is the arrangement of the incidents [i.e., plot], for tragedy is not a representation of men but of a piece of action, of life, of happiness and unhappiness, which come under the head of action, and the end aimed at is the representation not of qualities of character but of some action; and while character makes men what they are, it is their actions and experiences that make them happy or the opposite. [13] They do not therefore act to represent character, but character-study is included for the sake of the action. It follows that the incidents and the plot are the end at which tragedy aims, and in everything the end aimed at is of prime importance. [14] Moreover, you could not have a tragedy without action, but you can have one without character-study. . . . [19] The plot then is the first principle and as it were the soul of tragedy: character comes second. [20] It is much the same also in painting; if a man smeared a canvas with the loveliest colours at random, it would not give as much pleasure as an outline in black and white. [21] And it is mainly because a play is a representation of action that it also for that reason

16. Sternberg, *Poetics of Biblical Narrative*, 342–46.

represents people. . . . [24] Character is that which reveals choice, shows what sort of thing a man chooses or avoids in circumstances where the choice is not obvious, so those speeches convey no character in which there is nothing whatever which the speaker chooses or avoids. (*Poetics* 6:7-24)[17]

Aristotle's view of character as fixed and subordinate (even inessential) to the plot is well known. Rather than the modern idea that a person's character may develop through their actions and thought, and through external factors, for Aristotle, character is unchanging: "character is that which determines people's nature/qualities" (*Poetics* 6:8; cf. 6:12) and "character is that which reveals (moral) choice" (*Poetics* 6:24). Aristotle's "character" or ἦθος comes close to the modern notion of disposition—people's inherent qualities that influence their thought and actions.[18] Aristotle's notion of character corresponds to the modern category "flat" or "type."[19] Many Gospel critics have accepted this Aristotelian view of character as static, consistent ethical (stereo)types to represent the whole of ancient Greek thought—over against character development in ancient Hebrew narrative and modern fiction.[20] Christopher Gill states it succinctly:

It is often claimed that in the ancient world character was believed to be something fixed, given at birth and immutable during life. This belief is said to underlie the portrayal of individuals in ancient historiography and biography, particularly in the early Roman Empire; and to constitute the chief point of difference in psychological assumptions between ancient and modern biography.[21]

17. Aristotle, *The Poetics*, trans. W. Hamilton Fyfe (LCL 199; Cambridge, MA: Harvard University Press, 1982), 23–27.

18. According to BDAG (3rd ed.), ἦθος is "a pattern of behavior or practice that is habitual or characteristic of a group or an individual"—a custom, usage, or habit.

19. Theophrastus, a disciple of Aristotle, developed his master's ideas in his *Characters* (late fourth century BCE). *Traits* would actually be a better translation of this work since the Greek title χαρακτήρ means "a characteristic trait or manner" (BDAG [3rd ed.]), and ἦθος is normally used to translate "character" (although not with the modern psychological sense of character). *Characters* contains thirty chapters, each describing and elaborating on a single trait so that Theophrastus' "characters" are effectively types (cf. J. Rusten, "Introduction to Theophrastus," in *Characters*, ed. and trans. J. Rusten [LCL 225; Cambridge, MA: Harvard University Press, 2002], 5–13).

20. See, for example, Culpepper, *Anatomy of the Fourth Gospel*, 103; Tolbert, "Character," 347–49; Koester, *Symbolism*, 36–37; Outi Lehtipuu, "Characterization and Persuasion: The Rich Man and the Poor Man in Luke 16.19-31," in *Characterization in the Gospels: Reconceiving Narrative Criticism*, ed. David Rhoads and Kari Syreeni (JSNTS 184; Sheffield: Sheffield Academic Press, 1999), 75; Smith, "Tyranny," 263–64; Wright, "Greco-Roman Character Typing," 544–59; Myers, *Characterizing Jesus*, 55–60.

I will demonstrate, however, that Aristotle's view of character in Greek tragedy is not irrefutable or representative of ancient Greek literature at large, but that character could be more complex and take on more dimensions than Aristotle will have us believe.[22]

The earliest example of character advancing beyond the category "flat" or "type" is found in classical Attic tragedy of the fifth century BCE. In his analysis of Aeschylus' *Agamemnon*, Gowler brings out the complex characterization of Clytemnestra to show that she is not a standard type of character. Her character dominates the play and the emphasis is on her royal authority in her husband Agamemnon's absence. Clytemnestra does not conform to the accepted cultural order: for example, she takes on a public role, turns against her own husband, shows greater masculinity than he, and overpowers him both verbally and physically. Then, showing no shame, she glories in murdering Agamemnon and Cassandra, and clashes with the chorus.[23]

On examining Sophocles' tragedies *Ajax* and *Antigone*, Albin Lesky finds it unsatisfactory to label their respective protagonists Ajax and Antigone as "types," but the term "round" is also inadequate since they lack the abundance of individual features that can be seen of modern characters.[24] Lesky suggests the following way out of the dilemma:

> To understand the great figures of the Attic stage, especially those of Sophocles, we must realise that neither the usual concept "type" nor that of individual character brings us any nearer. . . . They are not determined by typical features that can be repeated at will, but entirely by their own fundamental qualities, and it is this which makes it a great experience to encounter them. We have rejected the terms "type" and "character" (in the modern sense); perhaps the best definition is the classical concept of "*personality*" as expressed by Herbert Cysarz: "Personality instead of just interesting individuality, a norm instead of the original and the bizarre."[25]

21. Christopher Gill, "The Question of Character-Development: Plutarch and Tacitus," *CQ* 33 (1983): 469.

22. Cf. Gowler, who states that while Aristotle's *Poetics* is an important voice in the analysis and critique of the characters of Greek tragedy, it remains a secondary source and cannot take the place of a firsthand analysis of the plays themselves (and there are thirty-three complete ancient Greek tragedies extant) (*Host, Guest, Enemy and Friend*, 88).

23. Gowler, *Host, Guest, Enemy and Friend*, 89–94.

24. Albin Lesky, *Greek Tragedy*, 2nd ed. (London: Ernest Benn, 1967), 123–24.

25. Lesky, *Greek Tragedy*, 124 (my emphasis).

Christopher Gill also ascribes "personality" to Sophocles' Ajax, in which he associates "personality" (i) with a response to people that is empathetic (i.e., understanding someone by placing oneself in the other person's position) rather than moral (i.e., evaluating a person from the outside in terms of vice and virtue), and (ii) with a concern with the person as an individual rather than as the bearer of character traits that are assessed by reference to general moral terms.[26]

Jacqueline de Romilly makes similar observations, arguing that Sophocles employs a vivid and nuanced characterization in which characters can take a variety of positions that are often in direct conflict with one another.[27] She says, for example, "Sophocles does not simply choose an ideal to embody in Antigone; he puts a living Antigone before us. Yet at every juncture of the plot he manages to reveal in her a set of principles and an ideal of proper conduct that together make up her unique personality."[28] As Simon Goldhill asserts, Greek tragedy may not have the same notion of character as the modern novel, but this does not mean that Greek tragedy has no interest in the inner life of its characters.[29] Patricia Easterling, arguing that Sophocles depicts his characters as life-like individuals, goes so far as saying, "[I]n the matter of characterization the differences between Sophocles and modern dramatists are ultimately unimportant . . . there is nothing in modern drama that does not have its counterpart in his plays."[30]

Although the Sophoclean characters could have "personality," Lesky argues that they were nevertheless unable to change since Sophocles adhered to the basic idea in ancient Greek culture that the inherent qualities of people (their φύσις) determined their character irreversibly. The idea of development or change in a character, Lesky continues, was only introduced by Euripides, after a revolution in ideas about human nature.[31] Goldhill differs however. According to him, Sophocles' Ajax for example is not stereotyped but undergoes change: rather than the fixed ἦθος that Ajax had proclaimed for himself, he goes

---

26. Christopher Gill, "The Character-Personality Distinction," in *Characterization and Individuality in Greek Literature*, ed. Christopher B. R. Pelling (Oxford: Clarendon, 1990), 2, 19–20.

27. Jacqueline de Romilly, *A Short History of Greek Literature* (Chicago: University of Chicago Press, 1985), 71–72.

28. De Romilly, *Short History*, 73. Cf. Patricia E. Easterling, who examines the interest in the "inner life" of the main characters of *Antigone* ("Constructing Character in Greek Tragedy," in *Characterization and Individuality in Greek Literature*, ed. Christopher B. R. Pelling [Oxford: Clarendon, 1990], 93–99).

29. Simon Goldhill, *Reading Greek Tragedy* (Cambridge: Cambridge University Press, 1986), 168–74.

30. Patricia E. Easterling, "Character in Sophocles," *GR* 24 (1977): 121–29 (quotation from p. 129).

31. Lesky, *Greek Tragedy*, 125–26.

beyond the norm, appears inconsistent, "out of character."[32] Although it is debatable whether we can speak of a real change or development in character in Sophocles, it appears that Sophoclean characters could fluctuate between flat and round, static and dynamic, and Lesky's suggested category of personality may be appropriate.

A related issue is the appearance of a hero in multiple plays by the same writer or different writers. Goldhill, for example, argues that Sophocles might have drawn on *and developed* the Ajax in Homer's *Iliad*. Characters of Greek drama draw on, define themselves through, and develop in relation to other texts.[33] Similarly, Creon appears in three of Sophocles' plays, and Burnett wonders how to compare the docile and passive Creon of the *Antigone* with the active and tyrannical Creon in *Oedipus Tyrannus* and the brazen liar Creon in *Oedipus at Colonus*. He then suggests that, for ancient audiences, oral traditions and private and public discussions about Creon may have contributed to Creon's change of character between plays.[34]

In Euripides' *Medea*, the central figure Medea displays a tragic conflict within herself and the intensity of her inner experiences, oscillating between furious passion (θυμός) and thoughtful reflection (βουλεύματα) (*Medea* 1079), is unequaled in Attic tragedy.[35] Medea's intense dialogue with herself in *Medea* 1019–80, for example, reveals her inner life with all its psychological reversals, not unlike a modern character.[36] In Euripides' later plays, such as *Electra* and *Orestes*, Kitto sees characters "who are regarded purely as individuals, not in any degree as types, or tragic and exemplary embodiments of some universal passion."[37] In his later plays, Euripides shows a radical new valuation of humankind: (i) in *Electra*, *Orestes*, and *Ion*, environment and education are the decisive factors that shape one's character rather than one's φύσις; (ii) in *Antiope*, the contrast between the two brothers Amphion and Zethus reflects the important split between thought and action—thought no longer being the servant of action.[38] The implication is that characters can change or develop:

---

32. Goldhill, *Greek Tragedy*, 181–89. Inconsistency goes against Aristotle's understanding of proper character (*Poetics* 15:6).

33. Goldhill, *Greek Tragedy*, 188.

34. Burnett, "Characterization," 13–14.

35. Lesky, *Greek Tragedy*, 146–47. Cf. Charles Garton, "Characterisation in Greek Tragedy," *JHS* 77 (1957): 254. Gowler asserts that "[t]he transition in Greek tragedy from portraying characters as types to depicting them as individuals reached its apex with Euripides" (*Host, Guest, Enemy and Friend*, 103). Gill also sees "personality" in Euripides' Medea ("Character-Personality Distinction," 27–28).

36. Cf. de Romilly, *Short History*, 79.

37. H. D. F. Kitto, *Greek Tragedy: A Literary Study*, 2nd ed. (London: Methuen, 1950), 258.

their external environment can influence inner thought and move them to a particular action rather than that they act solely out of their φύσις. Lesky thus concludes that "[t]his lively interplay between external changes and the characters' internal reactions represents a line of development that begins with the increased dramatic movement of Sophocles and brings us close to modern drama."[39]

We do not know much about postclassic Hellenistic tragedy of the fourth and third century BCE, but Lesky conjectures that the preoccupation with psychological portrayal of characters that we saw in Euripides continued or even increased.[40] Alongside tragedy, the genre of comedy emerged in the second half of the fifth century and into the fourth century BCE. In this new genre, there was a sporadic resemblance to character in tragedy. De Romilly observes that Menander, who belonged to New Comedy, replaced politics (characteristic of Old Comedy) with psychology, and although he mainly used typecast characters, they exhibited variety and subtle psychological nuances.[41]

Two new genres of Greek literature appeared in the Roman era: biography (βίος), which took its place beside history, and romance or the novel.[42] In a widely acclaimed study, Richard Burridge makes a convincing case for viewing the Gospels as Greco-Roman βίοι.[43] Examining ten Greco-Roman βίοι from the fourth century BCE to the third century CE, he observes that ancient characterization was much more indirect than its modern counterpart, revealing character primarily through the subject's words and deeds rather than by direct, psychological analysis.[44] Regarding early Greco-Roman βίοι, pre-dating the Gospels, Burridge argues that although there is interest in the individual (otherwise, there would be no βίος), most characters are stereotyped as examples of general, ethical qualities.[45] Regarding βίοι that came after the

---

38. Lesky, *Greek Tragedy*, 171–73, 188–89. Cf. Jasper Griffin, who finds that in the late Euripidean play *Iphigeneia* the characters are capable of contrasting emotions and abrupt changes of mind ("Characterization in Euripides: *Hippolytus* and *Iphigeneia in Aulis*," in *Characterization and Individuality in Greek Literature*, ed. Christopher B. R. Pelling [Oxford: Clarendon, 1990], 140–49).

39. Lesky, *Greek Tragedy*, 190.

40. Lesky, *Greek Tragedy*, 202–5.

41. De Romilly, *Short History*, 168–69. Cf. Lesky, *Greek Tragedy*, 207.

42. De Romilly, *Short History*, 191. Although the historians of the Roman age (e.g., Diodorus, Josephus, Tacitus, Dio Cassius, Eusebius) had considerable influence, they were inferior to the great Greek historians of the fifth century like Herodotus and Thucydides (de Romilly, *Short History*, 197–202).

43. Burridge, *What Are the Gospels?* (see n. 2, above, for details).

44. Burridge, *What Are the Gospels?*, 117, 139, 172.

45. Burridge, *What Are the Gospels?*, 144.

Gospels, he ventures that although we should not look for modern concepts of character in these βίοι, "we may find some quite carefully drawn characters—some stereotypical and others more realistic—emerging through the narratives."[46] Burridge asserts that in Plutarch's *Lives*, for example, there is evidence of character change.[47]

Comparing Plutarch's biographical theory and practice, Christopher Pelling makes similar observations. He observes that although the concern in Plutarch's *Lives* is character (ἦθος) and their ultimate purpose is protreptic and moral, in some of the *Lives* Plutarch displays real psychological interest in the characters.[48] Regarding *Antony*, for example, Pelling notes that, after the entrance of Cleopatra, Plutarch's moralism becomes rather different from crude remarks of praise and blame: "It is the moralism of a sympathetic insight into human frailty; the moralism which, like the tragic aspects of *Pompey*, points a truth of human nature."[49]

In the category of Greco-Roman biographies and historiographies, Christopher Gill examines the issue of character development in the first-century writings of Plutarch and Tacitus. Plutarch's ἦθος means "character" in an evaluative sense (like Aristotle's ἦθος) in that his point of view is highly evaluative, passing moral judgment on great people of the past and thus providing the reader with examples of behavior to imitate and avoid.[50] However, contra Aristotle, Plutarch's characters are not necessarily flat, static, or typecast. Quite the reverse. Like Pelling, Gill argues that Plutarch's moral essays clearly suggest the possibility of development of character, in that the journey of life can introduce changes in adult character.[51] Gill adds that in Tacitus we also find the idea of the development of the adult character.[52] Gowler too concludes

---

46. Burridge, *What Are the Gospels?*, 179.

47. Burridge, *What Are the Gospels?*, 178.

48. Christopher B. R. Pelling, "Plutarch's Adaptation of His Source-Material," *JHS* 100 (1980): 135–38.

49. Pelling, "Plutarch's Adaptation," 138. Regarding Suetonius' *Lives of the Caesars*, Gowler asserts that this biography shows a terse realism where the emperors remain individuals and resist attempts to typify them (*Host, Guest, Enemy and Friend*, 131).

50. Gill, "Character-Development," 472–73.

51. Gill, "Character-Development," 474–75. In fact, Plutarch seems to regard two kinds of character development acceptable: (i) the development of a child or youth toward a good or bad adult character; (ii) the process of an adult to improve his character, in some cases by conscious correction of deficiencies. What Plutarch finds problematic is when a good adult character turns bad (Gill, "Character-Development," 478). In turn, Christopher B. R. Pelling affirms Gill's findings and concludes that Plutarch had "a considerable interest in 'personality'" ("Childhood and Personality in Greek Biography," in *Characterization and Individuality in Greek Literature*, ed. Christopher B. R. Pelling [Oxford: Clarendon, 1990], 225–44 [quotation from p. 228]).

that in Tacitus' *Annals* the characters "can represent types—such as the sage, tyrant, or informer—but many come to be individuals in their own right."[53]

Gill warns against two extremities. On the one hand, though there was a general awareness in the Greco-Roman culture of that time that the adult character depended on a combination of factors (innate qualities as well as upbringing and influences of individuals and of society at large), and could therefore develop, this is not fully reflected in the historiography and biography of that time but merely lightly sketched. On the other hand, it would be a gross oversimplification to say that ancient writers were incapable of conceiving of a change of character.[54] Burnett argues in a similar vein that there is evidence from nonliterary sources of a move from the typical to the individual in the ancient Greek and Roman world, which would perhaps allow the reader to construct a character's individuality.[55] Nevertheless, Easterling warns that the Greeks were interested in individuals as part of a community rather than in the individual's unique private experience found in modern literature.[56]

Examining characterization in the ancient novel, Alain Billault observes that although novelists sometimes draw on characters in comedy, they also delineate new types of characters. Some characters are given personal features such as a name, and the novelists often make psychological remarks beyond the stereotyped categories "good" or "bad," thereby providing a character with a true psychological existence that comes close to ordinary people.[57] For example, Chariton and Heliodorus depict characters that are "a complex whole of various qualities and contradictions, which seems to be the real thing"; Longus subtly describes characters' psychology; and Achilles Tatius' protagonists often employ self-deprecating humor.[58] In addition, Billault observes that character development through suffering is a favorite theme in the ancient novel; some

---

52. Gill, "Character-Development," 475–76.

53. Gowler, *Host, Guest, Enemy and Friend*, 143.

54. Gill, "Character-Development," 476–77, 482.

55. Burnett, "Characterization," 11–12.

56. Easterling, "Character in Sophocles," 129. Cf. Bruce J. Malina's reminder that in ancient culture (and many non-Western cultures today), people identified themselves in terms of the social group to which they belonged, which can be called "group-oriented personality" or "collective personality" (*The New Testament World: Insights from Cultural Anthropology*, 3rd ed. [Louisville: Westminster John Knox, 2001], 61–62).

57. Alain Billault, "Characterization in the Ancient Novel," in *The Novel in the Ancient World*, ed. G. Schmeling (Leiden: Brill, 1996), 118, 122–25.

58. Billault, "Characterization," 125–26. Cf. Tomas Hägg, *The Novel in Antiquity* (Berkeley: University of California Press, 1983), 9, 16); Gowler, *Host, Guest, Enemy and Friend*, 167. Gowler concludes that Chariton presents in his *Chaereas and Callirhoe* four characters (Chaereas, Callirhoe, Dionysius, and

heroes are not the same in the end as they were in the beginning of the story.[59] Examples of characters that develop through suffering are Chaereas in Chariton's *Chaereas and Callirhoe*, Theagenes in Heliodorus' *Aethiopica*, Lucius in Apuleius' *The Golden Ass*, and Callisthenes in Achilles Tatius' *Leucippe and Clitophon*.[60]

From this survey, I conclude that character and characterization in ancient Greco-Roman literature is much more varied than most biblical scholars assume. David Gowler admits that the stereotypical view of ancient characters as types and immutable is not easy to overcome, but after a broad survey of Greek literature, he reasons:

> The varieties of characterization found in ancient narratives make it impossible to predict how a character may be presented in an individual ancient narrative. The best course seems to be one that would simply examine characters in individual narratives without taking any prefabricated frames and boxes in which to encase them. . . . The happy result for readers following this prescription will be an experience of the diversity of characters and characterization in ancient narratives.[61]

Likewise, Fred Burnett's conclusion is worth quoting at length:

> From modern views of characterization, which are interested in psychological description and change, indirect characterization in tragedy or in ancient biography and historiography appears to be simplistic. It appears to be minimal characterization, and thus it is easy to argue from a modern point of view that characters were only types and symbols. How audiences and readers inferred characters from the words, deeds, and relationships, and by what larger codes, however, still seems to be an open question. The discussions of the interest in the individual in portraiture and in tragedy, and the limited number of extant sources for both tragedies and biographical writing, should make Gospel critics reconsider the possibility from a narrative-critical viewpoint that ancient audiences and readers constructed much fuller characters than is usually thought.[62]

Artaxerxes) with "enough inconsistency in their portrayal to allow the possibility for change or development" (*Host, Guest, Enemy and Friend*, 167).

59. Billault, "Characterization," 127–28.

60. Billault, "Characterization," 128; Hägg, *Novel in Antiquity*, 53; cf. de Romilly, *Short History*, 205–6.

61. Gowler, *Host, Guest, Enemy and Friend*, 84.

62. Burnett, "Characterization," 13. Others who support Burnett's conclusion include Thompson (*Keeping the Church in Its Place*, 25) and Bauckham (*Jesus and the Eyewitnesss*, 174–75).

This more nuanced and measured understanding of character in ancient Greco-Roman literature also implies that the difference with characterization in the Hebrew Bible may not be so great.

2.3. Character in Modern Literature

Aristotle's concept of character as type and subordinate to plot has been advanced by Russian Formalists (e.g., V. Propp) and French Structuralists (e.g., A. J. Greimas), who argue that characters are merely plot functionaries. In Greimas's well-known actantial model, characters are subordinated to action, reducing them to mere actants or agents.[63] If the focus is on actions and plot, an actantial analysis may be beneficial, but for a study of characters, Greimas's approach is too reductionistic. To reduce, for example, all the Johannine characters to merely six actants will be to deny the complexity and variety of the cast of John's Gospel.[64] Seymour Chatman challenges this Aristotelian or structuralist approach to character, arguing that plot and character are equally important.[65] Similarly, Rimmon-Kenan suggests that character and plot are interdependent.[66]

Chatman carries on developing a so-called open theory of character. He disagrees that characters in fiction are mere words restricted to the text; rather, characters should be treated as autonomous beings we must try to figure out.[67] He maintains that to curb "a God-given right to infer and even to speculate about characters" would be "an impoverishment of aesthetic experience."[68] Chatman does not confuse fiction and reality: characters do not have "lives" beyond the text, but we endow them with "personality" only to the extent that they are familiar to us from real life.[69] Therefore, Chatman argues, we

63. Algirdas J. Greimas, *Sémantique structurale: Recherche de méthode* (Paris: Larousse, 1966).

64. Sheridan claims that I misread Greimas's actantial model (*Retelling Scripture*, 81 n. 151), but does not elaborate. It seems to me that Greimas's actantial model, where (by definition) characters are subordinated to the plot (rather than coordinated), produces "flattened" characters. I have used Greimas's actantial model in an earlier work (Cornelis Bennema, *The Power of Saving Wisdom: An Investigation of Spirit and Wisdom in Relation to the Soteriology of the Fourth Gospel* [WUNT II/148; Tübingen: Mohr Siebeck, 2002; repr., Eugene, OR: Wipf & Stock, 2007], 106–7), where it was useful to understand the characters' function in relation to the plot rather than to understand the characters themselves. See also Farelly's critique of Greimas's actantial model (*Disciples in the Fourth Gospel*, 166–67). For a critique of the structuralist view of character in general, see Shepherd, *Narrative Function*, 57–59.

65. Chatman, *Story and Discourse*, 108–16.

66. Rimmon-Kenan, *Narrative Fiction*, 34–36. Cf. Stephen D. Moore, *Literary Criticism and the Gospels: The Theoretical Challenge* (New Haven: Yale University Press, 1989), 15.

67. Chatman, *Story and Discourse*, 116–19. Cf. Rimmon-Kenan, *Narrative Fiction*, 33.

68. Chatman, *Story and Discourse*, 117.

reconstruct character by inferring traits from the information in the text.[70] Chatman points out two important features of trait: (i) often the trait is not explicitly named in the text but must be inferred; (ii) since readers rely upon their knowledge of the trait-name in the real world, traits are culturally coded.[71] This then leads Chatman to define character as "a paradigm of traits," in which trait is a "relatively stable or abiding personal quality."[72] Rimmon-Kenan agrees with Chatman to a great extent, but she points out that Chatman's character as "a paradigm of traits" may become too static a construct, and therefore she allows for a developmental dimension of character: "When, in the process of reconstruction, the reader reaches a point where he can no longer integrate an element within a constructed category, the implication would seem . . . that the character has changed."[73]

One of the earliest and most familiar classifications of characters in literary criticism is E. M. Forster's categories of "flat" and "round" character. Flat characters or types are built around a single trait and do not develop, whereas round characters are complex, have multiple traits, and can develop in the course of action. Forster's criterion for deciding whether a character is round or

69. Chatman, *Story and Discourse*, 137–38. Cf. Rimmon-Kenan, *Narrative Fiction*, 33; Billault, "Characterization," 115. Uri Margolin writes, "The IND [nonactual individual] is a member of some domain(s) of this possible world, and in it/them, it can be uniquely identified, located in a space/time region, and endowed with a variety of physical and mental attributes and relations, including social, locutionary, epistemic, cognitive, emotive, volitional, and perceptual. The IND may possess inner states, knowledge and belief sets, traits, intentions, wishes, dispositions, memories, and attitudes, that is, an interiority or personhood" ("Individuals in Narrative Worlds," *Poetics Today* 11 [1990]: 843–71).

70. Chatman, *Story and Discourse*, 119–20. Cf. Rimmon-Kenan, *Narrative Fiction*, 36, 59, 128–30. The reader's need to infer character-traits from the information dispersed in the text goes back to Wolfgang Iser ("The Reading Process: A Phenomenological Approach," *New Literary History* 3 [1972]: 284–85). Rimmon-Kenan contends that a gap in the text "need not entail a corresponding gap in the story" but in fact "enhances interest and curiosity, prolongs the reading process, and contributes to the reader's dynamic participation in making the text signify" (*Narrative Fiction*, 130).

71. Chatman, *Story and Discourse*, 123–25. For example, from John 13:36-38 and 18:10-11 we may infer that Peter speaks and acts before he thinks, and label this trait "impulsive" without the text ever mentioning this word. Or, if someone habitually produces an eructation after meals, we may assign the trait "impolite" whereas in some cultures this is entirely acceptable or even appreciated.

72. Chatman, *Story and Discourse*, 126. Elsewhere, Chatman defines trait more extensively as "a narrative adjective out of the vernacular labeling a personal quality of a character, as it persists over part or whole of the story" (*Story and Discourse*, 125).

73. Rimmon-Kenan, *Narrative Fiction*, 39. Although Chatman does not focus on the developing character, he does realize that a character's traits can change in that a new trait may emerge earlier or later in the course of the story, or it may disappear and be replaced by another trait (*Story and Discourse*, 126).

flat is whether it is capable of surprising the reader.[74] W. J. Harvey uses three or four categories of characters: (i) protagonists (the central characters in the narrative); (ii) intermediate figures, whom he divides into cards (characters who support and illuminate the protagonists) and ficelles (typical characters who serve certain plot functions); (iii) background characters (characters who serve a mechanical role in the plot or act as chorus).[75] Where Forster classifies characters according to traits and development, Harvey classifies them according to narrative presence or importance.[76] Thus Harvey's classification does not improve our understanding of the characters themselves but only of how active they are in the plot. If we accept Chatman's definition of character as "a paradigm of traits," Forster's "psychological" classification has scope but is still too reductionistic because not every character would neatly fit into either one of his categories.[77]

This has led some people to refine Forster's classification. Berlin, for example, uses the categories of full-fledged character (Forster's round character), type (Forster's flat character), and agent (the plot functionary), but she considers these categories as *degrees* of characterization rather than fixed categories.[78] Rimmon-Kenan draws attention to the more advanced classification of Yosef Ewen, who advocates three continua or axes upon which a character may be situated:

- *Complexity*: characters range from those displaying a single trait to those displaying a complex nexus of traits, with varying degrees of complexity in between.
- *Development*: characters range from those who show no development to those who are fully developed.
- *Penetration into the inner life*: characters range from those who are seen only from the outside (their minds remain opaque) to those whose consciousness is presented from within.[79]

74. E. M. Forster, *Aspects of the Novel* (New York: Penguin, 1976 [orig. 1927]), 73–81.

75. W. J. Harvey, *Character and the Novel* (London: Chatto & Windus, 1965), 52–73.

76. Cf. Daniel Marguerat and Yvan Bourquin, *How to Read Bible Stories: An Introduction to Narrative Criticism* (London: SCM, 1999), 60.

77. Cf. Gowler, *Host, Guest, Enemy and Friend*, 50. For a critique of Forster, see Rimmon-Kenan, *Narrative Fiction*, 40–41; Stibbe, *John as Storyteller*, 24; Tolmie, *Jesus' Farewell*, 122–23.

78. Berlin, *Poetics and Interpretation*, 23, 32. However, even Forster admits that a flat character could acquire "roundness" (*Aspects of the Novel*, 74–75, 112–13).

79. Rimmon-Kenan, *Narrative Fiction*, 41–42. Yosef Ewen's works, "The Theory of Character in Narrative Fiction," *Hasifrut* 3 (1971): 1–30 and *Character in Narrative* (Tel Aviv: Sifriyat Hapoalim, 1980), are only available in Hebrew (see Rimmon-Kenan, *Narrative Fiction*, 168).

Baruch Hochman has proposed the most comprehensive model for classifying characters to date. His classification consists of eight continua of polar opposites upon which a character may be located:

stylization	—————— naturalism
coherence	—————— incoherence
wholeness	—————— fragmentariness
literalness	—————— symbolism
complexity	—————— simplicity
transparency	—————— opacity
dynamism	—————— staticism
closure	—————— openness.[80]

Mieke Bal also suggests that we select relevant "semantic axes" on which to mark characters in order to map out the similarities and oppositions between them. However, instead of using polarized axes (e.g., an axis with the two poles "strong" and "weak"), she recommends grading axes either by degree, creating a sliding scale (very strong, reasonably strong, not strong enough, somewhat weak, weak), or by modality, creating nuance (certainly, probably, perhaps, probably not).[81]

Some biblical scholars take a similar position. Sternberg and Bar-Efrat, for example, view biblical characters as moving along a continuum rather than existing as two contingencies—flat or round.[82] While acknowledging the usefulness of Forster's "flat" and "round" categories, Malbon views them as extremes on a continuum rather than fixed categories.[83] Based on Jens Eder's work on character in film, Sönke Finnern proposes no less than ten *Gegensatzpaare* ("opposite/contrasting pairs") to analyze characters.[84] However, it is unclear whether he intends to use them as binary categories (a character is, for example, either static or dynamic) or as continua (a character can be

80. Baruch Hochman, *Character in Literature* (Ithaca, NY/London: Cornell University Press, 1985), 86–140. Gowler, for example, utilizes Hochman's model in his character study of the Pharisees in Luke–Acts, although he admits that this model is not entirely adequate to evaluate character in ancient narrative (*Host, Guest, Enemy and Friend*, 53–54, 306–17, 321, 327). Gowler also provides a helpful summary of Hochman's classification (*Host, Guest, Enemy and Friend*, 321–32). While Shepherd mentions Ewen's classification, he decides to adopt Hochman's because he seems to operate with the dictum "more is better" (*Narrative Function*, 70–71, 78). Although Conway refers to Hochman's classification, she does not utilize it herself (*Men and Women*, 58).

81. Bal, *Narratology*, 86–88.

82. Sternberg, *Poetics of Biblical Narrative*, 253–55 (cf. his chs. 9–10); Bar-Efrat, *Narrative Art*, 86–91.

83. Malbon, "Major Importance," 81 n. 6.

84. Finnern, *Narratologie*, 157–61.

positioned, for example, on a continuum that ranges from static to dynamic).[85]
Based on his extensive research on character in antiquity, Burnett concludes:

> [I]t does seem plausible that reading conventions that demanded that the reader
> infer character indirectly from words, deeds, and relationships could allow even
> for the typical character to fluctuate between type and individuality. If so, then it
> would seem wise to understand characterization, for any biblical text at least, on a
> continuum. This would imply for narratives like the Gospels that the focus should
> be on the *degree* of characterization rather than on characterization as primarily
> typical.[86]

The idea of plotting characters along a continuum or multiple continua is a
significant development, but there is no consensus on a model. In addition,
those scholars who have suggested classifying characters using multiple
categories or continua do not clarify what they will do with the results. Even
Hochman and Finnern, for example, do not indicate what we should we do
with the resulting eight or ten categories of their comprehensive models.

One last concept of character study is point of view. Any meaningful
communication, whether verbal or nonverbal, has a particular purpose, a
message that the sender wants to get across to the receiver. In line with its
purpose, a story is told or written from a particular perspective. This is called
"point of view."[87] Stephen Moore defines point of view as "the rhetorical
activity of an author as he or she attempts, from a position within some socially
shared system of assumptions and convictions, to impose a story-world upon
an audience by the manipulation of narrative perspective."[88] James Resseguie
states that "[i]t is the *mode* or *angle of vision* from which characters, dialogue,
actions, setting, and events are considered or observed. But also point of view
is the narrator's *attitude toward* or *evaluation of* characters, dialogue, actions,
setting and events."[89] We may call this *evaluative* point of view. The important
questions then are: How does the narrator communicate an ideology through

---

85. Most recently, Ruben Zimmermann employs Finnern's model to analyze "the Jews" in John's
Gospel and concludes that "[t]he binary-coded pairs pointed out by Finnern fall short in a determination
of the character conception of 'the Jews'" ("'The Jews': Unreliable Figures or Unreliable Narration?," in
Character Studies in the Fourth Gospel: Narrative Approaches to Seventy Figures in John, ed. Steven A. Hunt,
D. Francois Tolmie, and Ruben Zimmermann [WUNT 314; Tübingen: Mohr Siebeck, 2013], 107).

86. Burnett, "Characterization," 15 (original emphasis).

87. Others prefer the term *focalization* (Rimmon-Kenan, *Narrative Fiction*, 72; Bal, *Narratology*, 100;
Tolmie, *Jesus' Farewell*, 170).

88. Moore, *Literary Criticism*, 181.

point of view? What point of view does he want the reader to adopt?[90] Daniel Marguerat and Yvan Bourquin have best captured the dynamic behind point of view. They explain that since characters in a narrative offer the reader a possible form of life or existence, the narrative creates space for the reader to identify with the characters. This identification of the reader with the characters is secretly directed by the narrator. The narrator tries to influence for his own ends the interaction that occurs between the reader and the characters, counting on "a permanent mechanism of reading which is partly unconscious: the evaluation of the characters."[91] By implication, a narrative is not neutral since it has an inbuilt perspective. This perspective is communicated to the reader who can therefore also not remain neutral—he or she will either accept or reject the author's ideology.[92]

2.4. Deconstructing the Dominant Pattern/Paradigm of Character Reconstruction

Having examined aspects of character in ancient Hebrew and Greco-Roman literature as well as modern literature, we are now in a position to challenge the pattern or paradigm that scholars commonly use or assume to analyze characters in the New Testament. To recap, the pattern/paradigm of character reconstruction that we identified in Chapter 1 consists of three features: (i) characters in the Greco-Roman literature are "Aristotelian" (flat/types); (ii) characters in the Gospels and Acts are not like characters in modern narrative (round, individualistic, psychologized) but resemble Greco-Roman characters and hence are mostly flat/types; (iii) (yet) modern literary methods are used

---

89. Resseguie, *Strange Gospel*, 1 (original emphasis). Similarly, Mark Allan Powell states that point of view is "the general perspective that an implied author establishes as normative for a work" (*What Is Narrative Criticism?* [Minneapolis: Fortress Press, 1990], 53).

90. Resseguie, *Strange Gospel*, 1.

91. Marguerat and Bourquin, *Bible Stories*, 65–68 (quotation from p. 68).

92. Cf. Andrew T. Lincoln, *Truth on Trial: The Lawsuit Motif in the Fourth Gospel* (Peabody, MA: Hendrickson, 2000), 173–74; Farelly, *Disciples in the Fourth Gospel*, 9–10. Some view the concept "point of view" as more complex in that they distinguish between different kinds or levels of point of view. For example, Chatman employs perceptual point of view, conceptual point of view, and interest point of view (*Story and Discourse*, 151–53), while Boris Uspensky uses four/five levels of point of view (ideological, phraseological, spatial and temporal, psychological). For the application of Chatman and Uspensky's categories to biblical narratives, see Berlin, *Poetics and Interpretation*, 47–59. Berlin herself then continues to elaborate on the issue of multiple points of view in a narrative (*Poetics and Interpretation*, 59–82). Gary Yamasaki also explains and applies Boris Uspensky's "planes" of point of view ("Point of View in a Gospel Story: What Difference Does It Make? Luke 19:1-10 as a Test Case," *JBL* 125 [2006]: 89–105).

to analyze ancient characters. I will now seek to deconstruct this pattern or paradigm by means of four theses.

THESIS 1: THE NATURE OF CHARACTER IN ANTIQUITY AND MODERNITY IS COMPARABLE.

Regarding the nature of character, we observed that most people distinguish sharply between modern narrative and its psychological, individualistic approach to character, and ancient characterization where character lacks personality or individuality. Mary Ann Tolbert represents this position when she writes:

> Our modern textual practices often appear to be a poor "fit" for ancient or culturally distant texts. . . . [B]iblical scholars are only beginning to chart the gulf between modern Western modes of reading on the one hand and the styles used by the Greek-speaking authors of the New Testament some two thousand years ago on the other and to speculate about the differences those styles might suggest for our interpretations of the Gospels. Nowhere is this gulf between modern and ancient conventions of reading and writing more crucial than in the function and evaluation of characters. . . . Ancient characters existed as a "mouthpiece for the typical," and this usage was as true for biography as it was for drama. Ancient biographical writing was interested in the individual "as an exemplar of general, ethical qualities." Thus, one might describe ancient characterization as the practice of particularizing the universal or individualizing the general. Furthermore, it is this intentional blending of the typical with the individual that distinguishes ancient characters from both the profoundly inward, psychological, realistic characters of modern writing.[93]

In addition, within ancient literature, a common perception is that while character in the Hebrew Bible can develop and be round, character in ancient Greek literature is static or flat—largely based on Aristotle's view on character as fixed ethical types. Many biblical scholars assume that the Aristotelian view of character was representative of all ancient Greco-Roman literature and also influenced the Gospels.

Having examined aspects of character in ancient Hebrew and Greek literature, we have seen that it is impossible to maintain that Hebrew character can show development while Greek character is a static, ethical type. Our appraisal of ancient Greek literature revealed that Aristotle's analysis of character

---

93. Tolbert, "Character," 347–48.

is not necessarily representative. Instead, we have seen that from the fifth century BCE to the second century CE, whether it be classical tragedy, comedy, biography, historiography, or novel, there are notable instances of characters that can be complex, change, have inner life, and even show personality.[94] The Aristotelian notion of all character in ancient Greco-Roman literature as flat, static, and one-dimensional seems to be a caricature. Characterization in that period was more complex and varied, and capable of approaching modern notions of character at times.[95]

Petri Merenlahti makes a similar point when he examines the issue of how an agent becomes a person in biblical characterization.[96] On one hand, Merenlahti affirms the Aristotelian nature of biblical characters: "In antiquity [including the Gospels], characters had not so much 'personality' in the modern sense, as ethos—a static, unchanging set of virtues and vices."[97] On the other hand, he observes that "characters who on the atomistic level could be conceived as mere agents, plot functions, or actantial roles . . . gradually turn into more and more complex figures with genuine personality traits."[98] After further analysis, drawing especially on the work of Frank Kermode, he concludes:

> In the Gospels, characters are most often not yet quite complete. In the event of being read, some of them will increase, while others must decrease. Which way it will go, depends on how each character relates to the ideology of each Gospel and to the ideology of its readers. In this respect, biblical characters resemble living

---

94. Cf. Gowler's conclusion (*Host, Guest, Enemy and Friend*, 173). Based primarily on the work of Christopher Gill, Thompson comes to a similar conclusion, emphasizing that ancient literature often contains two categories of character portrayal—characters as typical figures and characters as individual personalities (*Keeping the Church in Its Place*, 22–25).

95. Cf. Lesky's final comment that "Greek tragedy's indirect influence on German, English and French literature, through the medium of the comedies, should not be underrated" (*Greek Tragedy*, 208). For further criticism of Aristotle's understanding of character, see Simon Goldhill, "Character and Action, Representation and Reading: Greek Tragedy and Its Critics," in *Characterization and Individuality in Greek Literature*, ed. Christopher B. R. Pelling (Oxford: Clarendon, 1990), 119–27; Christopher B. R. Pelling, "Conclusion," in *Characterization and Individuality in Greek Literature*, ed. Christopher B. R. Pelling (Oxford: Clarendon, 1990), 257–59.

96. Petri Merenlahti, "Characters in the Making: Individuality and Ideology in the Gospels," in *Characterization in the Gospels: Reconceiving Narrative Criticism*, ed. David Rhoads and Kari Syreeni (JSNTS 184; Sheffield: Sheffield Academic Press, 1999), 49–72.

97. Merenlahti, "Characters in the Making," 51.

98. Merenlahti, "Characters in the Making," 59.

organisms that mutate in order to adapt to their environments. This makes all static, comprehensive and harmonious interpretations of these characters problematic.[99]

While I disagree with Merenlahti's acceptance of the Aristotelian nature of biblical characters, I glean from his argument the important observation that most biblical characters are in "a process of learning,"[100] and hence developing.

Consequently, we can no longer maintain a sharp distinction between character in modern literary narrative and ancient literature.[101] We must, however, remain aware that characterization in ancient and modern literature is not identical but has different emphases: the ancient writers did not give character as much individual and psychological emphasis as the modern Western writers do.[102] Hence, differences in characterization in ancient and modern literature are differences in *emphases* rather than kind, and it is better to speak of *degrees* of characterization along a continuum.[103] Both ancient and modern literature portray flat and round, static and dynamic characters, although in modern narrative character is considerably more developed and "psychologized." Thus while the nature of character in antiquity and modernity is not identical, it is comparable.[104]

---

99. Merenlahti, "Characters in the Making," 71.

100. I borrow this term from Webb, *Mark at the Threshold*, 12.

101. See especially the essays in Christopher B. R. Pelling, ed., *Characterization and Individuality in Greek Literature* (Oxford: Clarendon, 1990). Bauckham reaches a similar understanding (*Jesus and the Eyewitnesses*, 174).

102. Cf. Pelling, "Childhood and Personality," 230–35; idem, "Conclusion," 247–51. See also Gowler's conclusion: "[A]ncient characters do not possess a modern (Western) introspective conscience, so their individuality and development will never approach those of characters in modern literature. Yet, character portrayals can be quite complex; persons may show development from a *character-viewpoint* (i.e., not a *personality-viewpoint*), and may also become individuals in a pre-Augustinian sense of the word" (*Host, Guest, Enemy and Friend*, 174 [original emphasis]).

103. Burnett has excellently argued this case ("Characterization," 6–15). Skinner supports Burnett's view (*John and Thomas*, 29).

104. Interestingly, although Malbon contends that Mark adheres to the convention in ancient (Greco-Roman) literature of characterization by "types," she admits that "twentieth-century readers of Mark's gospel are not, in fact, in a completely different realm from first-century hearers/readers of Mark in regard to perceiving 'typical' characters" ("Jewish Leaders," 278–79 n. 57). She refers to Baruch Hochman (*Character in Literature*, 41–47), who argues that our perception of people is typological, in both life and literature, because we tend to reduce people/characters to their essential meaning and place them in our preconceived systems. Only after that, if there are other indicators, do we view them in more unique or individual terms. I tend to agree with Hochman's observation, and we may, in subsequent rereadings of a narrative, reach "rounder" or "fuller" understandings of characters that we first perceived as "typical."

THESIS 2: THE APPLICATION OF MODERN LITERARY METHODS IS LEGITIMATE.

We are now in a position to address the issue of whether modern methods of fiction (the term many biblical scholars continue to use) can be applied to ancient biblical narratives. Before we set out, we must highlight two issues here: (i) the issue of category or genre (methods of fiction being applied to the historical narratives in the Bible); and (ii) the issue of alleged anachronism (modern methods being applied to ancient narratives). For those attuned to developments in modern literary criticism in the last half a century, it would seem that these issues are, in fact, nonissues. While modern literary methods were first developed based on the (fictional) novel, literary criticism soon broadened its scope and the now widely adopted term *narrative* encompasses a whole range of entities and realities.[105] As James Phelan writes,

> narrative theory now takes as its objects of study narrative of all kinds occurring in all kinds of media throughout history: personal, political, historical, legal, and medical narratives, to name just a few—in their ancient, medieval, early modern, modern, and postmodern guises, and in their oral, print, visual (film, sculpture, painting, performance), digital, and multi-media formats.[106]

Similarly, based on the extensive work of literary critics Northrop Frye, Robert Scholes and Robert Kellogg, Mikhail Bakhtin, structuralist Claude Lévi-Strauss, and historian Hayden White, William Shepherd delineates the important turn in literary theory from novel to narrative.[107] Shepherd argues that the commonalities of historical and fictional narratives have led both historians and literary critics to similar theories and methods, so that recent narrative theories deal with fiction and nonfiction, ancient as well as modern literature.[108] In short, "narrative has displaced the novel as the central concern of literary critics."[109]

The implication for our study may have become clear. The scope of our book is literary narrative, by which I mean those literary works that contain a story and a storyteller (see my clarification of terms in section 1.3), with a specific focus on New Testament narrative. Since literary narrative includes fiction and nonfiction, in both ancient and modern texts, the distinction

---

105. See esp. James Phelan's lengthy overview of narrative theory from 1966 to 2006 in Scholes, Phelan, and Kellogg, *Nature of Narrative*, 283–336.

106. Scholes, Phelan, and Kellogg, *Nature of Narrative*, 285.

107. Shepherd, *Narrative Function*, 44–49.

108. Shepherd, *Narrative Function*, 44.

109. Shepherd, *Narrative Function*, 49.

between novel and biblical narratives, regarding applying modern literary methods to the Bible, becomes blurred. As Stephen Moore asserts, "[T]he literary study of the Gospels and Acts, in consequence, need by no means be chained to the novel."[110] It follows that biblical narratives are a legitimate object of study in the discipline of literary criticism, and therefore Shepherd's conclusion that "[t]heories of character and characterization can appropriately be applied to biblical texts" is valid.[111]

Our findings in this chapter lead us to the same conclusion. We showed that there is reasonable evidence in ancient Hebrew and Greek literature of characters that could change, be complex, and even show personality. Therefore, character in ancient and modern literature is probably better viewed on a continuum than as distinct. I therefore contend that we can legitimately apply modern literary methods to ancient narratives as long as we take the necessary precautions. We must, for instance, be aware that by applying such methods we are fusing the modern and ancient horizon,[112] and using modern terminology to understand characters in ancient literature.

What then of the use of modern labels to name a character's traits? If we accept Chatman's definition of character as a "paradigm of traits" in which traits must be inferred from the deep structure of the text, it would be natural that the trait-names we assign are derived from what we know of real people in the real world. This means we would use contemporary language to reconstruct a character. Indeed, as Chatman argues, since the trait is not often named explicitly in the text but must be inferred, readers will usually rely upon their knowledge of the trait-name in the real world, so traits are culturally coded.[113] We must also note that the names for traits are "socially invented signs . . . Trait-names are not themselves traits."[114] Chatman states categorically that "characters as narrative constructs do require terms for description, and there is no point in rejecting those out of the general vocabulary of psychology, morality and any other relevant area of human experience."[115] This would hold true for the study of character in both modern literature and ancient narratives. It is therefore

110. Moore, *Literary Criticism*, xviii.

111. Shepherd, *Narrative Function*, 49.

112. This so-called new hermeneutic, rooted in the work of philosophers Martin Heidegger and Hans-Georg Gadamer, is developed extensively by Anthony C. Thiselton (*The Two Horizons* [Exeter, UK: Paternoster, 1980]; *New Horizons in Hermeneutics* [London: HarperCollins, 1992]).

113. Chatman, *Story and Discourse*, 123–25.

114. G. W. Allport and H. S. Odbert, *Trait-Names: A Psycholexical Study, Psychological Monographs* 47 (Princeton, 1936), 17, cited in Chatman, *Story and Discourse*, 124.

115. Chatman, *Story and Discourse*, 138.

inevitable that when we infer a character's traits from an ancient text we use trait-names that are familiar to the contemporary world.

Using modern terminology to analyze and describe characters in ancient literature is acceptable provided we remember that the terms or categories we use may be unknown to the ancient authors and audiences. Simon Goldhill, for example, points out that "[s]ince the description of character necessarily involves the mobilisation of (at least) implicit psychological models, it is unlikely that the criticism of Greek tragedy can expect wholly to avoid an engagement with psychological and psychoanalytic theory."[116] Robert Tannehill likewise defends the use of insights from modern narrative to ancient biblical narratives:

> [T]here are qualities which all narratives share and further qualities which various narratives may share, even when some make use of historical fact, if the author has a strong, creative role. Because of the importance of the novel in modern literature, qualities of narrative are often discussed in terms of the novel. With proper caution the biblical scholar can learn from this discussion.[117]

New Testament scholar Marianne Meye Thompson comments that in character reconstruction readers use their conceptions of real people (including emotional and imaginative responses) and often use language that belongs more to the realm of psychology and human development.[118]

As long as we are vigilant about the differences between a collectivist, ancient Mediterranean culture and an individualistic, modern Western culture, I maintain that it is possible to speak of an individual in antiquity without transposing a modern individualistic notion of identity onto the text. We can do so using the concept of a "collectivist identity" or "group-oriented personality," where the individual's identity is *embedded* in a larger group or community.[119] As Burnett points out, there is evidence of a move from the typical to the individual in the ancient Greek and Roman world, allowing for the reader to construct a character's individuality.[120] Similarly, Patricia Easterling notes that even though the Greeks were not interested in the

---

116. Simon Goldhill, "Modern Critical Approaches to Greek Tragedy," in *The Cambridge Companion to Greek Tragedy*, ed. Patricia E. Easterling (Cambridge: Cambridge University Press, 1997), 343.

117. Tannehill, "Disciples in Mark," 387.

118. Marianne Meye Thompson, "'God's Voice You Have Never Heard, God's Form You Have Never Seen': The Characterization of God in the Gospel of John," *Semeia* 63 (1993): 182–83.

119. Cf. Malina, *New Testament World*, 60–67.

120. Burnett, "Characterization," 11–12. Contra Tolbert, who insists on "the typological nature of all character depiction in ancient writing" ("Character," 348).

individual's unique private experience found in modern literature, they had an interest in individuals as part of a community.[121] Louise Lawrence too concludes that even the primarily collectivist Greco-Roman and Jewish cultures testify to the existence of individualistic traits.[122]

THESIS 3: THE DEVICE OF INFERENCE FOR CHARACTER RECONSTRUCTION IS INEVITABLE.

The main difficulty for developing a method of character reconstruction is that one can rarely read character from the surface of the text. Scholars have recognized that in ancient Hebrew and Greco-Roman literature characterization tends to be indirect—information about a character is conveyed primarily through the character's speech and actions rather than the narrator's statements. The reader is thus obliged to reconstruct the character from the text through *inference* or "filling in the gaps" (cf. section 2.1).[123] Developing a reading strategy for the Acts of the Apostles, Thompson stresses the need for inference in this way:

> The reader, not the text alone, decides which meaning will be realized and which possible meanings will be excluded. Since no text provides the reader with all the information or connections necessary for its realization, these textual indeterminacies or "gaps" stimulate the reader's imagination so that one fills in those gaps in ways that build a consistent reading.[124]

The practice of inference is employed in modern literature too—it is unavoidable. Seymour Chatman, for example, argues that we reconstruct character by inferring traits from the information in the text.[125] In fact, as Chatman asserts, to curb "a God-given right to infer and even to speculate

---

121. Easterling, "Character in Sophocles," 129.

122. Louise J. Lawrence, *An Ethnography of the Gospel of Matthew: A Critical Assessment of the Use of the Honour and Shame Model in New Testament Studies* (WUNT II/165; Tübingen: Mohr Siebeck, 2003), 249–59.

123. See especially Alter, *Art of Biblical Narrative*, ch. 6; Berlin, *Poetics and Interpretation*, 33–42; Sternberg, *Poetics of Biblical Narrative*, ch. 6; Bar-Efrat, *Narrative Art*, ch. 2. The reader's need to reconstruct character from the information dispersed in the text through a process of "filling in the gaps" goes back to Iser, "Reading Process," 284–85.

124. Thompson, *Keeping the Church in Its Place*, 16.

125. Chatman, *Story and Discourse*, 119–20. Cf. Rimmon-Kenan, *Narrative Fiction*, 36, 59, 128–30; Margolin, "Individuals," 847–49; Jonathan Culpeper, "Reflections on a Cognitive Stylistic Approach to Characterisation," in *Cognitive Poetics: Goals, Gains and Gaps*, ed. G. Brône and J. Vandaele (Applications of Cognitive Linguistics 10; Berlin/New York: De Gruyter, 2009), 139–49.

about characters" would be "an impoverishment of aesthetic experience."[126] Even in real life, as Bar-Efrat points out, we infer people's character both from what they say and do.[127] Thus in both ancient and modern literature, character is reconstructed from the information provided in the text. The only difference is that in ancient literature there is *less* direct characterization and readers must resort to the device of inference or gap-filling *more* than they would in modern literature.

In this process of inference, different readers may reconstruct characters differently from the same text, and while this could be a consequence of the narrative's reticence in characterization, it may also indicate that some characters are not simple, fixed, or types. Besides, even when readers reconstruct characters differently from the same text, just as scholars differ on the meaning of a text, this does not nullify the task of inference. Any interpretation involves an element of deduction because the reader-interpreter tries to make sense of the text in the absence of the author. In this process, the interpreter does not merely restate the author's *ipsissima verba* but engages in the task of understanding the meaning of the text—whether that meaning be "behind," "in," or "in front of" the text. In other words, the hermeneutical task involves a level of abstraction or aggregation—the interpreter explores the meaning of the text and this includes acts of analysis, comparison, extrapolation, inference, and so on. At the same time, rules of syntax and genre, relation to the wider text, and knowledge of the socio-cultural setting of the text provide the necessary hermeneutical parameters to control the process of interpretation. Thus while readers inevitably use inference to reconstruct characters from the text, they must do so by seeking to understand the text within its original literary and socio-cultural context (see further section 3.1).

We argued earlier that the use of modern terminology to describe characters is legitimate and inevitable (# Thesis 2). Similarly, as we reconstruct character from the text through inference, it follows that the language we use is unlikely to come from the text alone but from our knowledge of the real world and real people. As Hochman asserts, "our retrieval, or reading out, of character is guided by our consciousness of what people are and how people work. To read character adequately we must heighten our consciousness of the reciprocity between character in literature and people in life—between Homo Fictus and Homo Sapiens."[128] Stressing that we need "substantive rules of inference," Margolin suggests that these be borrowed from any real-world

---

126. Chatman, *Story and Discourse*, 117.

127. Bar-Efrat, *Narrative Art*, 89.

128. Hochman, *Character in Literature*, 59.

model of readers if the text world resembles or is at least compatible with it.[129] In essence, the language that we use to reconstruct characters is rooted in our knowledge of both the modern world and the ancient world.[130]

THESIS 4: THE CLASSIFICATION OF CHARACTERS ON A CONTINUUM IS ADVISABLE.

In the pattern or paradigm that I seek to deconstruct, ancient characters are usually classified by means of fixed categories—whether Forster's "round" and "flat" or Harvey's protagonist, card, ficelles, and background character. However, many characters in the New Testament do not fit easily into these rigid classifications, often leading to an understanding of character that is too reductionistic. Elizabeth Malbon, for example, recognizes the difficulty of putting New Testament characters into fixed categories. In her examination of Markan characters, she observes that while Mark adheres to ancient characterization by "types," he also violates this norm by constructing characters that do not fit the pattern. She suggests that "Mark offers the contrast of a typical character group and exceptional characters, who function not to 'round' out the 'flat' group but to prevent the type from becoming a stereotype."[131] In a later essay on Markan characters, Malbon admits that she has begun to see "flat" and "round" as opposite ends of a continuum.[132]

In section 2.3, we observed that a number of biblical scholars and literary critics have steered away from the idea of putting characters into fixed categories, toward an approach that views character as points along a continuum. Finding that characters in antiquity were not always typical but could fluctuate significantly, Fred Burnett concludes that "it would seem wise to understand characterization, for any biblical text at least, on a continuum. This would imply for narratives like the Gospels that the focus should be on the *degree* of characterization rather than on characterization as primarily typical."[133]

---

129. Margolin, "Individuals," 852–53.

130. I consider myself a "critical realist." On the one hand, I cannot claim to understand, for example, the Johannine characters exactly as a first-century Jewish or Greco-Roman reader would; on the other hand, my understanding of the Johannine characters is not an uncritical twenty-first-century Western reading of the text. As I carefully seek to consider the linguistic, literary, and socio-cultural aspects of the Johannine narrative, I maintain that my understanding of the Johannine characters is nevertheless a *Johannine* understanding.

131. Malbon, "Jewish Leaders," 279–80 (quotation from p. 280).

132. Malbon, "Major Importance," 81 n. 6. Tolbert also objects to using "flat" and "round" categories to classify ancient characters ("Character," 357 n. 9), but this obviously stems from her conviction that we should not apply modern literary methods to ancient narratives.

133. Burnett, "Characterization," 15 (original emphasis).

Although there is no consensus on how such a continuum should look—Ewen, for example, uses three continua, while Hochman proposes eight—the idea of positioning aspects of characters on various continua is a significant development because it circumvents the rigidity of fixed categories and the hazard of reductionism. I will return to this topic in section 3.2.

2.5. CONCLUSION

In this chapter, we examined character in ancient and modern literature, and observed that there is reasonable evidence in ancient Hebrew and Greco-Roman literature that character could, to a certain extent, be complex, change, and even show personality. Based on our findings, we presented four theses. First, the nature of character in ancient and modern literature is comparable and to be viewed as different degrees of characterization along a continuum. Second, it is therefore legitimate to apply aspects of modern literary theory to ancient literature, as long as we remain aware of the socio-cultural differences. Third, it is inevitable that we use the device of inference to reconstruct character from the text. Fourth, it is advisable to view characters on a continuum rather than fixed categories in order to avoid reductionism. I then argued that these theses essentially deconstruct a prevalent pattern or even paradigm of character reconstruction in New Testament scholarship. Even those who deny the existence of such a pattern or paradigm must admit that there is currently no comprehensive theory of character or agreed practice on how to reconstruct character from New Testament narrative. In either case, therefore, our investigation and theses provide the basis and necessary parameters for constructing a (new) paradigm for the study of New Testament character.

Before I turn to the New Testament, I return to Rohrbaugh's objection to my use of modern literary methods to study ancient characters (# Thesis 2) and the use of the device of inference, which he regards as speculative, imaginative, and oblivious of cultural differences (# Thesis 3). Should the sparse portrayal of character in ancient literature lead us to despair of reconstructing character or abandon the task altogether? No, but caution is essential. I contend that there is reasonable evidence that character in ancient Hebrew and Greek literature could be complex, change, and even show personality, suggesting that character in ancient and modern literature is better viewed on a continuum than being distinct. It would therefore be legitimate to use insights from modern narrative to study character in ancient literature. I maintain that we can apply aspects of modern literary methods to study character in ancient narratives as long as we take the necessary precautions. The interpreter must be aware, for instance, that by applying such methods she fuses the modern and ancient horizon, and uses modern terminology to understand characters in ancient literature. In the reconstruction of characters, therefore, the interpreter merges two horizons and bridges a vast cultural gap. On the one hand, I unequivocally agree with Rohrbaugh that knowledge of the social and cultural world of the New Testament is essential for understanding the personality, motive, and behavior of ancient characters. On the other hand, since ancient characterization is often indirect, we are compelled to infer aspects of character from the sparse information in the text with the assistance of modern terminology. And this is where the tension lies. I contend that the use of modern trait-names to describe ancient character must be governed by knowledge of the first-century world. This is precisely why the first aspect of my theory is the study of character in text *and context*, where the latter refers to the socio-cultural first-century environment (cf. section 3.1).[134]

In the next chapter, I will propose a (new) paradigm of character reconstruction, building on the work of, *inter alios*, Seymour Chatman, Shlomith Rimmon-Kenan, Yosef Ewen, Mieke Bal, John Darr, Fred Burnett, and Alicia Myers.

---

134. Ironically, because of his belief in the validity of cultural continuity, Malina concedes that he uses anthropological models of *contemporary* Mediterranean culture to understand cultures in the first century (*New Testament World*, xii; cf. Bruce J. Malina and Richard L. Rohrbaugh, *Social-Science Commentary on the Gospel of John* [Minneapolis: Fortress Press, 1998], 19–20). But how do we know that nothing has fundamentally changed in the last two millennia or the extent to which modern Spanish and Italian societies are comparable to first-century Palestinian society? I dare ask, then: Who engages in anachronism? Although elsewhere Richard Rohrbaugh addresses the issue of extending sociological models diachronically (e.g., he uses the concept of sacred space in relation to the temple before and after 70 CE), he only refers to a time continuum of fifty years ("Models and Muddles: Discussions of the Social Facets Seminar," *Forum* 3, no. 2 [1987]: 28–30). Of course, at higher levels of abstraction one can always find correspondence—sacred space, purity, honor/shame, and so forth exist in every culture and time—but the question is whether we can assume, for example, that the purity system in modern Italy is an appropriate model for that in first-century Palestine.

3

A Theory of Character in New Testament Narrative
Constructing a New Paradigm

In Chapter 1, we identified a minimum pattern or paradigm of character reconstruction in New Testament studies. In Chapter 2, based on an examination of the nature of character and the method of reconstructing character in ancient and modern literature, we dismantled this dominant pattern or paradigm. In the present chapter, I will proceed to the third step and propose a comprehensive, nonreductionist theory for studying character in New Testament narrative.

Besides the reasons stated in Chapter 2, there are also intrinsic reasons why most of the characters in the New Testament do not fit the dominant pattern or paradigm. The prevailing Aristotelian view of character as subordinate or secondary to action and plot is difficult to uphold for the narrative material in the New Testament because what the characters say is equally important to what they do. The Gospel of John, for example, seems a character-centered narrative where the characters' speeches often overshadow the events. Besides, if the consensus view is that the Gospels as a genre most closely resemble Greco-Roman biography in form and content, it has implications for the understanding of character in the Gospels.[1] For example, Burridge argues that, as in Greco-Roman βίοι, characterization in the Gospels is achieved primarily

---

1. While Burridge has argued most forcefully for viewing the Gospels as βίοι (*What Are the Gospels?*; see ch. 2, n. 2 for other supporters), the Gospels may also contain elements of Hebrew biblical narrative and Greek drama. Regarding the Gospel of John, for example, while Stibbe agrees that its form is that of the βίος, he suggests a more comprehensive account of its genre, including elements of Hebrew narrative and Greek comedy, romance, satire, and tragedy (*John as Storyteller*, ch. 2; *John's Gospel*, ch. 3 [but see Burridge's reply in *What Are the Gospels?*, 280]). Others attempt to understand John's Gospel against the backdrop of classical Greek tragedy (Brant, *Dialogue and Drama*, *passim*; Koester, *Symbolism*, 36–38).

through the indirect means of narrating the subject's words and deeds, and while characterization is often (stereo)typical, a more "real" picture of the characters emerges through the narratives themselves.[2] Nevertheless, many scholars view the characters in the Gospels in terms of a representative response to Jesus, effectively reducing them to types. I will argue, however, that a typical or representative belief-response need not reduce the character to a type, and that while some characters are indeed types, many others are complex, developing, and round.

In the remainder of the chapter, I will propose a (new) paradigm for character reconstruction in the New Testament that consists of three aspects or components. First, I study character in text and context. Second, I analyze and classify the characters along Ewen's three dimensions (complexity, development, inner life), and plot the resulting character on a continuum of degree of characterization (from agent to type to personality to individuality). Third, I evaluate the characters in relation to (i) the author's ideological point of view and (ii) the plot, after which I will seek to determine the characters' contemporary significance.

3.1. Character in Text and Context

We observed in the previous chapter that since ancient characterization is often indirect, we must infer aspects of character from the sparse information in the text and must often resort to modern terminology. This method can be problematic because character reconstruction through "filling the gaps" has the inherent tendency to be speculative, fanciful, and ignore cultural differences. I suggested that while the use of modern trait-names to identify the traits of ancient character is inevitable, it must be governed by knowledge of the first-century world. Knowledge of the social and cultural environment of the New Testament is essential for understanding the personality, motive, and behavior of ancient characters. This is why the first aspect of my theory is the study of character in text and context.

We must specifically address two issues. First, although we have argued in the previous chapter that insights from literary methods of narrative can be applied to parts of the Bible, we must clarify the nature of the narrative material in the New Testament and the implications for our approach to character. How would reading the narratives in the Gospels as fiction, nonfiction, or even a

---

2. Burridge, *What Are the Gospels?*, 205–6, 211–12, 222–23, 227. Although Burridge only examines Jesus, I have shown in my *Encountering Jesus* that a more "real" character also comes through in John's portraits of other characters, such as Peter, Pilate, Judas, the Samaritan woman, and the man born blind.

mixture of both, impinge on the reconstruction of character? For example, does it matter, for the reconstruction of his character, whether Nicodemus was a historical person or a fictitious character? Second, we must determine the kind of reader we are supposing and the sources that this reader has access to. How would a reader of John's Gospel reconstruct the character of Pilate if she also knew of other portrayals of Pilate from sources such as Mark's Gospel, Josephus, or Philo? To these issues we now turn.

The Nonfictional Nature of the New Testament and the Implication for Characterization

The truism "there are no characters without a text" indicates that characters are limited to the world of the text, and the interpreter's character reconstruction is based solely on the information in the text. I suggest that this is not an accurate deduction. While narrative critics tend to limit themselves to the text, I will argue for the need to go occasionally *beyond* the text for the reconstruction of character. On the one hand, characters do not have "lives" beyond the text and hence we reconstruct character from the information in the text. When it comes to the New Testament narrative material, the authors primarily employ indirect characterization, so we must infer character from the character's speech and actions, and what other characters say about that character, rather than the narrator's speech.[3] On the other hand, many scholars regard the narrative material of the New Testament as nonfictional in nature and as referring to real events and people in history. This means we can fill the gaps in the narrative from our knowledge of the socio-historical context of the first-century Mediterranean world (rather than our imagination). I will demonstrate this argument using the Gospel of John, and then show that we can do the same with the Gospel of Mark and the Acts of the Apostles.

John's Gospel claims to be a nonfictional narrative by a reliable eyewitness to the events recorded (19:35; 21:24). By implication, the *dramatis personae* are composites of historical people and must be viewed within the socio-historical context of first-century Judaism and not just on the basis of the text itself. This demands that we also look at sources outside John's Gospel that can assist us in reconstructing the Johannine characters. This historical data available to us from other sources will often supplement the data that the text provides about a character. Frank Kermode has said that in constructing character we (should) augment the text "by inferring from the repertoire of indices characteristics not immediately signalled in the text, but familiar from other texts and from life."[4]

---

3. Occasionally the author provides direct characterization. For example, the narrator's information about Judas's betrayal of Jesus and being a thief in John 12:4, 6 reveals traits of disloyalty and dishonesty.

Marianne Meye Thompson argues similarly: "'Actual readers' of the gospels may well have access to the characters in the narrative in other ways, whether through oral or written tradition, and these other 'narratives' surely influence the way they read."[5]

In comparing fictional and nonfictional narratives, Petri Merenlahti and Raimo Hakola state that in case of the latter, (i) the author vouches for the veracity of the narrative and assumes that the reader believes it; and (ii) the narrator represents the author and his point of view and therefore there is continuity between "reality" and the narrative world.[6] Indeed, John (or a later editor speaking for the author) explicitly states that his story is true and therefore can be believed (19:35; 21:24), and since there is no real distinction between the author and narrator in John's Gospel, the narrator reliably represents the author's voice and view.[7] Merenlahti and Hakola then clarify why nonfictional narratives must be seen *in context*:

> Because a non-fictional narrative claims to refer to events and circumstances of the "real" world, it is natural that the readers try to fill any gaps the narrative may have, making use of all available information about the events and circumstances in concern. What readers of a non-fictional narrative think of a character depends not only on what the narrator reveals but also on what else the readers may know about the person who is portrayed as a character in the narrative. . . . The natural way to read a Gospel would be to make connections between character groups of the story and the "real" groups which those characters intend to portray. . . . An "intrinsic," text-centered approach does not seem to match properly the nature of the Gospels as non-fictional narratives.[8]

These arguments can be readily applied to John's Gospel. One cannot simply assume, for example, that "the Jews" in John's Gospel are a homogeneous

---

4. Frank Kermode, *The Genesis of Secrecy: On the Interpretation of Narrative* (Cambridge, MA: Harvard University Press, 1979), 78. Based on Kermode's observation, Darr insists on taking into account "extratextual" factors (*On Character Building*, 48).

5. Thompson, "God's Voice," 181.

6. Petri Merenlahti and Raimo Hakola, "Reconceiving Narrative Criticism," in *Characterization in the Gospels: Reconceiving Narrative Criticism*, ed. David Rhoads and Kari Syreeni (JSNTS 184; Sheffield: Sheffield Academic Press, 1999), 35–38.

7. Cf. Culpepper, *Anatomy of the Fourth Gospel*, 42–43. Jeffrey L. Staley, however, argues that the Johannine narrator is not consistently reliable, resulting in the entrapment or victimization of the reader (*The Print's First Kiss: A Rhetorical Investigation of the Implied Reader in the Fourth Gospel* [SBLDS 82; Atlanta: Scholars, 1988]), but his case has not won much support.

8. Merenlahti and Hakola, "Narrative Criticism," 40–43.

group—either in composition or in their response to Jesus. Therefore, it is essential to study the "referent" of "the Jews," which means studying the identity and composition of "the Jews" as real people during the time of Jesus or the author.[9] For the character of Pilate, we would have to examine the works of Josephus and Philo since many scholars contend that these sources portray Pilate differently from John's Gospel. We would probably also look at the Markan portrayal of Pilate since a good case can be made that John knew Mark's Gospel and assumed that his audience was familiar with Mark.[10] This invites a comparison of how the various sources portray Pilate, but we must be careful that the character we reconstruct is in keeping with the particular perspective of the author. For example, John may have characterized Pilate in a particular way for a particular purpose, and if we reconstruct a Pilate by adding aspects from other sources such as Mark, Josephus, and Philo, the resulting Pilate may no longer be a "Johannine" Pilate. I will return to this issue shortly.

At the same time, in presenting his characters, John may have left out, changed, or added certain details from his sources—as historians and biographers often do. For example, John (the Baptist) appears in this Gospel as an eloquent witness to Jesus while the Synoptics present him as a rough-hewn figure preaching a baptism of repentance. The Beloved Disciple may well have been as perfect as this Gospel portrays him or could have been somewhat "idealized." If the Gospels belong to the genre of the ancient Greco-Roman biography, as many scholars contend today, they need not be viewed as "objective, factual" accounts akin to courtroom transcripts.[11] The Gospels would be expected to represent accurately the *ipsissima vox* rather than the *ipsissima verba Jesu*, and the speech of characters would often be paraphrases rather than the literal words. While the Gospel authors may have exercised this literary freedom, what matters is that the reader need not doubt their credibility; they would not have created fictitious characters. As Merenlahti and Hakola explain, while

---

9. I have undertaken this study elsewhere, arguing that the referent of "the Jews" *cannot* be resolved entirely narratologically (Cornelis Bennema, "The Identity and Composition of οἱ Ἰουδαῖοι in the Gospel of John," *TynBul* 60 [2009]: 239–63).

10. Cf. Richard Bauckham, "John for Readers of Mark," in *The Gospels for All Christians: Rethinking the Gospel Audiences*, ed. Richard Bauckham (Grand Rapids: Eerdmans, 1998), 147–71; Anderson, *Riddles of the Fourth Gospel*, 126–29. In my analysis of the Johannine Pilate elsewhere in this volume, I shall therefore also refer to the Markan Pilate. Rather than reading the Johannine Pilate through a Markan lens, I will simply assume that John knew Mark's characterization of Pilate and either confirms or augments his portrayal.

11. Cf. Lincoln, *Truth on Trial*, 369–97. He argues that John's Gospel belongs to the genre of the Greco-Roman βίος, where the purpose is to draw out the significance and interpretation of historical events, so John's Gospel need not necessarily be historically accurate in all its detail.

not everything in non-fictional narratives is necessarily historical, it does not make them fictional narratives since they do claim to describe the real world; what matters is that the reader not doubt the author's explicit or implicit truth claims.[12] Thus, the historicity of the characters in John's Gospel does not exclude the possibility that John used a legitimate degree of artistic freedom to portray them. Besides, the Gospel authors were theologians (rather than historians in a strict sense of the word). They wrote from a post-Easter perspective and interpreted the pre-Easter events with a specific agenda in mind, that is, they reflected on the Christ event and articulated its significance and implications for the early church. The primary concern of John is to assure his readers that his account of Jesus is a true and reliable testimony (cf. 19:35; 21:24).

Scholars have argued similarly for Mark's Gospel and the Acts of the Apostles. Kelly Iverson writes, "The social, historical, and cultural context of the first-century Mediterranean world is important for understanding the narrative of Mark's Gospel. Although the narrative depicted in Mark's Gospel will be the primary focus of study, I do not regard it as an autonomous story world that can be known in isolation from its socio-cultural context."[13] Regarding the Acts of the Apostles, John Darr asserts that a text is not seamless but "full of gaps, indeterminacies, tensions, inconsistencies, and ambiguities" and hence the reader seeks to "build a consistent, coherent narrative world" by piecing together textual and extratextual information.[14] Similarly, David Gowler proposes a "socio-narratological approach" to biblical narratives, where "a dialogue is necessary between literary analyses and analyses of the cultural contexts in which the narratives were created. A symbiotic relationship exists, for example, between characterization in a narrative and the narrative's cultural context; the cultural scripts inherent in any text are an important form of implicit communication between the implied reader and the implied author."[15]

This is an important shift in narrative criticism. Too often, narrative critics restrict themselves to the text of the Gospels and the narrative world these evoke, effectively reading the Gospels as fictional narratives that are

---

12. Merenlahti and Hakola, "Narrative Criticism," 38. Sternberg argues similarly for the Hebrew bible as historiography: "history-writing is not a record of fact—of what 'really happened'—but a discourse that claims to be a record of fact. Nor is fiction-writing a tissue of free inventions but a discourse that claims freedom of invention. The antithesis lies not in the presence or absence of truth value but of the commitment to truth value" (*Poetics of Biblical Narrative*, 24–35 [quotation taken from p. 25]).

13. Iverson, *Gentiles*, 4.

14. Darr, "Narrator as Character," 50–51. For a detailed account of John A. Darr's extratextual approach, see *On Character Building*, ch. 1 and *Herod the Fox: Audience Criticism and Lukan Characterization* (JSNTS 163; Sheffield: Sheffield Academic Press, 1998), 89–91.

15. Gowler, *Host, Guest, Enemy and Friend*, 9.

disconnected from reality.[16] Instead, we need a form of *historical narrative criticism* that takes a text-centered approach but examines aspects of the world outside or "behind" the text if the text invites us to do so.[17] In other words, we should reconstruct the characters from the information that the text of the Gospels provides *and* supplement it with relevant information from other sources.[18] Besides, since character is often inferred from the text, exegesis is the obvious and primary means for character reconstruction. However, it is not always clear which sources we can use to supplement the primary text for character reconstruction, so let us examine this issue next.

THE NATURE OF THE READER AND HIS SOURCES

In Chapter 1, I drew attention to John Lyons's essay on the Johannine character of Joseph of Arimathea (see ch. 1, n. 96). In his essay, he challenges how I use the sources (mainly the Synoptics and John) to reconstruct the identity of the Johannine Joseph of Arimathea. He argues that my use of multiple sources results in a composite Joseph of Arimathea that is more like a "historical" Joseph (i.e., a Joseph reconstructed by historical criticism) than a Johannine one. Instead, he presents two possible readings—one where the implied reader only has access to John's Gospel and another where the reader also knows Mark's Gospel. I concede Lyons's point. Consequently, we must consider (i) the kind of reader we suppose; (ii) the sources such reader has access to; and (iii) how these sources should be used in character reconstruction.[19] To facilitate the discussion, I will use the reconstruction of Pilate as an example because we have multiple

16. Although James Resseguie presents a more "mature" form of narrative criticism, stating that the narrative critic should be familiar with the cultural, linguistic, social, and historical assumptions of the audience envisioned by the implied author, he nevertheless contends that this information must be obtained *from the text itself* rather than from outside the text (*Narrative Criticism*, 32, 39).

17. Almost twenty years after *Narrative Fiction* was first published, Rimmon-Kenan points to new forms of narratology, including a cultural and historical narratology that is context-orientated, and historical and diachronous in orientation (*Narrative Fiction*, 140–42). Cf. Finnern, who labels it "postclassic narratology" (*Narratologie*, 35–36).

18. Mark Stibbe also asserts that "characters in the gospels need to be analyzed with reference to history, and not according to the laws of fiction" (*John as Storyteller*, 24). Martinus C. de Boer provides the best defense for a combined historical and narratological approach to John's Gospel ("Narrative Criticism, Historical Criticism, and the Gospel of John," *JSNT* 47 [1992]: 35–48). I do not go as far as Raymond E. Brown, who identifies seven historical groups of people behind the representative figures in the Gospel of John (*The Community of the Beloved Disciple* [New York: Paulist, 1979], 59–91).

19. This section does not deal with the role of the reader; for this, see the work of Northrop Frye, Wayne Booth, Wolfgang Iser, Seymour Chatman, Stanley Fish, Kevin Vanhoozer, and Robert Fowler. It is, however, well established that in the reading process, readers create or reconstruct character from the

sources (e.g., Mark, John, Josephus, Philo), and their portrayals of Pilate appear to vary greatly.

We can employ various kinds of reader to reconstruct characters from the text. Narrative criticism *pur sang* uses the concept of *implied reader*, whose knowledge is necessarily restricted by the world of the text because the implied reader itself is a construct of the text. However, since the implied reader is also a construct of the real reader, probably leaning toward an implied reader in the real reader's own image, by implication there are as many implied readers as there are actual readers. Alternatively, we could use the concept of *intended reader*, that is, the kind of reader that the real author had in mind when he wrote his narrative. However, it is debatable how much we can know of the real author, how accurately we can determine the intended reader, and how much such a reader knew. Regarding John's Gospel, for example, should we assume a first-century reader who is only familiar with the Johannine narrative or one who also knows the Markan one? Is it perhaps better to employ a *modern reader*, one who has access to all ancient sources? However, as Lyons argues, a modern reader's piecing together of a character from all available sources may simply correspond to what historians do and create, namely a "historical" Pilate rather than a Markan or Johannine one. While it is clear *that* the choice of reader will affect the reconstruction of characters, *how* it does so is unclear. Additionally, if we find contradictory information about a character in multiple sources, would it be legitimate to reconcile or synthesize them?

John Darr recognizes that the reader one postulates determines at least in part how characters are reconstructed. On the one hand, Darr admits that literary critics likely create readers in their own image, that is, the reader is usually a heuristic construct of the modern critic. On the other hand, he also values the reconstruction of a text-specific reader, that is, an approximation of the intended reader with a degree of knowledge of the socio-cultural conventions assumed by the original author. Darr's reader, then, is *a heuristic hybrid*, a fusion of ancient and modern cultural horizons.[20]

In line with Darr's hybrid reader, I propose a *plausible historically informed modern reader*. I will explain in two stages. First, by a *plausible historically informed* reader I mean a reader who has (i) a good (but not exhaustive) knowledge of the first-century Jewish and Greco-Roman world in which the New Testament documents were produced; and (ii) whose knowledge of a particular character

---

text. The issue here is the kind of reader we should suppose when we study character in New Testament narrative.

20. Darr, "Narrator as Character," 47–48.

comes primarily from the narrative he is reading but possibly also from other sources. In other words, I work with a first-century reader who reconstructs a character primarily from the text she is reading but who is also well informed about the socio-cultural world beyond the text. This could include information from other sources that might help in the reconstruction of that particular character. How such a reader would look depends, of course, on the particular narrative that is being read. Regarding the Gospel sources, for example, let us assume that someone works with both the Farrer-Goulder hypothesis (Mark was written first, Matthew used Mark, and Luke used both Mark and Matthew) and the hypothesis that John wrote for readers of Mark.[21] In that case, the following readers emerge: a reader of the Markan narrative knows the Old Testament and has informed knowledge of the first-century Jewish and Greco-Roman world; a reader of the Johannine narrative also knows the Markan narrative; a reader of the Acts of the Apostles knows the Gospel of Luke as well as the Gospels of Mark and Matthew. Finally, we must remember that since the modern critic does not have exhaustive or perfect knowledge of either the world of the ancient narrative or the author's intentions, the critic can only *approximate* this first-century reader, hence the use of "plausible" as a qualifier.

Nevertheless, even if the historically informed reader were a useful construct, problems remain with how we determine *what* sources were available to such a reader and *how* he would use them for character reconstruction. Applying Lyons's argument to the reconstruction of Pilate, the reader's amalgamation of information from all available sources would merely create a *historical* rather than, for example, a *Johannine* Pilate. Perhaps it is sufficient to acknowledge that the four portrayals of Pilate (those in Mark, John, Josephus, and Philo) are all valid first-century portrayals. Besides, what precisely is a "Johannine" Pilate? Depending again on the sources we assume the reader has access to, Pilate could be reconstructed solely from the Johannine text, from the Johannine and Markan texts, or from the Johannine, Markan, Josephian, and Philonic texts. So, we already have three possible readers and three possible Johannine Pilates. We can complicate the issue further. If we assume that John's audience was familiar with Mark's Gospel, the reader can reconstruct either a Johannine-Markan or hybrid Pilate (where the Johannine and Markan accounts carry equal weight) or a Johannine Pilate informed by the Markan one (the Markan account simply supports the Johannine account). I suggest that the

---

21. The best defense for the Farrer-Goulder hypothesis is provided by Mark Goodacre, *The Synoptic Problem: A Way through the Maze* (New York: T. & T. Clark, 2001). For the case that John wrote for readers of Mark, see the work of Richard Bauckham and Paul Anderson mentioned in n. 10, above.

safest route to reconstruct a *Johannine* Pilate is to prioritize the information in the Johannine text and then compare the resulting character with portraits of Pilate in other narratives. We can then consider whether the Johannine Pilate affirms, enhances, supersedes, corrects, or subverts, for example, the Markan Pilate. So, instead of reading the Johannine account of Pilate through a Markan lens, I would simply assume that the reader is familiar with the Markan Pilate and seeks to discern whether the Johannine Pilate confirms or augments the Markan one. The issue of who is the "real" or "historical" Pilate and the extent to which each portrayal contributes and corresponds to the whole is another task, one we can delegate to historians.[22]

I now turn to the second descriptor for my proposed reader, namely the *modern* reader. We can no longer know for certain how a first-century reader would have read a first-century New Testament narrative. Reading an ancient narrative today necessarily implies a fusion of ancient and modern horizons. Thus while the modern reader must be sensitive to the socio-historical realities of the ancient narrative, he remains a *modern* reader nonetheless. It must be obvious that the knowledgeable first-century reader I speak of is me. That is, *I* construct and am this plausible historically informed reader. I create this reader through the particular choices I make—I decide what sources I use and how much knowledge I need about the socio-cultural world "behind" the narrative—and subsequently, I read the ancient narrative as this constructed reader. Hence, the critic's construction of a plausible historically informed reader is not entirely an objective exercise because I am this particular reader.

I will briefly discuss two dialogical features arising from the modern reader's attempt to be a historically informed reader: (i) the effect of the modern reader bringing his world to an ancient narrative; and vice versa (ii) the effect of the ancient narrative world on the modern reader. Inevitably, the modern critic will bring aspects of himself and his world to the construction of his reader but precisely how this affects the reading process and the reconstruction of character is still unclear. How will issues such as gender, ethnic identity, social class, geographical and cultural location, and life experiences affect the reading of a text? How, for instance, will the reconstruction of the Samaritan woman in John 4 be affected if the reader is a male, white, educated American living in Boston, over against an uneducated Hispanic in San Diego, or, to be more extreme, a Tutsi woman from Rwanda living in a Ugandan refugee camp? It is difficult to say except there will be three very different readings

---

22. See, for example, the excellent work by Helen K. Bond (*Pontius Pilate in History and Interpretation* [SNTSMS 100; Cambridge: Cambridge University Press, 1998]).

and hence character portrayals. Besides, the task of reconstructing characters is open-ended, for there is no definitive way of reading characters. Added to the fact that different readers will reconstruct characters differently, readers themselves may develop in their thinking and approaches, in turn, affecting their reconstruction of characters. As Geoff Webb states, "Characters . . . remain unfinalisable in the sense that each reading and re-reading of the text will 'shape' the character in new and unforeseen ways."[23] While this does not imply that each reading produces an entirely new or different reconstruction of character, it does allow for changes or adaptations.

At the same time, the modern reader infers from the ancient story world meaning for his own world. Just as the reader enters the story world (the world "of" the text) as faithfully as possible, being informed by the original socio-historical setting (the world "behind" the text), so the characters in the story enter the world of the reader (the world "in front of" the text).[24] In which case, it is reasonable and legitimate that the reader uses tools available to him to interpret these characters further, for example, by placing a modern grid on the ancient narrative. Hence, in section 3.2, I will suggest modern categories of character analysis and classification to add a meta-layer of information about ancient character. In doing so, I do not suggest that ancient readers would have read the narrative this way, but that this is a valid and fruitful way for the modern reader to examine ancient characters.

This somewhat extended explanation of the nature of the reader and his sources may not resolve all the issues raised. While I have clarified the kind of reader we may assume, I cannot determine with certainty the written sources such a reader has access to. Whether a plausible historically informed modern reader has access to all sources or only a limited number of sources are perhaps both legitimate assumptions. One source that the New Testament authors would automatically assume their readers had access to is, of course, the Hebrew Bible or Old Testament. To return to Lyons's argument, he considers a reading where the implied reader only has access to John's Gospel and another reading where the implied reader also knows Mark's Gospel as equally valid readings. Similarly, I might consider another equally valid reading, namely one where the Johannine reader has access to the three Synoptic Gospels and Acts. In short, *perhaps all an interpreter must do is to give a plausible explanation for the ancient sources he presumes his reader has access to.*

23. Webb, *Mark at the Threshold*, 10.

24. Cf. Malbon, "Characters in Mark's Story," 58; Dorothy A. Lee, "Martha and Mary: Levels of Characterization in Luke and John," in *Characters and Characterization in the Gospel of John*, ed. Christopher W. Skinner (LNTS 461; New York: T. & T. Clark, 2013), 214.

Bringing it all together, I suggest the following process for the character reconstruction of the Johannine Pilate: (i) clarify the sources that John might have assumed for his original audience; (ii) reconstruct the character of Pilate from the information in the Johannine text; (iii) simultaneously, use information from the assumed sources and the first-century world to fill the gaps in the Johannine narrative (e.g., knowledge of Roman trial procedures may indicate that the scourging in John 19:1 is judicial not punitive in nature);[25] (iv) compare the Johannine Pilate with those from other sources that were available in John's time (whether or not assumed by John) (e.g., Mark, Josephus, and Philo). The result will be a Johannine Pilate who fits realistically into the first-century world but is nevertheless a Pilate viewed from a particular perspective, one who can be compared to other portrayals of Pilate.[26]

3.2. Character Analysis and Classification

The second aspect of my theory for character reconstruction involves the analysis and classification of character. Using a systematic and uniform approach to reconstruct characters enables us to look at characters consistently through the same lenses and thus compare the various characters—both within a narrative and across narratives. In this section, I will propose using the nonreductionist model of Yosef Ewen to analyze the New Testament characters. Based on this character analysis, we can classify the characters on a resulting continuum that indicates their degree of characterization. First, however, I briefly recap part of section 2.3 to show how and why we have arrived at Ewen's classification.

The classification of characters into the categories of "flat" and "round," introduced by Forster in 1927, is probably the most well known in literary criticism, and is still widely used in biblical studies. Also familiar are Harvey's categories of protagonists, cards, ficelles, and background characters. We found Harvey's classification unsuitable for our study because his grouping of characters according to narrative presence or importance does not improve our understanding of the characters themselves. Forster's psychologically oriented classification, though rudimentary, at least focuses on the characters' traits and

---

25. So Jennifer A. Glancy, "Torture: Flesh, Truth, and the Fourth Gospel," *BibInt* 13 (2005): 107–36.

26. Although this goes beyond the scope of this book, I contend that more can be gained if we engage with the recent discipline of relevance theory. Based on the referential theory of H. P. Grice and speech act theory, relevance theory examines the process of communication in order to understand how a listener or reader cognitively processes a narrative. For the application of relevance theory to biblical interpretation, see Stephen W. Pattemore, *The People of God in the Apocalypse: Discourse, Structure, and Exegesis* (SNTSMS 128; Cambridge: Cambridge University Press, 2005), ch. 2.

development. However, his classification is too reductionistic, and many New Testament characters do not fit neatly into either of his categories.[27] This has prompted scholars such as Berlin, Sternberg, Bar-Efrat, Bal, and Burnett to view characters not in fixed categories but on a continuum. This new approach of focusing on the degree of characterization has potential for the study of character in New Testament narrative because it is less reductionistic and rigid. However, while the analysis and classification of characters as points along a continuum or multiple continua is a significant development, the question of how such a model should look has not been resolved. I highlighted Yosef Ewen's sophisticated, nonreductionist classification of character where he delineates three continua upon which a character may be situated. I suggest that his model of character analysis has the potential to be applied to New Testament narrative albeit with some clarifications and modifications.[28] I also suggest that a character analysis based on Ewen's model must be supplemented with an aggregated continuum that compiles the results of individual continua to indicate the character's total degree of characterization.

CHARACTER ANALYSIS: THE CONTINUUM OF COMPLEXITY

The continuum of complexity ranges, according to Ewen, from characters with a single trait to those who have multiple traits, with varying degrees of complexity in between. Traits include the cognitive, behavioral, and emotional qualities of a character. According to Chatman, trait is a "relatively stable or abiding quality."[29] Character traits are revealed by "showing" and "telling," that is, they are surmised from the character's interaction with other characters and from the information mentioned by the narrator.[30] Stephen Smith, for example, provides an example based on the Gospel of Mark. The author can

27. Lehtipuu contends that Forster's distinction of round and flat characters is based on psychological criteria, which cannot be applied to the Gospels as they are apsychological, plot-centered narratives (over against psychological, character-centered narratives) ("Characterization and Persuasion," 79; cf. Tolbert, "Character," 348–49). However, the Gospel of John, for example, seems a character-centered narrative—the characters' speeches greatly outweigh the events—and we cannot simply subordinate the characters to the Gospel's plot.

28. While the models of Hochman and Finnern consist of eight and ten categories or continua respectively, and Ewen only three, more is not necessarily better. In my view, the models of Hochman and Finnern are unnecessarily complex and the results of a character analysis on eight or ten continua cannot easily be aggregated on a resulting continuum, which is what I seek to do with my character analysis according to Ewen's model at the end of this section.

29. Chatman, *Story and Discourse*, 126.

30. Cf. Wayne Booth, *The Rhetoric of Fiction*, 2nd ed. (Chicago: University of Chicago Press, 1983), 3–9; Resseguie, *Narrative Criticism*, 126–28.

communicate a character's trait either directly ("telling") through the narrator or character, or indirectly ("showing") through a particular action (Jesus' action in the temple in Mark 11:15 reveals traits such as a sense of justice and religious sincerity), a character's speech (James and John's request in Mark 10:37 shows misunderstanding), the description of a character's physical appearance (Jesus' metamorphosis in Mark 9:2-3 may reveal that he is "god-like"), or the description of the environment or setting (Jesus' being "in the house" in Mark 7:17; 9:33; 10:10 shows intimacy).[31] As we observed in the previous chapter, we must infer a character's traits from the text and we often have to resort to modern trait-names. Besides, this hermeneutical process of inference is not without difficulties and we must remain aware of using modern categories to identify features of ancient character.

An additional difficulty is the issue of what constitutes a trait. For example, if a character shows a particular quality only once, does that constitute a trait? If not, then how often does a certain feature need to occur before we can call it an "abiding personal quality" or trait? Smith asserts that a character trait is not established by the mere disclosure of some act or thought or reaction but by what we learn throughout the narrative as a whole.[32] Nevertheless, while certain personal qualities or behavioral features of a character may recur in the narrative, others occur just once and one could question whether these constitute a trait. What if a character only has limited appearances in the narrative and has little or no opportunity to show certain characteristics again? I would suggest that a character trait can be established by different means. Sometimes a character may show a particular feature once but, within the theological framework of the narrative, this feature may be significant and therefore identified as a trait. For example, in the Gospel of Mark, although it is only mentioned once that Peter's mother-in-law serves Jesus and some of his disciples (1:31), in the light of Mark's emphasis on service in the rest of his Gospel (9:33-37; 10:45; 15:40-41), it would be safe to suggest that her service, in response to Jesus' miracle, is not a random action but constitutes an inherent quality—a trait. At other times, a trait can be mentioned explicitly as well as implied. Take the Johannine Judas. For example, he betrays Jesus just once, so one could refute that this constitutes a trait. Nevertheless, it probably does because the narrator keeps referring to it.[33] Besides, Judas's dishonesty in his role as the treasurer of the group (he is characterized as a habitual thief) implies a regular betrayal of the other disciples' trust. Thus betrayal is a recurring

---

31. Smith, *Lion with Wings*, 53–54.

32. Smith, *Lion with Wings*, 55.

33. I thank Steven Hunt for this insight.

trait of Judas, but expressed in different ways. Based on Rimmon-Kenan, who also states that a character trait can be established by various means,[34] Smith contends, for example, that the impetuous nature of the brothers James and John in the Gospel of Mark can be inferred from both their name Boanerges, "sons of thunder" (Mark 3:17), and their speech/actions (Mark 9:38; 10:35-41).[35] Despite these considerations, there will undoubtedly be disagreement among scholars over when or whether a particular feature constitutes a trait.

Contra the majority view, much of the New Testament narrative material shows a remarkably broad spectrum of complex characters. In the Gospel of Mark, although many of the so-called minor characters, that is, those characters that only feature in a single episode in the Markan story, demonstrate one aspect of discipleship, it does not mean that they have no other traits. In fact, I have argued elsewhere that even though Mark primarily uses the minor characters to show positive responses to Jesus and to reveal various aspects of discipleship, they are not necessarily types or flat.[36] While Peter's mother-in-law only embodies service and hence is a type, minor characters like the woman with chronic haemorrhages, Jairus, the Syrophoenician woman, and Bartimaeus exhibit multiple traits, such as showing initiative, persistence, courage, insight, and faith. Beyond the minor characters, Peter is probably the most complex, multi-trait character in Mark.

Examples of Johannine characters with a single trait are Andrew (he finds people and brings them to Jesus) and Nathanael (he is skeptical but responsive). Others have a dominant trait combined with secondary traits, like John (the Baptist) whose primary trait is to be a witness to Jesus, but who also displays the traits of a baptizer, herald, teacher, best man, and a light.[37] Judas's dominant trait is betrayal, but he also displays a lack of care, dishonesty, and disloyalty. Other characters that have primary and secondary traits are Nicodemus (he is mainly ambiguous but also shows an interest in Jesus and courage), the Samaritan woman, and the man born blind (both are perceptive in their understanding of Jesus but also show traits of testifying, courage, and open-mindedness). Complex, multi-trait characters include Pilate and Peter.

The Acts of the Apostles also has characters that range across the entire complexity spectrum. There are certainly characters with a single trait: for example, Ananias and Sapphira are deceptive; John Mark is unreliable (at least

---

34. Rimmon-Kenan, *Narrative Fiction*, 67–70.

35. Smith, *Lion with Wings*, 54–55.

36. Bennema, "Figurenanalyse." Cf. Williams, *Other Followers*.

37. In fact, John's secondary traits clarify and define his primary trait of being a witness to Jesus. See further, Cornelis Bennema, "The Character of John in the Fourth Gospel," *JETS* 52 (2009): 271–84.

from Paul's perspective); the slave girl in Philippi has the ability to tell fortunes; and Timothy is helpful. Some characters have limited traits: Simon the sorcerer is boastful and able to astonish people; Philip proclaims Jesus and shows obedience; James shows insight and authority/decisiveness. Still others, such as Stephen, Cornelius, and Barnabas show a mixture of a primary trait and secondary traits, while characters such as Peter and Paul are complex, exhibiting multiple traits. Sometimes minor characters can be surprisingly complex. For example, Lydia, although uncomplicated, nevertheless exhibits multiple traits: she is enterprising, attentive, responsive, influential, hospitable, and persuasive (see the analysis of Lydia in section 4.3).

CHARACTER ANALYSIS: THE CONTINUUM OF DEVELOPMENT

On the continuum of development, characters range from those with no development (they are static, unchanging), to those who display some development, to those who change dramatically. I make two comments. First, the development can sometimes be traced in the text but at other times it is implied.[38] In the Gospel of John, Judas is an example of one who displays both implicit and explicit development. When the narrator mentions that Judas is a thief (12:6), we may infer that he did not join Jesus' fellowship as a thief but became one along the way—an implicit development. Then, the narrator makes Judas's development explicit: from being influenced by the devil (13:2), to being indwelt by the devil (13:27), to finally leaving the fellowship of Jesus and entering into the darkness (13:30)—in short, the catastrophic development from a disciple of Jesus to a disciple of Satan.[39]

Second, development is *not* simply the reader becoming aware of an additional trait of a character later in the narrative or a character's progress in his or her understanding of Jesus. Instead, development occurs when a new trait replaces an old one or does not fit neatly into the existing set of traits, implying that the character has changed.[40] This coheres with Forster's criterion of a character's ability to surprise the reader. We can therefore speak of development when there is apparent tension within a character's set of traits. For example, the revelation in John 6:70-71 that Judas will betray Jesus is meant to shock the reader, and though there is no explanation the implication is that Judas has developed (or will develop) from one of Jesus' intimate friends to a betrayer. In 13:21, when Jesus reveals that one of his twelve disciples will betray

---

38. Rimmon-Kenan, *Narrative Fiction*, 42.

39. Contra Resseguie, who describes Judas as "a flat character who does not develop" (*Narrative Criticism*, 159).

40. Cf. Rimmon-Kenan, *Narrative Fiction*, 39.

him soon, they are shocked, and even after Jesus provides a clue about the betrayer's identity, the disciples are too stunned to comprehend it (13:26-29). The disciples' perplexity implicitly indicates the development that Judas has undergone. The reader too is expected to be surprised by these changes in Judas and will notice the replacement of traits. From 12:6 the reader knows that Judas is the treasurer of the group (a position of trust) but also a thief, so traits of honesty and reliability have been replaced by dishonesty and unreliability. Then, with the switch in allegiance from Jesus to Satan, traits of intimacy and following Jesus disappear, and alienation and defection emerge.

Other Johannine characters are also capable of surprising the reader and showing development. The Samaritan woman, for instance, is unafraid to violate social norms by entering into a dialogue with a Jewish man. She also proves to be a sharp, theological thinker, able to grasp enough of Jesus' revelation to testify to her kinsfolk (in sharp contrast to Nicodemus). The man blind from birth, a beggar, and presumably uneducated, not only progresses remarkably in his understanding of Jesus but does so *as* he boldly defends Jesus while facing persecution from the religious authorities. Seemingly disadvantaged and marginalized, the Samaritan woman and the blind man surprise us with their cognitive abilities and the way they reach an authentic understanding of Jesus. Nicodemus initially shows some true knowledge of Jesus (3:2), creating the expectation that he will progress in his understanding of Jesus in the subsequent dialogue, but the opposite occurs. Jesus expresses dismay that this leading theologian cannot grasp the spiritual realities he is speaking of (3:10). Later in the narrative, Peter's denial and cowardice in 18:15-27 shockingly contradicts his remarkable christological confession in 6:68-69 and impulsive bravado in 13:37 and 18:10. The reader may also be surprised that the cruel Pilate, toward the end of the trial, dramatically tries to release Jesus (19:12).

In the Gospel of Mark we also find examples of character development. The wit of the Syrophoenician woman in countering Jesus' rejection of her request is surprising (7:28). In Mark too, Judas undergoes development. Although the narrator informs the reader with Judas's first appearance in the narrative that he is going to betray Jesus (3:19), when Jesus informs his disciples, they are severely distressed, indicating an unexpected development at the story level (14:18-19). The twelve disciples, as a corporate character, are a seeming contradiction with regard to traits. On the one hand, they respond quickly to Jesus' call (1:16-20) and remain firmly on Jesus' side through most of the narrative, occasionally acting as his representatives (6:7-13) and showing insight about his identity (8:27-29). On the other hand, they frequently display behavior not befitting disciples, such as fear, bewilderment, lack of understanding or faith, and even disloyalty (4:40; 6:49-52; 9:18, 28-29, 33-35; 14:27-31). In this regard, the self-serving request of the brothers James and John in 10:35-45 serves as an example. It is a surprising and disappointing turnaround from their initial response to Jesus (1:20) and mocks the privileged position they had within the group (1:29; 5:37; 9:2; 14:33).

In the Acts of the Apostles, it is surprising that Peter takes a leading role from the start and that the other disciples apparently accept this (1:15-26; 2:14-39) because Luke's Gospel, a familiar source for a reader of Acts, does not resolve Peter's denial of Jesus. Likewise, the "conversion" of Paul from a zealous persecutor of Jesus' followers to one who zealously proclaims Jesus as the Christ should come as a surprise to the reader. The seeming tension in the portrayal of Apollos may indicate some development. For someone who the narrator says has extensive knowledge of the Scriptures and has been instructed about Jesus on at least two occasions (and been able to disseminate this information successfully), Apollos is surprisingly ignorant about a vital issue such as the baptism in the name of Jesus (18:24–19:5). Finally, the row between Paul and Barnabas and their consequent split (15:36-41) is rather surprising in the light of the unity among the early Christians.

CHARACTER ANALYSIS: THE CONTINUUM OF PENETRATION INTO THE INNER LIFE

The continuum of penetration into the inner life ranges from characters whose minds remain opaque to those who allow us a peek inside their minds. The inner life of characters gives the reader insight into their thoughts, emotions, and motivations, and is usually conveyed by the narrator and sometimes by other characters.[41] Evidence of inner life is one factor that moves a character toward roundness or individuality. This continuum has few takers. Scholes and Kellogg, for example, claim that "[t]he inward life is assumed but not presented in primitive literature, whether Hebraic or Hellenic."[42] With regard to the characters in the Gospels, it appears at first that we are not privy to their inner thoughts, emotions, or motivations—only Jesus' inner life is well portrayed. Whitney Taylor Shiner, for example, asserts that "an inner life is conspicuous by its absence in the Gospel of Mark. The characters in Mark fulfill roles, but their inner life, even when recorded in a perfunctory manner, is largely irrelevant to the story."[43] Similarly with regard to the Gospel of John, Francois Tolmie

---

41. Berlin, *Poetics and Interpretation*, 38. Cf. Bar-Efrat, who provides numerous examples of the inner life of characters in the Hebrew Bible (*Narrative Art*, 58–64).

42. Scholes, Phelan, and Kellogg, *Nature of Narrative*, 166.

43. Shiner, *Follow Me*, 10.

concludes that no inner life of the Johannine characters is revealed.[44] This, I contend, is a mistaken notion. The New Testament narratives do portray the inner life of many characters, which affects their characterization.

In the Gospel of Mark, it is the narrator who conveys most aspects of the characters' inner life. Regarding Jesus, the narrator reveals that he is compassionate toward others (1:41; 6:34), knows what people are thinking (2:8; 8:17; 12:15), is angry and disturbed about others' attitude (3:5; 8:12; 10:14), realizes that someone had tapped into his power (5:30), is amazed at people's lack of faith (6:6), has knowledge of his own destiny and that of others (8:31; 9:1, 31; 10:33-34), loves the rich young man (10:21), is hungry (11:12), and deeply distressed as his death approaches (14:33). Regarding other characters, the narrator mentions that people are regularly amazed that Jesus teaches and acts with authority (1:22, 27; 2:12; 5:42; 6:2; 7:37; 11:18) and sometimes even offended (6:3); evil spirits know who Jesus is (1:34; 3:11; cf. 5:7); the Jewish authorities are offended by Jesus' claims (2:6; 12:12), stubborn (3:5), have murderous intents toward Jesus (3:6; 11:18; 14:1), are delighted that Judas is willing to betray Jesus (14:11), and mock Jesus (15:31); the disciples are terrified (4:41; 6:50; 9:6), amazed (6:51; 10:24, 26, 32), misunderstand or fail to understand (6:52; 9:6, 32), forgetful (8:14), indignant (10:41), and distressed (14:19); the Gerasene demoniac shows first severe agony (5:5) but later has a sound mind (5:15); the town people of the demoniac are afraid when they see the "cured" demoniac (5:15); people in the Decapolis region are amazed at the formerly demoniac's testimony (5:20); the woman with haemorrhages has suffered a great deal (5:26), then experiences healing after touching Jesus' robe (5:29), but is afraid to testify about it (5:33); Herodias has a grudge against John the Baptist (6:19); Herod respects John the Baptist, has knowledge of him but is also perplexed and distressed (6:20, 26); people are satisfied when they are fed miraculously (6:42; 8:8); Peter has knowledge of Jesus' identity (8:29), remembers what Jesus has said (11:21; 14:72), and weeps (14:72); the rich young man is sad at hearing Jesus' challenge (10:22); Pilate is aware of the motivation of Jesus' opponents, seeks to please the crowd (15:10, 15), and is surprised by Jesus' swift death (15:44); the soldiers mock Jesus (15:20); Mary Magdalene and two other women are bewildered and terrified by the message of the angel (16:8).

---

44. Tolmie, *Jesus' Farewell*, 142. Except for Jesus and the disciples, whose inner life is revealed "a little" (without providing examples), he considers the inner life of all other characters as "none." Part of the problem is that Tolmie only examines a section of the narrative (John 13–17) to reconstruct characters. If he had considered the entire Johannine narrative, his analysis would undoubtedly have rendered different results.

Some Markan characters reveal their own inner life: John the Baptizer professes his unworthiness (1:7); unclean/evil spirits reveal their knowledge of Jesus (1:24); Jesus declares that he is willing to heal (1:41) and shows that he has compassion (8:2); Jesus' family and the authorities presume to know Jesus' mental state (3:21-22); the woman with haemorrhages reveals her inner thoughts (5:28); the disciples know what others think of Jesus (8:28); Peter professes knowledge of Jesus' identity (8:29); the father of a demon-possessed boy expresses his mixture of belief and unbelief (9:24); the musings of the Jewish authorities function as a soliloquy or "inner monologue," revealing their indecisiveness and fear (11:31-33), and they feign knowledge of Jesus (12:14).

The Markan Jesus also reveals information about people's inner life, but much less so than in the Gospel of John: Jesus perceives when his disciples are afraid, lack faith or understanding, and become disloyal; and that one will betray him (4:40; 6:50; 7:18; 8:17-21; 14:17, 20-21, 27-30). While the narrator reveals many aspects of Jesus' inner life (see above), Jesus expresses his own emotions only twice—severe distress when he knows his end is imminent, and a sense of abandonment at the cross (14:34; 15:34).

In the Gospel of John, the narrator conveys aspects of the inner life of various characters. Regarding Jesus, the narrator mentions that he is zealous about his Father's affairs (2:17); has insight into people's lives (2:24-25); can be tired (4:6), agitated (11:33, 38), sad (11:35), troubled (12:27; 13:21), and joyful (11:15, 15:11; 17:13); he loves people (11:5; 13:1, 23, 34); he knows his betrayer (6:70; 13:11, 21).[45] As for other characters, the narrator reveals that the disciples remember certain things (2:17, 22; 12:16), are amazed (4:27), afraid (6:19; 20:19), make assumptions (11:13; 13:29), are at a loss (13:22), do not understand (12:16; 13:28; 21:4), and lack courage (21:12); the royal official believes and knows (4:50, 53); the invalid at the pool lacks knowledge (5:13); the crowd follows Jesus and draws its conclusions when it sees his signs (6:2, 14), it exhibits inner thought processes and logic (6:22-24), and can be afraid (7:13); the religious authorities do not understand (8:27; 10:6), assume (11:31), are afraid (12:42), love human praise (12:43), and want to kill Jesus (5:18; 11:53); Judas is inconsiderate and dishonest (12:6), is influenced by the devil (13:2), is set to betray Jesus (6:71; 12:4), and knows where Jesus often goes (18:3); the man born blind has some knowledge of God (9:31); Pilate is afraid (19:8) and wants to release Jesus (19:12); Joseph of Arimathea is afraid (19:38); the Beloved Disciple sees and believes (20:8); Mary Magdalene lacks knowledge and makes an assumption (20:14-15).

45. See also Stephen Voorwinde, *Jesus' Emotions in the Fourth Gospel: Human or Divine?* (LNTS 284; London: T. & T. Clark, 2005).

Apart from the narrator, Jesus also reveals peoples' inner thoughts and motivations. Regarding the Jewish authorities, he reveals that they make assumptions, neither love nor know God, do not accept him but seek people's praise, have no understanding, are unbelieving, sinners, enslaved, murderous, and belong to the devil rather than to God (5:39-47; 8:31-55). He also exposes the false motives and unbelief of the crowd (6:26, 36); the inner thoughts of those disciples who could no longer accept his teaching (6:61, 64); the imminent betrayal of Judas (6:70; 13:21); the bravado of Peter (13:37-38); and the sorrow of his inner circle of disciples (14:1; 16:6). Compared to Mark's Gospel, Jesus' insight into people's inner lives is remarkable but not surprising considering he is depicted in John's Gospel as the revealer *par excellence*, the one who knows all people and what is in them (2:24-25; cf. 6:64; 13:11; 16:30; 21:17).

Occasionally characters reveal their own inner life. For example, John (the Baptist) admits his initial ignorance of the Messiah's identity and how he acquired that knowledge (1:33); Nathanael's rhetorical question betrays his skepticism (1:46); Nicodemus claims knowledge of Jesus (3:2); the Jewish leaders also claim to know Jesus (9:24, 29) and sometimes their style of speech is comparable to an individual's self-talk—an "inner monologue" (7:35-36; 9:16; cf. the crowd in 7:12, 40-43). On the odd occasion occasion, the structure of a passage reveals a character's inner life. For example, Jesus' trial before Pilate in 18:28–19:16a consists of seven rounds, and in each round Pilate alternates between coming out of and going into his palace, reflecting how Pilate goes back and forth in his mind (see further the analysis of Pilate in section 4.2). John thus employs a variety of means to convey aspects of the inner life of his characters.[46]

In the Acts of the Apostles too, it is the narrator who primarily conveys information about the inner life of characters, while characters themselves do so occasionally. Here are a few examples. The narrator informs us that the crowd is amazed and perplexed about what happens at Pentecost and when a crippled beggar gets healed (1:6-7, 12; 3:10), and that they are "cut to the heart" after hearing Peter's speech (2:37); the authorities are disturbed and astonished by

---

46. Contra Culpepper, who only mentions what the *narrator* conveys about the characters' inner life. Besides, he regards the narrator's inside views as "brief" and "shallow," concluding that John shows "no interest in exploring the more complex psychological motivations of his characters" (*Anatomy of the Fourth Gospel*, 22–26 [quotation from p. 26]). However, despite many inside views being brief, they can convey profound understanding of a character. The brief insights about Judas's dishonesty and that he is influenced by the devil can hardly be called shallow. We can obviously not expect the same amount and kind of inner life as in a modern novel.

the apostles' proclamation (4:2, 13) and jealous of them (5:17); the captain of the temple police is puzzled and afraid of the people (5:24, 26); the apostles rejoice in sharing in Christ's suffering (5:41) and so does the Ethiopian eunuch when he receives the good news about Jesus (8:39); the apostles are initially afraid of Paul (9:26); some Jewish believers are astonished about the events in Cornelius's home, while others are initially critical but later praise God (10:45; 11:2, 18); Barnabas is glad when he sees what is happening in Antioch (11:23); the church in Antioch rejoices when they hear the resolution of the Jerusalem council, and some of their prophets seek to encourage and strengthen the congregation (15:31-32); many Jews are jealous, obstinate, and abusive toward Paul (13:45; 17:5, 13; 18:6; 19:9); the Lord opens the heart of Lydia (16:14); the Philippian jailer is full of joy over his newfound belief (16:34); the Berean Jews are noble and show great eagerness for Paul's proclamation (17:11); Paul is distressed in Athens and reasons with people (17:16-17); Apollos speaks with great enthusiasm and vigor (18:25, 28); the Ephesian elders weep and grieve at their farewell to Paul (20:37-38).

Sometimes characters reveal aspects of their own inner lives. Peter states that he is confident (2:29), knows the miraculous power available to him (3:6; 9:34), and recognizes God's intentions (10:34). On various occasions, Peter even displays a knowledge of the inner life of other people (2:22; 3:17; 5:3-4, 9; 8:23). James declares that he has made a decision regarding the influx of the Gentiles into the people of God (15:19). Paul, before the Ephesian elders, claims to have served Jesus with humility, tears, and without reserve, knows that he is guided by the Spirit, considers his life worthless compared to his calling, and foretells events (20:19-31). In addition, Paul shows insight into the inner life of others (13:10; 14:9-10; 17:22-23).

From this brief survey, it is clear that the New Testament narratives portray the inner life of many characters by various means.

ADDITIONAL CONTINUA OF CHARACTER ANALYSIS?

I do not consider Ewen's model of three continua to be exhaustive. The number of continua along which to analyze characters could well be extended. For example, Baruch Hochman and Sönke Finnern use eight and ten continua respectively upon which a character may be located, although their models have yet to demonstrate their value and feasibility (cf. the remarks by Gowler and Zimmermann in ch. 2, nn. 80 and 85). In my view, the models of Hochman and Finnern are unnecessarily complex, and the results of a character analysis on so many continua cannot easily be aggregated on a resulting continuum, as I seek to do later in this section. At this point, I return to the works of Susan Hylen and Chris Skinner that I mentioned in Chapter 1 (cf. nn. 76–77 for details) because their findings of a particular trait that (Johannine) characters possess in varying degrees might be the basis for an additional continuum on which to plot characters.

Hylen presents an alternative strategy for understanding characters in John's Gospel. Rather than viewing many Johannine characters as "flat" or one-dimensional, she argues that John's characters display various kinds of ambiguity.[47] Although Hylen does not use the term *continuum* in relation to ambiguity (she views ambiguity as a trait), she contends that all Johannine characters possess this trait, so ambiguity effectively functions as a continuum on which the various Johannine characters can be positioned. I applaud her attempts to avoid treating the Johannine characters in a reductionist way, but I have a few critical observations. First, I am uncertain how Hylen differs from Colleen Conway, who also challenges the "flattening" of Johannine characters, arguing that the Johannine characters portray varying degrees of ambiguity, causing instability and resulting in responses to Jesus that resist or undermine the Gospel's binary categories of belief and unbelief.[48] Second, Hylen rightly observes that certain characters are not perfect in their belief and understanding, but this "imperfection" she labels "ambiguity." However, can imperfect faith not be adequate (i.e., sufficiently authentic) without being called ambiguous? Besides, does an ambiguous action make one an ambiguous character? Since no one is perfect, holds perfect beliefs, or is completely consistent through life, everyone would be ambiguous. Thus the concept as Hylen uses it loses meaning. Third, I wonder whether Hylen attributes more ambiguity to the Johannine characters than the author intended. Would the author have built ambiguity into each of his characters? We should not confuse diversity in modern interpretations with the author's (supposedly) intended ambiguity. Otherwise, we could conclude that the entire Bible is intentionally ambiguous. Ambiguity, as evident from the variety of interpretations, may be more the result of modern hermeneutical enterprise than the author's intentional design.

Despite my questions about Hylen's work, I agree that many Johannine characters show various degrees of ambiguity and I have considered whether we can add a continuum of ambiguity to the other three continua. Should we perhaps extend Ewen's model to include a *continuum of stability* (to use a positive category) on which to position the various Johannine characters? I have decided, however, against this move. To me, plotting characters on a

---

47. Hylen, *Imperfect Believers*, ch. 1.

48. Conway, "Ambiguity," 324–41. For my own critique of Conway, see our section 3.3 or Bennema, *Encountering Jesus*, 210–11.

continuum of stability will not correspond or contribute directly to the degree of characterization. Let me explain. While a greater degree of complexity, development, or inner life results in a greater degree of characterization (moving the character toward individuality), we cannot say the same for stability. More stability (or less ambiguity) does not necessarily point toward personality or individuality. Conversely, a greater degree of instability or ambiguity does not necessarily make the character a type. For example, both Peter and the man born blind have a high degree of characterization (individual and personality respectively).[49] But while Peter displays instability on many occasions—he has knowledge of Jesus but often misunderstands him; he denies Jesus contrary to his earlier bold claims; he defects but is restored later—the blind man shows a remarkable degree of stability under relentless pressure from his interrogators. Likewise, many types appear stable (often because the text simply gives minimal information about them), but Thomas, also a type, displays instability, fluctuating between courage/commitment (11:16) and misunderstanding (14:5), between unbelief (20:24-25) and belief a week later (20:28). In essence, while it is possible to plot the various characters on a continuum of stability or ambiguity, such a continuum will *not* contribute to our understanding of character and the degree of characterization.

The same would apply to Skinner's examination of the Johannine characters through the lens of misunderstanding. While Skinner does not use the term *continuum*, he contends that every Johannine character is uncomprehending to a degree.[50] On the premise that the Johannine prologue is the greatest source of information about Jesus, Skinner states that "[e]ach character in the narrative approaches Jesus with varying levels of understanding but no one approaches him fully comprehending the truths that have been revealed to the reader in the prologue. Thus, it is possible for the reader to evaluate the correctness of every character's interaction with Jesus on the basis of what has been revealed in the prologue."[51] Agreeing with Skinner that all Johannine characters show misunderstanding to various extents, I did consider creating a *continuum of understanding* (to use a positive category). However, plotting characters on a continuum of understanding will be difficult if not impossible because it is hard to measure the extent or degree of a character's understanding. Does Thomas, for example, misunderstand Jesus to a greater extent than Peter? Besides, even if we could plot characters on a continuum of understanding, it would not contribute to the degree of characterization.

49. Cf. Bennema, *Encountering Jesus*, 204.

50. Skinner, *John and Thomas*, 40.

51. Skinner, *John and Thomas*, 37.

For example, characters such as Thomas, the crowd, and Peter frequently misunderstand, but they have different degrees of characterization—Thomas is a type, the crowd has personality, and Peter is an individual. Conversely, both the Beloved Disciple and Thomas have a low degree of characterization (type), but the former exhibits near perfect understanding while the latter often misunderstands.[52]

In sum, although we could turn a trait that most (Johannine) characters possess (whether ambiguity, misunderstanding, or something else) into a continuum, the question is whether it would contribute to our understanding of character and the degree of characterization. In fact, the choice of using a continuum of complexity with reference to a character's traits virtually excludes the option of using individual traits to create other continua.[53]

CHARACTER CLASSIFICATION: AN AGGREGATE CONTINUUM OF DEGREE OF CHARACTERIZATION

While Ewen's classification is a big step forward, I suggest we go further. First, I will apply Mieke Bal's suggestion for refinement, namely to divide each continuum according to *degree*, thus creating a sliding scale instead of a polar scale (see section 2.3). This will help us decide *how* we can position a character on each of Ewen's continua. For example, instead of having a continuum of complexity with two opposite poles, "simple" and "complex," I will use a continuum that indicates the degree of complexity: "none," "little," "some," and "much."[54] This refinement or precision will facilitate an evaluation of how the various characters relate to each other.

Second, we noted in section 2.3 that various scholars have suggested classifying characters on multiple continua, but they do not clarify how their

---

52. Bennema, *Encountering Jesus*, 203–5. When it comes to evaluating a character's response to Jesus (see further section 3.3), misunderstanding may be an inadequate response but misunderstanding itself does not determine whether the character's overall response is adequate or inadequate—other factors are responsible for that. In John's Gospel, for example, the crowd's frequent misunderstanding of Jesus taken *together with* being divided, fearful, dismissive, and unbelieving causes its overall response to be inadequate. Conversely, the Twelve frequently misunderstand Jesus but remain at his side; the Samaritan woman and the man born blind struggle to understand but are open-minded and eventually reach sufficient understanding to make an adequate belief-response to Jesus.

53. My decision not to expand my model is in no way a negative appraisal of Hylen and Skinner's excellent work. The social sciences are perhaps better suited to providing appropriate continua to extend Ewen's model. Although it is impossible to explore here, additional continua could include "status (in the group)" or "degree of testimony." See further Jerome H. Neyrey, *The Gospel of John* (NCBC; Cambridge: Cambridge University Press, 2007), 7–9, 313–15, 321–24.

54. While Ewen probably had sliding scales in mind, Mieke Bal makes it explicit (*Narratology*, 86–88).

results can be used. Take the most comprehensive models of Hochman and Finnern, for example. What should we do with eight or ten continua of results? Even with Ewen's model, I find we cannot stop with a mere analysis of characters, lest we are left with three detached continua. I suggest instead that we supplement Ewen's model with an *aggregate* continuum that collates the data from the individual continua to indicate or measure the character's total degree of characterization. In other words, after plotting a character along the three continua of complexity, development, and inner life, we must classify or plot the resulting character on *an aggregate continuum of degree of characterization* as (i) an agent, actant, or walk-on; (ii) a type, stock, or flat character; (iii) a character with personality; or (iv) an individual or person. It must be noted that in classifying ancient characters, I do not use the categories "personality" and "individual/person" in the modern sense of an autonomous individual but refer to a "collectivist identity" or "group-oriented personality" where the individual identity is *embedded* in a larger group or community (cf. ch. 2, n. 119). My proposed classification of character could potentially be expanded, but the basic structure of the model remains, namely a resulting continuum of degree of characterization that is informed by a number of subcontinua.

The results of the character analysis can be collected in the following table:

Character	Complexity	Development	Inner Life	Degree of Characterization
Character 1	0	0	0	agent
Character 2	–	0	0	type
Character 3	–/+	0	–	personality
Character 4	+	+	–	personality
Character 5	++	+	+	toward individual
Character 6	++	++	+	individual

Key: 0 = none, – = little, + = some, ++ = much

I avoid spelling out the terms *little*, *some*, and *much* but position a character on each continuum *in relation to* other characters. While some may question such an "intuitive" approach and prefer more precise definitions or "objective" criteria for what constitutes "little," "some," and "much,"[55] I do not think this is achievable or desirable. I place each character on a particular continuum proportionate to the other characters, and therefore the character's positioning is always relative.[56] Besides, what constitutes "little," "some," and "much" is not only relative within a particular narrative but also between one narrative and another if a character appears in multiple narratives, depending on the amount of information each author disseminates about the characters. Let me provide an example.

In section 4.4, the table that presents the results of our character analyses shows that the amount of information about Pilate in the Johannine narrative and in Acts differs greatly for each of our three subcontinua and thus results in an entirely different degree of characterization. In the diagram, we can also note that the "distance" between Pilate and Peter's characterization in John's Gospel is much smaller than it is in Acts. In other words, while the Johannine Pilate and Peter are consistently positioned close to each other on each subcontinuum and thus achieve a similar high degree of characterization, in Acts they are virtually polarized on the continua of complexity and inner life and hence obtain a radically different degree of characterization. In conclusion, the use of the terms *none*, *little*, *some*, and *much* is simply to create recognizable markers on each continuum rather than to provide absolute, objective quantifiers. Arguably, there is greater clarity or precision when we place all the characters simultaneously on a particular continuum so that we can perceive the relative "distance" from one character to the other, such as we can see below:

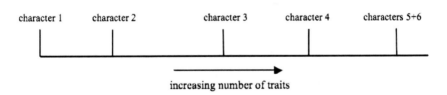

increasing number of traits

Continuum of Complexity

Having suggested this twofold improvement of Ewen's model, I will put it to the test using the Gospel of John. In this Gospel, examples of agents include the master of ceremonies in 2:9-10 and the servants of the royal official in 4:51-52—they simply fulfill a function in the plot and do not produce a response to Jesus. Examples of types—characters who have a single trait and

55. Cf. Redman, "Eyewitness Testimony," 62.

56. Cf. Malbon, who thinks of "flat" and "round" as relative or relational terms, i.e., these character distinctions are to be determined in relation to other characters ("Major Importance," 82 n. 6).

show no development—are Andrew and Nathanael. The character of John (the Baptist) is somewhere between type and personality. Characters with personality—displaying development and a measure of complexity but not completely round—are Nicodemus, the Samaritan woman, and the man born blind. Pilate has a higher level of characterization but not quite that of an individual. Characters such as Judas and Peter are most developed and complex within the Johannine narrative and can be classified as individuals or persons.[57] We can tabulate the results as follows:[58]

Character	Complexity	Development	Inner Life	Degree of Characterization
Master of ceremonies	0	0	0	agent
Servants of the royal official	0	0	0	agent
Nathanael	–	0	–	type
Andrew	–	–	0	type
John (the Baptist)	–/+	0	–	type/personality
Samaritan woman	+	+	–	personality
Nicodemus	++	+	–	personality
Blind man	+	+	+	personality
Pilate	++	+	+	toward individual
Judas	++	+	++	individual
Peter	++	++	+	individual

Key: 0 = none, – = little, + = some, ++ = much

Alan Culpepper and Francois Tolmie are the only scholars to have classified the Johannine characters, and before we go on I will review their work. Culpepper's analysis of character in John's Gospel, though thirty years old is undoubtedly the most detailed and significant to date. He uses Forster's classification in part, stating that the Johannine characters are types and do not have much of a personality: for example, Thomas doubts, Peter is impulsive, and the Beloved Disciple is perceptive.[59] He also employs Harvey's classification,

---

57. For a justification of these evaluations, see the respective chapters in Bennema, *Encountering Jesus*.

58. For the full results of my analysis of Johannine characters, see Bennema, *Encountering Jesus*, 203–4.

seeing Jesus as the protagonist and most other characters as ficelles—"typical characters easily recognizable by the readers" and fulfilling specific plot functions.[60] Although Culpepper describes almost all the relevant Johannine characters, he does not classify them (they are all ficelles or types), only their belief-responses. In doing so, he effectively reduces the characters to their respective responses. Even if the Johannine characters are plot-functionaries who represent various responses to Jesus, we cannot simply reduce them to their respective responses, making types without personality. I suggest that John is subtler than that.[61] It is not so much the characters that are types as their *responses* to Jesus. Many characters gain "roundness" in the Johannine narrative and move toward personality or even individuality on the degree of characterization continuum, but their responses are typical. For example, Nicodemus achieves a certain roundness—sympathetic toward Jesus but slow when it comes to spiritual matters, willing to be associated with Jesus and ready to face scorn and possible retaliation from his colleagues but not taking a clear stand. However, his dominant response of ambiguity (it remains unclear whether he accepts Jesus) is typical. It is therefore imperative that we classify *both* the characters *and* their responses toward Jesus.

In his narratological analysis of John 13–17, Tolmie also examines its characters. The weakness of his study, however, is in the way he employs the classifications of Forster, Harvey, Greimas, and Ewen.[62] He uses Greimas's actantial model best, but we have already pointed out that this is *not* the ideal model for understanding characters since it concentrates on plot, thereby subordinating characters to it and reducing them to mere actants. The characters in the Gospel of John have a much more important role.[63] As for the other classifications, Tolmie fails to use them adequately. He regards Forster's classification as inadequate because all the characters in John 13–17 would have to be classified as flat since none of them is able to surprise the reader. Tolmie

---

59. Culpepper, *Anatomy of the Fourth Gospel*, 102, 145.

60. Culpepper, *Anatomy of the Fourth Gospel*, 104. Elsewhere he uses the term *minor characters* as analogous to types or ficelles (*Anatomy of the Fourth Gospel*, 102, 132, 145).

61. Recently, while still viewing the Johannine characters as mainly plot functionaries, Culpepper also admits that the Johannine characters are more than their responses ("Weave of the Tapestry," 34–35).

62. Tolmie, *Jesus' Farewell*, 120–24; 141–43.

63. It is therefore surprising that Tolmie concludes that Greimas's model is one of the two most suitable models for classifying Johannine characters (*Jesus' Farewell*, p. 144). Other scholars who have used an actantial analysis of the plot of John's Gospel are: Mark W. G. Stibbe, "'Return to Sender': A Structuralist Approach to John's Gospel," *BibInt* 1 (1993): 189–206; idem, *John's Gospel*, 38–53; Lincoln, *Truth on Trial*, 162–66; Bennema, *Power of Saving Wisdom*, 106–7 (but see my critique of Stibbe and Tolmie there).

does not clarify why it would be inadequate to classify all the characters as flat if indeed they cannot surprise the reader. More importantly, I contend that it is methodologically incorrect to examine only a section of the narrative (John 13–17 in Tolmie's case) to reconstruct characters. Over the entire Johannine narrative, some of the characters that Tolmie analyzes are indeed able to surprise the reader (e.g., Judas Iscariot and Peter). As for Harvey's classification, Tolmie simply observes that Jesus is the protagonist and all the other characters are ficelles, but he does not elaborate. This is unsurprising because, as we had pointed out, Harvey's classification of characters according to their importance or presence in the narrative does not provide much understanding of the characters themselves. Finally, using Ewen's classification, Tolmie evaluates all characters (except God, Jesus, and the Spirit-Paraclete) as not complex or having a single trait, showing no development, and revealing no inner life. It is ironic that using Ewen's nonreductionist classification, Tolmie still arrives at a reductionist understanding of the Johannine characters. Again, if Tolmie had analyzed all characters along the entire text continuum of John's Gospel, his results might have been different.

Essentially, the task of organizing all the characters under an accepted classification has not yet been accomplished. Regarding the Gospels and Acts, besides the characters themselves, their responses too must be classified and this brings us to the subject of evaluation of characters.

3.3. Character Evaluation and Significance

The third and final aspect of my theory for character reconstruction in the New Testament involves two elements: (i) the evaluation of characters in relation to point of view and the plot; and (ii) the understanding of the characters' representative value for today. For this part of my theory, rather than explaining it entirely at a conceptual level, I will use the Gospel of John as a case in point, and to a lesser degree the Gospel of Mark and the Acts of the Apostles.[64]

CHARACTER EVALUATION: POINT OF VIEW

Besides analyzing and classifying characters, I contend that we must *evaluate* them from the author's ideological point of view. We noted in section 2.3 that any meaningful communication, whether verbal or nonverbal, has a specific message that the sender tries to convey to the receiver. Authors thus have an

---

64. For a good introduction to the concept of point of view and perspective criticism, see Gary Yamasaki, *Perspective Criticism: Point of View and Evaluative Guidance in Biblical Narrative* (Eugene, OR: Wipf & Stock/Cascade, 2012).

agenda, implicit or explicit, and tell their story from a particular perspective called "point of view." The point-of-view dynamics can contribute toward readers sympathizing with or becoming distanced from a particular character.[65] As Rhoads, Dewey, and Michie explain, readers are led to evaluate the characters according to the narrative's "standards of judgment" (their term for point of view), that is, those values and beliefs embedded in a narrative, which "represent the moral fabric of a narrative—the positive values that the narrative promotes and the negative behavior that the narrative condemns."[66] Consequently, a narrative is not neutral because it has an *inbuilt* perspective that is communicated to the readers, and so they must evaluate the characters in the light of the author's evaluative point of view. I will explain this further with reference to the Gospel of John.

Many scholars who have studied the Johannine characters do not discuss the ideological or evaluative point of view of John's Gospel, and consequently fail to evaluate the characters. A few, however, do connect the Johannine characters with the Gospel's worldview and evaluative point of view. Alan Culpepper argues that the Johannine characters are "typical characters easily recognizable by the readers" and that "[t]he characters are . . . particular sorts of choosers. Given the pervasive dualism of the Fourth Gospel, the choice is either/ or. All situations are reduced to two clear-cut alternatives, and all the characters eventually make their choice."[67] He then produces an extensive taxonomy of belief-responses in keeping with the author's ideological point of view.[68] Culpepper is the only one who produces a continuum of belief-responses (and a commendable one at that), but he does not classify the characters themselves, only their responses, thereby reducing the characters to their typical responses and hence to types. His resultant analysis is therefore reductionistic and raises questions. Does Nicodemus make a clear choice? Are Peter and Pilate types, easily recognizable? Is Thomas simply the doubter?

James Resseguie's monograph on point of view in the Gospel of John studies eleven characters (besides Jesus) to show that they "represent distinct points of view that elaborate, reinforce, or in some way highlight ideological perspectives of the gospel."[69] He concludes, for instance, that the lame man and the blind man represent the marginalized in society; and that Nicodemus, the royal official, the world, and the Jewish authorities represent the dominant

---

65. Yamasaki, *Perspective Criticism*, 106.

66. Rhoads, Dewey, and Michie, *Mark as Story*, 102.

67. Culpepper, *Anatomy of the Fourth Gospel*, 104.

68. Culpepper, *Anatomy of the Fourth Gospel*, 145–48.

69. Resseguie, *Strange Gospel*, ch. 3 (quotation from p. 109).

culture.[70] Although Resseguie mentions the characters' faith-stance, he evaluates the characters primarily from a material or sociological perspective rather than from John's overall purpose and worldview, which, we will see, are clearly soteriological.

Other scholars, however, contend that the evaluation of characters is not feasible. Colleen Conway, for example, argues that the Johannine characters portray varying degrees of ambiguity, causing instability and resulting in responses to Jesus that resist or undermine the Gospel's binary categories of belief and unbelief.[71] By implication, the Johannine characters cannot clearly be evaluated. Conway's stimulating article has much to commend it, so her conclusion that John cannot fit his characters' varied responses into his dualistic worldview is surprising. Later in this section, I will suggest how this can be resolved.

Jo-Ann Brant deliberately refrains from any evaluation since she contends that "the Fourth Gospel does not invite us to line up the characters into categories of good and evil, saved and damned."[72] Drawing on ancient Greek tragedy, she argues that readers are not members of a jury, evaluating characters as right or wrong, innocent or guilty, or answering christological questions about Jesus' identity, but are called to join John in commemorating Jesus' life.[73] According to Brant, "[i]nstead of asking, 'Who are the children of God?'—that is, inquiring about who is in and who is out—the question that the Fourth Gospel addresses seems to be, 'What does it mean to be children of God?'"[74] If she had considered John's evaluative point of view and purpose, Brant might have seen that the narrative itself calls for the evaluation or judgment of the characters' responses toward Jesus. The narrative and its inbuilt perspective *demands* that the reader reflect on and assess the characters. The author's aim is not simply that the reader judge characters for their own sake but that in this process of evaluation the reader will judge his or her *own* response toward Jesus. Brant wrongly assumes that John's purpose in writing this Gospel is only to deepen the existing faith of believers. The Gospel is also meant to persuade

---

70. Resseguie, *Strange Gospel*, 167. See also Resseguie, *Narrative Criticism*, 137–65.

71. Conway, "Ambiguity," 328–41.

72. Brant, *Dialogue and Drama*, 225. Earlier, Brant admits that "[p]erhaps it is simply a reflection of my position as a modern reader conscious of the historical contingency of my faith that I seek to find some sort of awareness that the disbelief of the crowd or the Jews is not to be treated as a corporate character flaw but as a twist of plot or an accident of history" (*Dialogue and Drama*, 225). It is however dangerous to be guided by one's own views rather than by those of John.

73. Brant, *Dialogue and Drama*, 225–26, 259–60.

74. Brant, *Dialogue and Drama*, 231.

nonbelievers to come to believe in Jesus and in doing so to participate in the eternal life available in him.[75] The lack of consensus among Johannine scholars about character evaluation (but the same holds true for Mark and Acts) shows that we must tread carefully on this issue.

Before evaluating a character, we must determine what we are evaluating and how; that is, we need guidelines or criteria for evaluation. For instance, what is the central theme against which we might evaluate characters? In the case of John's Gospel, I suggest that we evaluate characters primarily in terms of their *response* to Jesus. The author of John's Gospel explicitly states the purpose for writing his narrative in 20:30-31: "Now Jesus did many other signs in the presence of his disciples, which are not written in this book. But these are written *so that* you may (come to or continue to) believe that Jesus is the Messiah, the Son of God, and that through believing you may have (eternal) life in his name."[76] So, the author's purpose in writing his Gospel—to evoke and strengthen belief in Jesus among his readers—indicates that what counts is the *reader's* response to Jesus. The author's strategy for achieving his purpose is to put various characters on the stage and show their interaction with Jesus. He wants his readers to evaluate the characters' responses to Jesus, join his point of view, and make an adequate belief-response themselves.

It follows that in order to evaluate the character's (belief-)response to Jesus according to the *author's* point of view, the reader must understand what the author views as adequate belief. I have defined an adequate belief-response to Jesus in John's Gospel as a sufficiently true, Spirit-provided understanding of Jesus in terms of his identity, mission, and relationship with his Father, resulting in a personal allegiance to Jesus.[77] It is impossible, however, to quantify such a belief-response or to determine how much authentic understanding is adequate. Instead, I estimate whether a character's response is adequate by discerning the author's (implicit or explicit) evaluation of this response, which relates to his evaluative point of view. Once we know what, for the author, constitutes an adequate belief-response, we can evaluate the character's response to Jesus. For this, we must also take into account the author's worldview. The author of John's Gospel operates with a dualistic worldview within which people ultimately accept or reject Jesus. This implies that for the author the characters' responses are either adequate or inadequate. In short, *we must evaluate*

---

75. Cf. Bennema, *Power of Saving Wisdom*, 107–9.

76. For a discussion of the textual variant πιστεύ[σ]ητε in 20:31, see any major commentary.

77. Bennema, *Power of Saving Wisdom*, 124–33; idem, "Christ, the Spirit and the Knowledge of God: A Study in Johannine Epistemology," in *The Bible and Epistemology: Biblical Soundings on the Knowledge of God*, ed. Mary Healy and Robin Parry (Milton Keynes, UK: Paternoster, 2007), 119–20.

the Johannine characters in terms of their response to Jesus, in keeping with the author's
evaluative point of view, purpose, concept of belief, and dualistic worldview. Let me
explain this further.

In our analysis of the Johannine characters, we must be conscious of the
author's evaluative point of view, that is, his appraisive commentary on the
story, which operates at the level of narrative. As the Johannine characters
interact with Jesus, the author or narrator communicates his ideology and
point of view to the reader with the intention of winning over the reader.[78]
Since John has written his Gospel with a specific purpose in mind (20:31), his
evaluative point of view is directly related to the purpose and worldview of the
Gospel. Stephen Moore succinctly captures the dynamic between purpose and
point of view in John's Gospel:

> Johannine characterization . . . is entirely christocentric. Jesus is a static character in
> the Fourth Gospel. . . . The functions of the other characters are to draw out various
> aspects of Jesus' character by supplying personalities and situations with which he
> can interact, and to illustrate a spectrum of alternative responses to him. . . . Such
> characterizations are strategically oriented toward the reader, pushing him or her
> also toward a decisive response to Jesus.[79]

Similarly, Mark Stibbe asserts that

> [t]he narrator works obviously . . . to coax the reader round to the point of view or
> ideological stance which he embraces. That point of view is the enlightened post-
> resurrectional understanding of Jesus as the Messiah, the Son of God, and it is this
> understanding which undergirds the narrator's rhetorical strategy expressed in John
> 20.31.[80]

The author communicates and recommends his values and norms to the
reader, particularly in the way he portrays his characters and evaluates them.
Through his portrayal of various characters, the author encourages the reader
to identify with those characters or responses that are worthy of imitation and
to dissociate from characters or responses that are not.[81] The reader, therefore,

---

78. Cf. Culpepper, *Anatomy of the Fourth Gospel*, 32–33, 89, 97–98.

79. Moore, *Literary Criticism*, 49.

80. Stibbe, *John as Storyteller*, 28.

81. According to Beck, anonymity facilitates readers' identification with, and imitation of, characters
in John's Gospel. Beck concludes that the unnamed characters most closely model the paradigm of
discipleship, of appropriate response to Jesus, whereas named characters, even those with a degree of

must evaluate both the characters and the extent to which each character's response to Jesus is adequate. As the reader identifies with the characters, she must also evaluate her own belief-response. The author reveals his point of view through the narrative rhetoric and demands from the reader a self-evaluation and response, implicitly recommending one that corresponds to the purpose of his Gospel stated in 20:30-31.[82] As Culpepper aptly puts it:

> The affective power of the plot pushes the reader toward a response to Jesus. The characters, who illustrate a variety of responses, allow the reader to examine the alternatives. The shape of the narrative and the voice of the narrator lead the reader to identify or interact variously with each character . . . readers may place themselves in the role of each character successively while searching for the response they will choose. Through the construction of the gospel as narrative, therefore, the evangelist leads the reader toward his own ideological point of view, the response he deems preferable.[83]

The author's evaluative point of view thus corresponds to the soteriological purpose for which he has written his narrative—to elicit faith in Jesus as the Messiah, which results in eternal life—and to his dualistic worldview in which there is scope for only two responses to Jesus—acceptance or rejection. The author's evaluative point of view thus has two corresponding options—adequate and inadequate. In other words, the characters' responses to Jesus are part of a larger soteriological framework that is informed by the purpose and worldview of John's Gospel. But there is a tension. On the one hand, the author's dualistic worldview only allows for acceptance or rejection of Jesus, and hence all responses to be either adequate or inadequate. On the other hand, the characters' responses to Jesus are varied and form a broad spectrum. So how do

approval, are inappropriate models for reader identification and imitation (*Discipleship Paradigm*, 137–42; cf. his earlier essay, "Narrative Function," 143–58). Beck, however, overstates his case, consequently misreading some characters. For example, contra Beck, the invalid at the pool is not a model to be emulated since he does not heed Jesus' warning and instead reports Jesus to the Jewish authorities, resulting in Jesus' being persecuted (5:14-16). On the other hand, Nathanael, Martha, and Thomas do display an appropriate belief-response (contra Beck, *Discipleship Paradigm*, 139–40)—especially since their confessions closely resemble the ideal Johannine confession in 20:31. Finally, characters such as John (the Baptist), Andrew, Peter, and Mary exemplify various aspects of true discipleship. Beck's character analysis is flawed and too categorical in concluding that *only* the anonymous characters represent a paradigm of discipleship.

82. See further, Tannehill, "Disciples in Mark," 387–96. Conway also notes that John's Gospel "pushes the reader toward a decision" ("Ambiguity," 324).

83. Culpepper, *Anatomy of the Fourth Gospel*, 148.

they correspond with the dualistic scheme that John's Gospel presents? Can such diverse responses fit into the binary categories of belief and unbelief, adequate and inadequate? We saw earlier in this section that Conway, for example, does not believe that John's dualism can contain such a range of responses (cf. n. 71, above), while Brant contends that we should not even try to fit this spectrum of responses into it (cf. n. 72, above).

I suggest that the characters' responses can (and should) fit into the dualistic worldview of John's Gospel. Here is how: the Johannine characters reflect the *human* perspective, presenting the whole gamut of responses that people make in life, but from a *divine* perspective these responses are (ultimately) categorized as acceptance or rejection. The divine reality is that the world and its people are enveloped in darkness and do not know God—they are "from below" (cf. 1:5; 8:23). In order to dispel this darkness or lack of divine knowledge, Jesus came to the world to reveal God and to bring people into an everlasting, life-giving relationship with himself and God. People who encounter Jesus may either reject or accept him, and consequently remain part of the world below or enter the world above through a spiritual birth. The reality is that human responses to Jesus vary—they may be instant or gradual, positive or negative, consistent or haphazard, ambiguous or evident. Faced with this reality we must attempt to evaluate what John thinks would qualify someone for the new birth that brings a person into the realm of God, what kind of responses would bring (and keep) someone in a life-giving relationship with Jesus.[84]

Judith Redman objects to the evaluation of Johannine characters.[85] Supporting Conway's argument that the Johannine characters cannot be contained in binary categories and hence there is no clarity about what they

---

84. For an overview of my evaluation of the responses of the Johannine characters to Jesus, see Bennema, *Encountering Jesus*, 204–6. In a recent review, David Ball criticizes my theory, saying it is "weakened by categorizing all belief responses as 'adequate' or 'inadequate.' This does not effectively account for the complexity of characters such as Nicodemus" (Review of Cornelis Bennema, *Encountering Jesus: Character Studies in the Gospel of John, JSNT* 33 [2011]: 70). Unfortunately, Ball has misunderstood me on this point. We must distinguish between what happens at the story level and the narrative level. At the story level, the author does not resolve whether Nicodemus makes an adequate belief-response—while he is clearly attracted to Jesus, Nicodemus neither accepts nor rejects him, remaining ambiguous throughout. At the narrative level, however, the author informs his reader that as a belief-response such an attitude falls short. The author is not negative about Nicodemus per se but about his response; he wants his readers to evaluate the character's *response* to Jesus rather than the character. Hence, the categories adequate/inadequate have nothing to do with the character's complexity (or lack of it) but with the representative value of his response for the reader. For an analysis of Nicodemus, see Bennema, *Encountering Jesus*, 77–85.

85. Redman, "Eyewitness Testimony," 63–67.

represent, Redman asserts that John never intended for his characters to be evaluated (contra Culpepper and myself), and consequently the Johannine characters cannot be used as yardsticks against which to evaluate people's belief. She also takes issue with my use of the categories "adequate" and "inadequate" because in her view the Johannine narrative does not provide objective criteria for assessing whether a response is adequate or inadequate. Instead, she contends that the Johannine characters are there to "provide examples for the reader of what a belief in Jesus that brings life might look like in real life."[86] While I agree with Redman's assertion that the Johannine characters are examples for the readers (then and now), I disagree that John does not intend his readers to evaluate them. I have argued that every story has an inbuilt evaluative point of view, which the reader must discern. It can hardly be the case that the author depicts Nicodemus as an ambiguous character simply because in real life there are also ambiguous people, or that it is acceptable to be a "secret" believer because the author shows that such people exist. What is more, the Johannine narrative does, in fact, indicate what adequate (but not perfect) belief looks like (see my definition above), thus providing the "objective" criteria Redman requires. It is this *Johannine* understanding of adequate belief that is the yardstick against which the reader can (and should) evaluate the characters' responses, and also their own.[87]

One final comment. While evaluating the various responses as either "adequate" or "inadequate," I refrain from plotting the characters' responses along a continuum of faith because that would be presumptuous. Who can decide whether testifying about Jesus, following him, or remaining with him is closer to the ideal, whether belief in Jesus' words or belief in Jesus' signs is "better," or whether antipathy is worse than apathy? This is the difficulty I have with Culpepper's taxonomy, which ranks the belief-responses of the characters.[88] I now turn to the Johannine narrative and examine the responses of some Johannine characters, bearing in mind that a character's response to Jesus can be explicit or implicit, verbal or nonverbal.[89]

---

86. Redman, "Eyewitness Testimony," 76.

87. Redman's argument that only Martha lives up to the norm in 11:27 because her confession is the only one that literally matches the criterion in 20:31 ("Eyewitness Testimony," 66) is too simplistic. The life-giving belief that 20:31 speaks of must be unpacked and understood in the light of the entire Johannine narrative. If we do so, we observe that while many characters do not reach "ideal" or "perfect" faith, they do express adequate belief, which the reader can discern through their speech and actions, or what other characters say about them.

88. Culpepper, *Anatomy of the Fourth Gospel*, 146–48.

89. For a detailed account of these characters and their responses, see the respective chapters in Bennema, *Encountering Jesus*.

Examples of explicit belief-responses are Nathanael's "Rabbi, you are the Son of God, you are the king of Israel" (1:49; "king of Israel" is a messianic title) and Martha's "Yes, Lord, I believe that you are the Messiah, the Son of God" (11:27). I evaluate these responses as adequate since they closely parallel the ideal Johannine confession that "Jesus is the Messiah, the Son of God" (20:31). Regarding Nicodemus, contra many scholars who force a decision upon him, we contend that Nicodemus remains sympathetic but noncommittal toward Jesus throughout the narrative. His dominant trait is that of ambiguity. But we cannot stop there; his response must be evaluated, and from John's evaluative point of view, we should conclude that remaining ambiguous as a belief-response is inadequate. The Samaritan woman's response to Jesus is implicit rather than explicit, and I evaluate it as adequate: (i) she leaves the water jar behind (4:28), possibly symbolizing that her thirst has been quenched; (ii) she invites her fellow-villagers to "come and see" this man, Jesus, whom she tentatively believes is the Messiah (4:28-29; cf. 1:46);[90] (iii) many Samaritans believe in Jesus on the basis of the woman's testimony (4:39); and (iv) their climactic confession of Jesus as the Savior of the world (4:42) very likely includes the woman's confession. The blind man's explicit response to Jesus is both verbal and nonverbal: he exclaims, "Lord, I believe" and falls prostrate before Jesus in an act of worship. Considering the man's progress from not knowing the identity of his benefactor to gaining profound understanding of Jesus during his interrogation, his response is remarkable and adequate. Judas's responses are clearly inadequate: (i) he surrenders to the devil's influence (13:2); (ii) in response to Jesus' final attempt to reach out to him, Judas silently accepts the piece of bread and seals his lot (13:26-27); (iii) in another wordless but telling response, Judas leaves the fellowship of Jesus and enters the darkness (13:30); (iv) he betrays Jesus (18:2-3). As for the "secret belief"-response of Joseph of Arimathea (19:38), there are indicators that point to the inadequacy of such a response. First, some of the Jewish authorities have a response similar to Joseph's (12:42), and 12:43 explains that, besides fear, the authorities' desire for human praise contributes to their lack of open confession—an attitude that Jesus has criticized earlier (5:44). Second, John has been implicitly critical of the blind man's parents, who fail to testify because of "the fear of the Jews," which stands in sharp contrast to their son's bold testimony. Third, at Jesus' burial, the fearful Joseph of Arimathea is linked up with the ambiguous Nicodemus, whose response we have evaluated as inadequate.

---

90. Considering her progressive understanding of Jesus, 4:29 should probably be translated as "Is he perhaps the Christ?," cautiously suggesting an affirmative answer rather than serious doubt.

We must note that although characters' responses can be typical, a response is not necessarily bound to one character (e.g., the response of defection is displayed by some disciples in 6:60–66, as well as by Peter and Judas); likewise, a character is not restricted to one response (e.g., Peter responds with understanding and misunderstanding, belief and defection). We can now compile the results in two tables:

Character	Response toward Jesus
Nathanael, Martha	resembling the ideal confession of Jesus as Messiah and Son of God
Nicodemus	ambiguous, sympathetic but uncommitted/indecisive
Samaritan woman	progressive understanding resulting in an adequate belief-response as she testifies to her kinsfolk
Blind man	progression from blindness to spiritual (in)sight, from not knowing Jesus to understanding that he is from God to confessing belief in him
Judas	defection, apostasy, betrayal
Peter	belief, defection, insight, misunderstanding
Joseph of Arimathea	"secret belief" instigated by fear

Type of Response	Evaluation	Character Typifying the Response
ambiguity	inadequate	Nicodemus
misunderstanding	inadequate	Nicodemus, Peter, Samaritan woman
"secret belief"	inadequate	Joseph of Arimathea, perhaps Nicodemus
defection	inadequate	Peter, Judas
apostasy	inadequate	Judas
betrayal	inadequate	Judas
confession of Jesus' identity	adequate	Nathanael, Martha, Peter, Samaritan woman, blind man
understanding Jesus' identity	adequate	Samaritan woman, blind man
testifying about Jesus	adequate	Samaritan woman, blind man

Having dealt with the evaluation of characters in John's Gospel, I will now briefly look at character evaluation in the Gospel of Mark and the Acts of the Apostles. Mark's point of view, the first criterion for character evaluation, is similar to John's, although expressed more implicitly. Like John, Mark aims to persuade his audience to believe that Jesus is the Christ and Son of God—Mark 1:1 finds its climactic expression in the confessions of Peter in 8:29 and the Roman centurion in 15:39 respectively—and to engage in discipleship. Mark wants his audience to evaluate the characters' responses to Jesus (in terms of faith and discipleship), join his point of view, and become disciples of Jesus themselves.[91] As Rhoads, Dewey, and Michie conclude, "the story of Mark seeks to create ideal readers who will receive the rule of God with faith and have the courage to follow Jesus whatever the consequences."[92] Similarly, Iverson asserts that "Mark's Gospel intends to shape the beliefs, attitudes, and actions of its readers. . . . Mark's Gospel engages the reader at the cognitive and affective levels in order to elicit the reader's response."[93] I suggest, therefore, that Mark's purpose for writing his Gospel is to reveal Jesus' identity and mission in order to promote faith and discipleship among his readers through the characters' interactions with and responses to Jesus. Like the Gospel of John, Mark's narrative reflects a worldview that is characterized by a moral dualism—living on God's terms versus living on human terms—and characters embody one or the other.[94] For example, the minor characters mostly act on God's terms, the authorities on human terms, and the disciples vacillate between the two.[95]

Regarding the Acts of the Apostles, many scholars contend that Acts 1:8 is programmatic for the entire book, that is, the purpose of Acts is to narrate

91. Cf. Williams, *Other Followers*, 89; Malbon, "Major Importance," 81.

92. Rhoads, Dewey, and Michie, *Mark as Story*, 138 (original emphasis removed).

93. Iverson, *Gentiles*, 5.

94. Cf. the programmatic parable in Mark 4:1-20. Instead of viewing the parable as speaking of four types of soils/hearing, perhaps the point is to indicate that, ultimately, there are only two types of responses—fruitless and fruitful ones.

95. Rhoads, Dewey, and Michie, *Mark as Story*, 102. See also Petersen, "Point of View," 97–121. Differently, Smith employs the theories of Boris Uspensky (who identifies four/five levels or planes of perception) and Gérard Genette (who focuses on mood and voice) to determine Mark's point of view (*Lion with Wings*, 167–91). As a result, however, Smith merely mentions aspects of Mark's point of view using the various categories of Uspensky and Genette rather than spelling out the Markan point of view. My understanding of point of view actually corresponds to Uspensky's "ideological point of view," while Uspensky's "psychological point of view" relates to our continuum of penetration into the character's inner life. Joanna Dewey, who also examines Mark's point of view using Genette's categories of mood and voice, concludes that Genette's theory is irrelevant to the study of Mark's narrative ("Point of View and the Disciples in Mark," in *Society of Biblical Literature 1982 Seminar Papers*, ed. Kent Harold Richards [Chico, CA: Scholars, 1982], 105).

the growth of the church in Jerusalem (Acts 2–7), Judea and Samaria (Acts 8–12), and to the ends of the earth (Acts 13–28). In his account of the church's development, Luke is not disinterested but intentionally chooses to follow the spread of Christianity westward through the apostle Paul. Many other scholars, however, say that Luke's purpose for writing Acts was more than just to recount the spread of Christianity. In fact, a good case can be made that Luke describes the spread of Christianity from Jerusalem to Rome in order to encourage Christians about the advancement of God's word amidst conflict and persecution.[96] Somewhat differently, Darr contends that the Acts narrative focuses attention on whether or not the (secondary) characters recognize and respond correctly to the divine will as it is manifested through the protagonists.[97] Similarly, Beverly Gaventa states, "Luke presents and assesses these human characters in relationship to their place in and reception of the larger story of God. What makes human characters interesting or important for Luke pertains to their response or resistance to God."[98] In the Gospels, it is crucial how characters respond to the protagonist Jesus. In Acts, however, Peter and Paul, by virtue of being spokespersons of the divine, are now the primary protagonists (although in some pericopae we should also consider characters such as Stephen, Philip, Barnabas, and James). Hence, the decisive factor is now how the other characters respond to them. Thus I suggest that the main criterion for evaluating the characters in Acts is how they respond to the various protagonists (especially Peter and Paul) regarding the divine message and how they subsequently perform as witnesses of Jesus and contribute to the growth of the church.[99]

96. David Peterson, "Luke's Theological Enterprise: Integration and Intent," in *Witness to the Gospel: The Theology of Acts*, ed. I. Howard Marshall and David Peterson (Grand Rapids: Eerdmans, 1998), 534–44.

97. Darr, *On Character Building*, 55–57.

98. Beverly Roberts Gaventa, *The Acts of the Apostles* (ANTC; Nashville: Abingdon, 2003), 27.

99. While Richard Thompson asserts that ancient narratives often provide little explicit information about the characters and hence "the reader must actively make judgments and decisions about those characters from the information that the text provides" (*Keeping the Church in Its Place*, 20), he does not provide the criteria by which the reader can evaluate the characters in Acts. He seems to suggest merely that the reader is invited to evaluate the various characters insofar as they constitute or relate to Luke's picture of the church as those Jews and Gentiles who truly belong to God (*Keeping the Church in Its Place*, 241–48). However, it seems more appropriate to ask the reader to evaluate how the various characters in Acts *contribute* to the development of the church rather than how they *comprise* the church.

CHARACTER EVALUATION: PLOT

After this elaborate explanation of the author's point of view as the first criterion for character evaluation, I turn briefly to a second criterion for evaluating characters, namely their relation to the plot.[100] As we noted in section 2.3, for a long time character has been perceived as subordinated to the plot. The idea that characters are mere plot functionaries is due to two influences: (i) many scholars use an Aristotelian approach to character; (ii) Greimas's actantial model has been influential (see, e.g., the works of Stibbe and Tolmie). The result is that characters have often been unnaturally "flattened." However, many literary critics, such as Chatman, Rimmon-Kenan, and Moore, have stressed that plot and character are equally important and interdependent. More recently, in his discussion on the relationship between plot and character, Farelly also argues that characters are more than mere plot functionaries. He concludes that although "characters do 'exist' to serve specific plot functions . . . they do not lose their impact as constructed persons."[101] There is therefore value in examining the character's role in the plot.

While it is by no means beyond debate, simply defined, "plot" is the logical and causal order of events in a narrative.[102] The plot of the Gospel of Mark revolves around conflict, caused by the proclamation of "the good news" of Jesus' identity and mission, and the various responses of people.[103] The Gospel's plot is shaped by the author's aim of persuading the audience to believe the good news that Jesus is the Christ and Son of God (1:1, 14-15) and commit to discipleship. The minor characters, for example, significantly advance the plot of Mark's narrative because they function as primary examples of faith and discipleship, and the extent to which these characters respond to Jesus and reveal aspects of true discipleship is the extent to which they advance the plot.[104]

---

100. In *Encountering Jesus*, I had not related the Johannine characters to the narrative's plot and I thank David Ball for drawing my attention to this ("Review of Cornelis Bennema," 70).

101. Farelly, *Disciples in the Fourth Gospel*, 164–67 (quotation from p. 167).

102. For more detailed discussions of plot, see Kieran Egan, "What Is a Plot?," *New Literary History* 9 (1978): 455–73; Smith, *Lion with Wings*, 82–88; Farelly, *Disciples in the Fourth Gospel*, 164–67.

103. For more informed discussions on the Markan plot, see Kingsbury, *Conflict in Mark*, 27–29; Rhoads, Dewey, and Michie, *Mark as Story*, 73–97; Robert R. Beck, *Nonviolent Story: Narrative Conflict Resolution in the Gospel of Mark* (Maryknoll, NY: Orbis, 1996), 39–62; Smith, *Lion with Wings*, 82–123; Francis J. Moloney, *Mark: Storyteller, Interpreter, Evangelist* (Peabody, MA: Hendrickson, 2004), 48–54.

104. Differently, Christopher D. Marshall argues that "[i]n the healing and exorcism narratives, there is no progressive development in plot or character from one account to the next. Each story is complete in itself; the need is raised and resolved in the same episode. . . . The pattern is not progressive but iterative" (*Faith as Theme in Mark's Narrative* [SNTSMS 64; Cambridge: Cambridge University Press, 1989], 76). Smith, however, argues against the idea that Mark is too episodic to have plotted story (*Lion with Wings*,

Similarly, the Johannine plot revolves around the revelation of the Father and Son (in terms of their identity, character, mission, and relationship), people's response to this revelation, and the subsequent conflict this causes.[105] The Gospel's plot is shaped by the author's aim of persuading the reader to believe that Jesus is the Christ and the source of everlasting life or salvation (20:31).[106] Hence, the extent to which the Johannine characters reveal Jesus' identity and respond to him is the extent to which they advance the plot. In the Acts of the Apostles, the plot also revolves around proclamation and conflict, namely the conflict caused by the proclamation of the gospel that the crucified Jesus is God's Messiah and Lord, and the fulfillment of Israel's (and indeed the entire world's) hopes.

In addition to describing their role in the plot, we could hypothetically quantify the characters' plot involvement by positioning them on a continuum, with the usual indicators "none," "little," "some," and "much." In practice, however, it is near impossible to distinguish between the roles of the various characters in the plot. We simply lack the criteria to determine whether, for example, the Samaritan woman, Peter, or Pilate has a larger or more crucial plot involvement in John's Gospel. What is possible, however, is to indicate *where* the various characters peak in the Johannine plot and narrative. So, in the episode of the Samaritan woman, the peak comes in 4:28-30 when she testifies about Jesus to her fellow people, who then come to Jesus (and 4:42 possibly marks a post-peak). Peter peaks twice—first with his confession in 6:68-69 and then with his denial in 18:17, 25-27 (and the resolution is delayed to 21:15-19). After being manipulated by "the Jews," 19:15 marks the peak of the Pilate story when, in turn, Pilate manipulates "the Jews" into admitting their allegiance to Rome. We must distinguish between where individual characters peak in the Johannine plot and where the Johannine plot itself peaks. For example, while the peak in the episode of the Samaritan woman occurs early on in the Johannine plot, the peaks in the Peter and Pilate stories coincide with the peak of the entire Johannine plot, which comes in John 18–19, describing Jesus' arrest, trial, death, and burial (with the resurrection as the resolution).

111–12). Besides, while the minor characters each exemplify various aspects of discipleship, collectively, they communicate to the reader Mark's composite understanding of discipleship and hence advance the plot.

105. Cf. Culpepper, *Anatomy of the Fourth Gospel*, 79–98; Andrew T. Lincoln, *The Gospel according to Saint John* (BNTC 4; Peabody, MA: Hendrickson, 2005), 11–12; Farelly, *Disciples in the Fourth Gospel*, 168–76.

106. Cf. Culpepper, *Anatomy of the Fourth Gospel*, 98.

CHARACTER SIGNIFICANCE: THE REPRESENTATIVE VALUE OF THE CHARACTER

The process of reconstructing characters from the text is a hermeneutical process that merges two horizons—that of the historical-narratological world of the text and that of the contemporary world of the reader. This creates the possibility for two-way communication where the characters can "influence" the reader and thus have a role or impact beyond the narrative. In short, characters have a representative value for today. In turn, as the reader evaluates the characters in the narrative according to the author's point of view and purpose, it might lead the reader to seek to emulate some characters (those who align themselves with the author's perspective) and avoid others (those whose behavior is unacceptable from the author's perspective).[107] Alternatively, we can use terms such as empathy, sympathy, and antipathy to express the reader's identification with characters in the narrative.[108] I will, once again, use to the Gospel of John to elaborate.

Once we have evaluated the Johannine characters in terms of their response to Jesus and their role in the plot, we must determine each character's significance for today. In other words, we must reflect on how these characters and their responses have representative value for readers in other contexts and times. It was Raymond Collins who, in 1976, dubbed the characters in John's Gospel as "representative figures." He argued that John has definitely typecast the various characters (they have characteristic traits) in order to represent a particular type of belief-response to Jesus.[109] Culpepper advanced the paradigmatic function of Johannine characters, producing an extensive continuum of belief-responses.[110] Although Collins and Culpepper have rightly highlighted the representative value of the Johannine characters, they have, as I have shown, wrongly concluded that John reduces his characters to their belief-responses and hence to types.[111]

I propose that while a character's belief-response may be typical, this does not necessarily reduce the entire character to a type. I have, I believe, amply demonstrated in my book *Encountering Jesus* that many Johannine characters

---

107. Cf. Rhoads, Dewey, and Michie, *Mark as Story*, 103–4.

108. Powell, *Narrative Criticism*, 56.

109. Collins, "Representative Figures," 8.

110. Culpepper, *Anatomy of the Fourth Gospel*, 101–48.

111. Many still subscribe to the views of Collins and Culpepper. Neyrey, for example, writes that "[i]t is now accepted wisdom to examine the Johannine characters as representative of some trait important to the group or along some continuum of responses to Jesus or according to the choices made concerning Jesus" (*Gospel of John*, 6).

are complex, able to change, and show personality or even individuality. Yet, while many Johannine characters cannot be reduced to "types," their belief-responses can—it is the character's *response* to Jesus that is "typical."[112] I contend that the Johannine author has presented an array of responses to Jesus that are applicable in any time and context—they are typical, human responses.[113] Burnett points out that a character may display individuality but need not be idiosyncratic: "A biblical character may leave the reader with the impression of individuality because of that character's situation or response to events, yet he or she can still be representative of a generic ethos."[114] In other words, characters like Nicodemus, the Samaritan woman, Peter, or Pilate may acquire personality or even individuality on the continuum of degree of characterization, while their responses to Jesus remain representative or typical. In short, *a character's typical belief-response need not reduce the character to a type.*[115] Even so, I contend that the representative value across cultures and time lies in the *totality* of each character—traits, development, *and* response.

This implies that we must carefully distinguish between evaluating the character's response and gauging the representative value of the overall character. That is, we evaluate the character's response rather than the entire character. The author urges the reader to evaluate the character's typical response to Jesus as either adequate or inadequate, not the character itself. For example, the author is not warning us to dissociate from Nicodemus as a character as much as his response to Jesus. Nor are we to judge Peter harshly. Though he is far from perfect, shifting between adequate responses (e.g., in 6:68-69 and 21:15-17) and inadequate ones (his misunderstandings in 13:6-10; 18:10-11; his denial; his petulant query about the Beloved Disciple in 21:20-22), Peter is (and remains) firmly at Jesus' side (cf. his restoration in 21:15-19 after his defection). Admittedly, in the cases of Judas and "the Jews" it would be difficult to differentiate between character and response since both are negative or inadequate throughout the Gospel with little evidence of change. Thus we may not always be able to clinically separate characters from

---

112. We noted earlier that a typical response is not necessarily restricted to one character and, conversely, a character is not limited to one response.

113. Even the highly contextual response of Joseph of Arimathea as secret belief instigated by "the fear of the Jews" (19:38) remains relevant today since many people do not dare to confess their allegiance to Jesus openly lest they be ostracized or persecuted. Similarly, Nicodemus's ambiguity—seemingly sympathetic to Jesus without making a decisive commitment—is a common attitude today.

114. Burnett, "Characterization," 19 n. 7.

115. Cf. Koester's assertion that the characters' "representative roles do not negate their individuality but actually develop their most distinctive traits" (*Symbolism*, 35).

their responses—a character's response corresponds with who that character is. Recently, Ruth Sheridan has suggested that, in my book *Encountering Jesus*, I may have "cordoned off" too neatly the characters' responses from the characters themselves.[116] This is not my intention. What I suggest is that we approach characters holistically, and if there is anything "typical" it is their response rather than their totality—the latter is in most cases too complex to typify.

In sum, the Johannine characters are representative figures who have a symbolic or illustrative value beyond the narrative but not in a reductionist, "typical" sense. The reader is invited to identify with (aspects of) one or more of the characters, learn from them, and then make her own response to Jesus—preferably one that the author had in mind. Conversely, the reader may already have made a response to Jesus and can now evaluate that response against those of the characters.[117]

3.4. Revisiting Ancient Characterization

Before we turn to the final task of applying our theory, I will look at Alicia Myers's recent monograph in which she exclusively uses ancient Greco-Roman characterization techniques to analyze the Johannine Jesus (see ch. 1, n. 88). Myers is mildly critical of my use of modern categories to analyze and classify ancient characters rather than the characterization techniques and *topoi* from Greco-Roman rhetoric.[118] While she admits that a character may exhibit personality traits as an individual, she maintains that ancient characters "behave in a consistent manner that reflects their primary traits. . . . It is these typical traits that pave the way for the ancients to use characters from history and legend as 'types' and ethical examples for their own audiences to emulate or avoid even if they can also acknowledge the individual personalities of certain historical and legendary figures."[119] Although I have challenged the consistent flattening of characters in New Testament narrative either through an Aristotelian or actantial approach, I do not object to Myers's use of ancient Greco-Roman rhetoric. After all, my categories correspond to some ancient *topoi* (as Myers herself admits). Besides, there is little difference between her

---

116. Sheridan, *Retelling Scripture*, 82.

117. I have attempted to show the contemporary representative value of the various Johannine characters in Bennema, *Encountering Jesus*, 209–10. Cf. Farelly, who discusses the readers' participation in the narrative through identification with the characters, which includes both involvement and distancing because the world of the narrative is like and unlike the world of the readers (*Disciples in the Fourth Gospel*, 184–95).

118. Myers, *Characterizing Jesus*, 6–7 n. 20.

119. Myers, *Characterizing Jesus*, 7 n. 20.

assertion that ancient authors use characters as ethical examples for their audiences and my claim that characters function as representative figures for the reader. Besides, my evaluation of a character according to the author's point of view as either "adequate" or "inadequate" has some correspondence to Myer's contention that ancient authors wanted their audience to either emulate or avoid a character. The difference may be that I allow for more variation in their characterization than Myers, who insists that they are predictable.[120]

While I acknowledge that Myers makes a significant contribution to New Testament character studies, I also contend that her approach has weaknesses. First, her proposal to analyze characters in the Gospel of John (and I assume other New Testament narratives) by the exclusive means of ancient Greco-Roman characterization techniques ignores one obvious reality, that New Testament characterization is also influenced by Old Testament characterization. Why should we examine the Gospels' characters against Greco-Roman character handbooks rather than Old Testament narratives? Let me clarify. An important characteristic of the Bible is that it is progressive in nature—its grand story gradually unfolds, revealing God's dealings with humanity and the world (some use terms such as "progressive revelation" or "salvation history"). This incremental aspect is also reflected in many individual stories and the characters in them, which is unsurprising since these stories make up the overall story of the Bible. Various characters in the biblical narratives develop in their understanding of God and consequently exhibit change. This occurs both in the Old Testament (think, for example, of Abraham, Jacob, Samson, Saul, and David) and in the New Testament (for example, Peter, Judas, and Paul). Whereas characters in ancient Greco-Roman literature are often (but by no means always) fixed, ethical types, examples to emulate or avoid, characters in the biblical narratives are often in "the process of becoming"[121] or "a process of learning,"[122] and hence develop and serve as examples of what real life with God (and Jesus) is about (cf. Merenlahti's argument in section 2.4 under # Thesis 1). To rephrase, while Greco-Roman characters often represent ethical "ideals," biblical characters appear to be more "realistic." Again, this is not an immutable distinction. Just as the Old Testament narratives contain many types, and Greco-Roman literature knows of "round" characters, so characterization in these two corpora of literature should be seen as reflecting

---

120. In a recent essay, which is perhaps more in line with Myers's approach, I have examined the extent to which select Johannine characters promote the Greco-Roman cardinal virtues of prudence, justice, temperance, and courage (Bennema, "Virtue Ethics," 167–81).

121. Scholes, Phelan, and Kellogg, *Nature of Narrative*, 123.

122. Webb, *Mark at the Threshold*, 12.

different degrees of emphases on the Hebraic-Hellenic characterization continuum.

Second, while Myers competently analyzes the character of Jesus according to the various *topoi* found in ancient Greco-Roman rhetorical handbooks and *progymnasmata*, her account of the sum total of Jesus' characterization does not seem to go beyond what we can achieve with "standard" exegesis, nor does she indicate how Jesus' character can be classified (and hence relates to other characters in the Johannine narrative).[123] She also fails to show whether her approach works equally well on other Johannine characters or to provide criteria for deciding which characters should be emulated or avoided. If we were to reconstruct a character from the text using her list of *topoi*, how would the result look? Besides, as Myers herself admits, there is a (considerable) correspondence between her *topoi* of origins (ancestry, parentage, birth), upbringing (education, training, disposition), words and deeds, external goods (reputation, offices held, friends), manner of death, and events after death, and the "*topoi*" or character descriptors that I used in my 2009 work on Johannine character studies (titles, occupation, socio-economic status, place of residence, relatives, group affiliation, speech and actions).[124] Nevertheless, in the next section, I will propose a modified version of my earlier table of "*topoi*" in order to achieve a greater degree of correspondence with ancient lists of *topoi*. The main difference in our approach is that I add *aggregate information* about the characters in terms of their complexity, development, and inner life (qualities Myers essentially denies to the biblical characters), and their resulting degree of characterization. This meta-level of characterization is crucial to determine how characters relate to each other within a narrative. Admittedly, this more highly organized data about character is extracted from the ancient text by modern literary methods (no ancient reader would have thought in these categories), but it is nevertheless information that is present *in* the text.

Third, I maintain that since characters resemble people, and people across time are more alike than different, it is legitimate and fruitful to apply insights of modern literary methods to ancient narratives. Many of the *topoi* Myers uses still apply today—in both life and literature. Origins (family, ethnicity, nationality), upbringing (social class, education), words and deeds (behavior, virtues), external goods (reputation, offices held, friends, fortune), and even

---

123. Myers, *Characterizing Jesus*, 76, 131–32, 181–83. Myers states that I overlook "ancient systems of classification" (*Characterizing Jesus*, 6 n. 20), but she does not refer to these herself.

124. Bennema, *Encountering Jesus*, 19. While Myers acknowledges that my categories correspond to some *topoi* (*Characterizing Jesus*, 6 n. 20), I contend that the overlap is considerable.

noble death all play crucial roles in how we perceive people in life and reconstruct characters in literature. Besides, in reading the Bible (or any ancient narrative) today, we inevitably fuse the ancient and modern horizons. If meaning, which includes the reconstruction of character, is created in the meeting of text and reader, we inevitably use modern categories to understand ancient narratives. Many hermeneutical methods do so, whether historical criticism, narrative criticism, social-science criticism, or any other approach. As I explained in section 3.1, while I seek to be a plausible historically informed reader, I still remain a modern reader. Moreover, I also seek to study the potential or relevance of a text for today. As much as we seek to understand the characters in their original socio-historical context, I contend it is also legitimate, inevitable, and fruitful to use a modern lens to look at these characters.

Despite these differences, I view Myers's approach and mine as complementary or supplementary rather than contradictory. Myers's approach contains three aspects of ancient characterization: (i) rhetorical *topoi* of characterization; (ii) rhetorical techniques of characterization; (iii) rhetorical expectations of characterization. I have no objection to her list of *topoi*, which fits in with my list of character descriptors, although I have argued that it must be supplemented with other information such as character classification and character significance. I also see no problem with her use of rhetorical techniques of characterization since my work focuses on how readers can reconstruct character from the text rather than how the author disperses information about the character in the text. My disagreement is with the third aspect, that in Greco-Roman antiquity characters had to be consistent, predictable, unchanging in order to be persuasive.[125] This might hold true for the protagonist of the story but arguably less so for other characters. Besides, it is not always clear what Myers means by "consistent" characterization. If the typical betrayer is someone who changes sides, who goes from being loyal to becoming disloyal, then the character is both consistent (this is how a betrayer is expected to behave) and showing development (he does change). Even when the narrator provides insight into a character, it does not make the character predictable. For example, while the Johannine narrator informs the reader in John 6:71 that Judas is going to betray Jesus, it does not rule out the significant development Judas undergoes in John 13. Moreover, consistency does not negate the possibility of change or development (cf. my discussion of Hylen in section 3.2 where I considered creating a continuum of consistency or stability).

---

125. Myers, *Characterizing Jesus*, 55–60.

According to my analysis, most Johannine characters are consistent or stable; yet, seven out of twenty-three Johannine characters (i.e., a third) show some degree of development.[126]

3.5. Conclusion

In this chapter, I have proposed a comprehensive, nonreductionist theory of character for the narrative material in the New Testament. This theory consists of three aspects. First, since the New Testament narratives are neither fiction nor created in a vacuum, I study character in text and context, supplementing the text with information from other sources. Building on Darr's reader as a heuristic hybrid, I use the concept of a plausible historically informed modern reader, that is, a modern reader who has considerable knowledge of the first-century Jewish and Greco-Roman world and can give a plausible explanation for the ancient sources he draws on. Second, I analyze and classify a character along Ewen's three continua (complexity, development, inner life), and then plot the resulting character on a continuum of degree of characterization (from agent to type to personality to individual). Third, I evaluate the characters according to two aspects (the author's ideological point of view and the plot) and then determine the characters' significance beyond the narrative for today.

Assuming the role of the above-mentioned reader, I will engage in a close reading of the text while being informed by extratextual information. Since character is often inferred from the text, exegesis will be the primary means for character reconstruction. In other words, the main method for character reconstruction is a historical-narratological exegesis of the text in its original socio-historical context (cf. section 3.1). I will collate the results of our reading and character reconstruction in the following table of character descriptors.

---

126. Bennema, *Encountering Jesus*, 203–4. While Myers admits that *some* change in a character can occur, she contends that certain parameters, such as a standard list of *topoi* and ancient expectations of characters being consistent, are often placed upon this development (*Characterizing Jesus*, 59–60).

Name of Character	
Narrative Appearances	
Origin	Birth, Gender, Ethnicity, Nation/City
	Family (Ancestors, Relatives)
Upbringing	Nurture, Education
External Goods	Epithets, Reputation
	Age, Marital Status
	Socio-Economic Status, Wealth
	Place of Residence/Operation
	Occupation, Positions Held
	Group Affiliation, Friends
Speech and Actions	In Interaction with Protagonist
	In Interaction with Other Characters
Death	Manner of Death, Events after Death
Character Analysis	Complexity
	Development
	Inner Life
Character Classification	Degree of Characterization
Character Evaluation	Relative to Point of View
	Relative to Role in the Plot
Character Significance	Representative Value

The top half of the table (from "narrative appearances" to "death") contains various character descriptors that correspond to the *topoi* found in ancient Greco-Roman rhetorical handbooks and *progymnasmata*.[127] This information

127. After engaging with Myers's work (see section 3.4), I decided to adapt the table of character descriptors or "*topoi*" that I used in my 2009 study on Johannine characters (Bennema, *Encountering Jesus*, 19) in order to achieve a greater degree of correspondence with ancient lists of *topoi*. Except for the categories "upbringing" and "death," most adaptations to the top half of the table are merely rephrasing and reordering earlier categories. It is beyond the scope of this book to discuss whether we should follow

will be gathered as the first step of studying character in text and context through a close reading or exegesis. The rest of the table contains aggregate information about the characters in terms of their complexity, development, inner life, degree of characterization, evaluation, and significance as I outlined in sections 3.2 and 3.3. This meta-level of characterization is essential for determining how characters relate to each other within a narrative. Though this more analytical data about character is distilled from the ancient text by modern literary methods, it nevertheless arises from the text. Thus the two parts of the table show the fusion of the ancient and modern horizons in the reconstruction of character.[128]

In this chapter, I have regularly provided examples from the Gospel of Mark, the Gospel of John, and the Acts of the Apostles to clarify and illustrate the theory, but I have not demonstrated the validity of the theory by applying it to select characters in these New Testament narratives. This is our task for the next chapter.

---

a particular list of *topoi* in antiquity or combine various lists. For the various ancient lists of rhetorical *topoi*, see George A. Kennedy, trans., *Progymnasmata: Greek Textbooks of Prose Composition and Rhetoric* (Writings from the Greco-Roman World 10; Leiden: Brill, 2003); Jerome H. Neyrey, "Encomium versus Vituperation: Contrasting Portraits of Jesus in the Fourth Gospel," *JBL* 126 (2007): 529–52; Michael W. Martin, "Progymnastic Topic Lists: A Compositional Template for Luke and Other Bioi?," *NTS* 54 (2008): 18–41; Myers, *Characterizing Jesus*, 43–46.

128. While Ruben Zimmermann appreciates my theory of character, he contends that a weakness of my "formalistic" approach is that it leaves little room for specific particularities ("Figurenanalyse im Johannesevangelium: Ein Beitrag zur narratologischen Exegese," *ZNW* 105 [forthcoming 2014]: section 1.1). I disagree. I prefer the term *uniform* instead of the more negative term *formalistic*, and my uniform approach does certainly not result in uniform results. Besides, I start with a close reading of the text to analyze each character, taking into account the specific particularities, and only then use a uniform grid to collect meta-information about the characters.

4

Application of the Theory
Validating the New Paradigm

A theory is only as good as it works. Hence, in order to validate the new paradigm, I will put our theory to the test and demonstrate its value. From the various New Testament narratives, I have selected the following cross-section of characters: from the Gospel of Mark, Peter, Jesus' mother, the woman with haemorrhages, and Bartimaeus; from the Gospel of John, Peter, Jesus' mother, Nicodemus, and Pilate; from the Acts of the Apostles, Peter, Pilate, Barnabas, and Lydia. I have intentionally chosen some characters that appear in multiple narratives (Peter, Jesus' mother, Pilate) in order to determine how the various authors portray these characters differently. In line with our discussion about the kind of reader I assume (see section 3.1), a reader of Mark's Gospel knows the Old Testament, a reader of John's Gospel knows the Old Testament and the Markan narrative, and a reader of Acts will be familiar with the Old Testament, Mark, Luke, and either Matthew or Q.[1]

As we stated earlier, a close reading of the text and exegesis are the main means for character reconstruction. We have two main sources of information for the analysis and reconstruction of characters in New Testament narrative: the character text (what characters say about themselves and others) and the narrator text (the author's commentary about the characters). We will examine the following aspects: (i) the character's actions; (ii) the character's speech; (iii) what other characters say about that character; (iv) the narrator's speech. In analyzing the speech of the character and the narrator, we study both the

---

1. The reader of Acts will obviously be familiar with Luke's Gospel. Then, depending on the hypothesis one adheres to with regard to the Synoptic problem, the reader of Acts will also know Mark (the majority of scholars prefer Markan priority over Matthean) and either Matthew (according to the Farrer-Goulder hypothesis) or Q (according to the two-source hypothesis).

content and style of that speech since *what* is said is sometimes determined by *how* it is said. It is therefore vital to recognize the author's literary techniques, such as irony, misunderstanding, metaphor, symbolism, and double entendre in order to get the point he wants to make.

I will seek to validate our theory by applying it consistently to the selected characters. I will use the table of character descriptors that we outlined in section 3.5 to collect the information about each character. The following character studies are by no means exhaustive but are sufficiently detailed to illustrate our theory.

4.1. Characters in the Gospel of Mark

As I mentioned in section 3.3, the evaluation of characters occurs according to the author's or narrative's point of view and their role in the plot. In this regard, Mark aims at persuading the readers to believe the good news that Jesus is the Christ and Son of God, and to engage in discipleship. Hence, we will evaluate the responses of the characters to Jesus in terms of faith and discipleship. The plot of the Markan narrative revolves around the proclamation of "the good news" in terms of Jesus' identity and mission, the conflict this causes, and the various responses of people.

Peter

Peter is the best-known disciple in Mark's Gospel. He is also the most complex one. Mark provides a good deal of information about Peter's identity. His original name is Simon, but Jesus renames him Peter (3:16), although neither Jesus nor the narrator explains his new name (but cf. Matt. 16:18 and John 1:42).[2] Peter is a Galilean (14:70), has a (family) home in Capernaum, is married, and has a brother named Andrew (1:16, 29-30). Peter and Andrew are fishermen, and while they apparently do not possess a boat or have hired personnel (like the Zebedee brothers [1:19-20]), they are not hired men either but probably self-employed. Therefore, from a socio-economic perspective, Peter might have belonged to the lower middle stratum of society or "lower middle class."[3] In fact, the Sea of Galilee was known to teem with fish and hence

---

2. Tolbert contends that the nickname "Peter" (Πέτρος) is explained in the parable of the sower by the "rocky ground" (πετρώδης)—Peter "typifies hard and rocky ground, where seed has little chance of growing deep roots" (*Sowing the Gospel*, 145–46 [quotation from p. 146]).

3. Cf. Larry W. Hurtado, *Mark* (NIBC 2; Peabody, MA: Hendrickson, 1989), 25. For the socio-economic stratification of first-century Palestinian society, see Kenneth C. Hanson and Douglas E. Oakman, *Palestine in the Time of Jesus* (Minneapolis: Fortress Press, 1998), 117.

being a fisherman could be lucrative.[4] Peter, together with the Zebedee brothers James and John, is privileged by Jesus on various occasions, and they constitute Jesus' so-called inner circle (5:37; 9:2; 14:33). I will now briefly examine the character of Peter in the Markan text and context.

Peter's Call, Response, and Leadership. Peter and Andrew are the first disciples whom Jesus calls (1:16-17).[5] Jesus' radical call to follow him is matched by a radical response—they immediately leave their trade and follow him (cf. 10:28).[6] Jesus' promise to Peter and Andrew is to make them fishers of people instead. The Old Testament uses the analogy with fishing in the context of judgment (Jer. 16:16; Ezek. 29:4-6; 38:4; Amos 4:2; Hab. 1:14-17), which perhaps suggests that Jesus' promise to make them fishers of people has the connotation of rescuing people from eschatological judgment.[7] Anyway, it is clear that Peter is responsive to Jesus and follows him. "To follow" Jesus has clear connotations of discipleship in Mark (e.g., 8:34), and so Peter picks up a new trait here. During his time with Jesus, Peter often takes initiative in that he regularly speaks first (8:29, 32; 9:5; 10:28; 14:29) or is named first (e.g., 1:16, 29, 36; 3:16; 5:37; 9:2; 14:33; cf. 16:7), indicating that he probably functions as the spokesman or leader of the Twelve. In this role, he is sometimes impulsive, asserting himself too quickly, as 8:32-33; 9:5-6; 14:29-31 show.

Peter's Understanding of Jesus. Mark's story is primarily concerned about the revelation of Jesus' true identity, his mission, and people's responses to him. Many scholars consider Peter's confession of Jesus' identity in 8:27-30 as the turning point in Mark's Gospel.[8] Following this episode, for example, 8:31–10:52 constitutes Mark's largest segment on discipleship, including Jesus' predictions of his imminent passion. After Jesus finds out from his disciples what other people think of him, he asks them who they think he is (8:27-29a). On behalf of the group, Peter then proclaims that he is the Christ (8:29b). We

---

4. Ben Witherington, *The Gospel of Mark: A Socio-Rhetorical Commentary* (Grand Rapids: Eerdmans, 2001), 84.

5. For an elucidation of the Markan call stories, see Shiner, *Follow Me*, 171–98.

6. Whereas Jewish rabbis and their disciples continued to practice a trade, Jesus challenges his first disciples to stop it (Robert H. Gundry, *Mark: A Commentary on His Apology for the Cross* [Grand Rapids: Eerdmans, 1993], 67). Marshall's effort to identify Peter and Andrew's response to Jesus here as "faith" is overstated (*Faith*, 136–39).

7. Witherington, *Gospel of Mark*, 85–86. Shiner is more cautious, stating that this meaning can only be established in hindsight, in the light of the missionary activity of the church (*Follow Me*, 175–76). For the possible meanings of the phrase "fishers of people," see Joel Marcus, *Mark 1–8* (AB 27; New York: Doubleday, 2000), 184–85.

8. E.g., W. R. Telford, *The Theology of the Gospel of Mark* (New Testament Theology; Cambridge: Cambridge University Press, 1999), 104; Moloney, *Mark*, 48–49.

must observe that Peter's claim gains significance in the Markan story because this particular confession echoes the opening of Mark's Gospel, where Mark announces that his story is the good news about Jesus Christ (1:1). In fact, Mark 1:1 highlights two important aspects of Jesus' identity—Christ and Son of God—and while Peter confesses the first aspect, the Roman centurion at the foot of the cross confesses the second (15:39). Besides, this is the only occurrence in Mark where a character confesses Jesus as the Christ. Peter thus shows a profound understanding of Jesus' identity, albeit without indication of what he precisely means by "Christ," and 8:31-33 shows that his understanding is only partially correct.[9] Nevertheless, Peter's confession here may count as an adequate faith-response to Jesus.[10]

Peter's Misunderstandings. Almost immediately after having professed who Jesus is, Peter lapses. In 8:31 we find Jesus' first passion prediction (the other two are found in 9:31 and 10:33-34), where Jesus informs his disciples of his imminent suffering, death, and resurrection. This information probably does not fit Peter's understanding of the Messiah and he begins to rebuke Jesus (8:32). In reply, Jesus rebukes Peter for his lack of understanding (8:33).[11] Thus, although Peter shows profound insight into Jesus' identity (8:29), his understanding is marred by misunderstanding because he is unable to reconcile his picture of the Messiah with suffering and death.[12] Rooted primarily in Isa.

---

9. Cf. Hurtado, *Mark*, 135–36; Francis J. Moloney, *The Gospel of Mark: A Commentary* (Peabody, MA: Hendrickson, 2002), 166–67.

10. Cf. Joel Marcus, *Mark 8–16* (AYB 27a; New Haven: Yale University Press, 2009), 612. Morna D. Hooker is more critical of Peter's confession, stating that it is only now in Mark's story that he at last grasps what Mark's readers undoubtedly have understood much earlier (*The Gospel according to St Mark* [BNTC; London: Black, 1991], 202–3). However, this assessment seems unfair as Hooker mixes what can be known at the level of story and at the level of narrative. The reader has two distinct advantages over the characters in the story: (i) the reader is privileged by the narrator's information (e.g., that Jesus is the Christ and Son of God in 1:1); (ii) the reader has the opportunity to learn from the misunderstandings, mistakes, and failures of the characters in the story. Edwin K. Broadhead also considers Peter's confession inadequate because Jesus' silencing his confession (8:30) echoes Jesus' silencing the rantings of demons (*Mark* [Sheffield: Sheffield Academic Press, 2001], 79). In the light of the two-stage healing of the blind man in 8:22-26, Ernest Best considers 8:29 as the first stage of Peter's sight, with 8:33 indicating that Peter is still partially blind ("Peter in the Gospel according to Mark," *CBQ* 40 [1978]: 549).

11. Shiner considers that the conjunction of ἐπιτιμᾶν with the use of "Satan" may suggest that Jesus' rebuke is either a literal or a figurative exorcism of Peter (*Follow Me*, 260). Moloney comments that Jesus' command "get behind me" indicates that Peter (and the others) must keep their place "behind him" and not block his path to Jerusalem with their all-too-human understanding (*Gospel of Mark*, 174).

12. Shiner contends that although Peter's response is inappropriate, it does not reflect negatively on him because other characters also misunderstand and apparently Peter's position in the group has not been affected, as 9:2 shows (*Follow Me*, 263–64). However, even though Peter's inadequate response on

11:1-9 and 42:1-4, first-century Palestinian apocalypticism generally depicts a victorious messiah who would defeat God's enemies and inaugurate the new age (e.g., in *Pss. Sol.*, *Similitudes of Enoch*, *2 Baruch*, *4 Ezra*, Revelation, and various Qumranic writings).[13] Yet, other Isaianic Servant passages speak of suffering and death (50:6; 53:3-9), and perhaps Jesus expects Peter to have made that connection. Another of Peter's misunderstandings occurs in 9:5-6. Jesus' transfiguration was obviously a confusing experience for Peter, James, and John. Peter's offer of making shelters for Jesus, Moses, and Elijah shows that he has not understood the significance of the event; in fact, he just blurts out something because, as the narrator reveals, he does not know what to say (9:6).[14]

Peter's Failures. Peter is one of the first disciples whom Jesus calls. Peter immediately responds by following Jesus and proves to be a loyal disciple. Unfortunately, Peter's story is marred by serious failures. In 14:26-28, just before his arrest, Jesus foretells that his disciples will all fall away (or even, stop believing), although the message that he will go ahead of them to Galilee after he is raised up seems to indicate some restoration or continuity (cf. Matt. 28:16-20). Replying to Jesus' scandalous announcement, Peter boldly proclaims that this will not happen to him (14:29). Jesus, however, predicts a worse scenario, telling Peter that he will deny him three times (14:30). Peter then vehemently claims that even the prospect of death would not cause him to deny Jesus (14:31).[15] Jesus and his disciples then move to Gethsemane where Jesus will plead with his Father. Taking Peter, James, and John with him, Jesus urges them to stay alert (14:34). They are, however, unable to do so. Jesus even addresses

---

this occasion is not a verdict on the totality of his character, it does contribute toward it. Marcus calls Peter "a man in the middle, a disciple in whose heart the forces of God and Satan contend fiercely with each other" (*Mark 8–16*, 615).

13. Cornelis Bennema, "The Sword of the Messiah and the Concept of Liberation in the Fourth Gospel," *Biblica* 86 (2005): 37–49. As an exception, *4 Ezra* 7:28-29 says that the Messiah will be revealed and live for four hundred years after which he will die. Another messianic category is the so-called messianic pretenders, whose aim was to overthrow Herodian and Roman domination through militant action. Examples of messianic pretenders are Theudas, Judas (Acts 5:36-37), "the Egyptian" (Acts 21:38), the son of Ezekias, and Simon, servant of king Herod. See further Richard A. Horsley and John S. Hanson, *Bandits, Prophets & Messiahs: Popular Movements in the Time of Jesus* (Harrisburg, PA: Trinity, 1999), 111–34.

14. Marcus suggests that the nature of Peter's misunderstanding was his desire to linger on the Edenic mountain instead of descending with Jesus into the valley of human weakness, need, and pain (*Mark 8–16*, 639).

15. While Peter has at least learned that "being with Jesus" (cf. 3:14) may mean "dying with him," he has yet to learn that this co-dying is a divine gift and cannot be accomplished by human zealousness (Marcus, *Mark 8–16*, 973).

Peter by his old name "Simon" and challenges him again to be alert and pray, lest he is tempted, but Peter fails to follow through (14:37-41).[16] As the story continues, and Jesus is arrested, all the disciples do indeed desert Jesus (14:50), as he foretold (14:27). Peter, however, continues to follow Jesus (as a loyal disciple) (14:54). Unfortunately, Jesus had been right earlier because when challenged, Peter denies knowing Jesus (14:66-71).[17] With this, Peter denies his belonging to Jesus and thus negates his discipleship. Peter is unable to follow through on his earlier claim to remain loyal to Jesus unto death. Mark does not resolve this dilemma.

Peter's Character Analysis and Classification. This brief analysis of Peter shows that he is a complex character, with multiple (often contradictory) traits: on the one hand, he is responsive, takes initiative, shows understanding, and is loyal to Jesus; on the other hand, he is impulsive, fails to understand Jesus, and eventually becomes disloyal to him. In terms of development, Peter surprises the reader throughout the Markan narrative as aspects of discipleship and nondiscipleship regularly interchange in his life: he shows understanding and misunderstanding, following and desertion, loyalty and disloyalty. Regarding Peter's inner life, various aspects are revealed: he is afraid (9:6), claims to have been sacrificial (10:28), feigns ignorance and even curses (14:68, 71), remembers what Jesus had said earlier (11:21; 14:72), and laments his failure (14:72). Peter thus appears to be a very unstable character. Considering his location on the continua of complexity (complex), development (much), and inner life (some), I suggest that Peter is depicted as an individual.

Peter's Character Evaluation and Significance. Regarding the first criterion of Markan character evaluation, Peter's response to Jesus is both adequate and inadequate. On the one hand, Peter makes adequate faith-responses to Jesus in that he follows Jesus as a loyal disciple and confesses Jesus' identity; on the other hand, Peter makes inadequate responses in that he sometimes misunderstands and fails, and eventually stops being a disciple of Jesus. Although Peter's nondiscipleship behavior is not resolved within the Markan narrative, the

---

16. Best contends that the use of "Simon" simply reflects pre-Markan material rather than a relapse ("Peter," 550).

17. Contrasting Jesus' trial and that of Peter, Broadhead observes the ultimate irony: "The lying Peter goes out free and without harm. Jesus, who speaks the truth, is bound and tortured" (*Mark*, 121). Broadhead also points out the temporal device of the cockcrow: Peter's denial, framed around the two notices of the cockcrow, serves to warn the reader to be faithful in witness (13:9-12) and to be alert (13:35) because the master may return at the cockcrow (13:35) (*Mark*, 120–22). David Brady remarks that Peter's triple denial was in fact anticipated by his triple failure to be alert in 14:32-41 ("The Alarm to Peter in Mark's Gospel," *JSNT* 4 [1979]: 57).

young man's message to the women to report to the disciples *and Peter* to go to Galilee to meet their risen Lord (16:7) probably indicates that he is still on Jesus' side.[18] Indeed, all disciples had deserted Jesus when he was arrested and their relationship with Jesus needed renewal.[19] Regarding the second criterion of Markan character evaluation, Peter significantly advances the plot. First, Peter's confession of Jesus as the Christ (8:29) and the Roman centurion's confession of Jesus as God's Son (15:39) are key events in the Markan plot and, taken together, accomplish the purpose of Mark's story about Jesus as the Christ, the Son of God (1:1). Second, Peter's impulsive responses often provide further revelatory teaching of Jesus about himself and his mission, which ultimately benefits the reader. Third, Peter's denial of his belonging to Jesus fulfills Jesus' prediction based on what was written about him in the Old Testament (14:27). When we come to his significance for today, Peter may represent those who are quick to respond to Jesus and are zealous for him, but who sometimes fail miserably in their discipleship. In other words, Peter represents those who love Jesus but are unstable and sometimes unable to follow through on their claims of loyalty to Jesus.

Simon Peter		
Narrative Appearances	1:16–18, 29–30, 36–37; 3:16; 5:37; 8:29-33; 9:2-6; 10:28; 11:21; 13:3-4; 14:29-31, 33, 37, 54, 66-72; 16:7	
Origin	Birth, Gender, Ethnicity, Nation/City	male, Galilean
	Family (Ancestors, Relatives)	brother Andrew, mother-in-law
Upbringing	Nurture, Education	fisherman
External Goods	Epithets, Reputation	Peter, spokesperson
	Age, Marital Status	married
	Socio-Economic Status, Wealth	lower middle class
	Place of Residence/Operation	Capernaum, but travels with Jesus

18. Cf. Best, "Peter," 550; Moloney, *Gospel of Mark*, 309. However, Best's assertion that Peter's *weeping* "to some extent cancels his previous behaviour as it indicates his repentance and therefore his re-acceptance" ("Peter," 554) seems overstated.

19. Hence, Malbon labels the disciples as "fallible followers" ("Fallible Followers," 30–31).

	Occupation, Positions Held	fisherman, leader of the Twelve
	Group Affiliation, Friends	the Twelve
Speech and Actions	In Interaction with Jesus	responsive, impulsive, understands Jesus' identity, often misunderstanding, loyal, disloyal
	In Interaction with Other Characters	often appears with James, John, and Andrew; denies his belonging to Jesus to a servant girl
Death	Manner of Death, Events after Death	[Peter claims to be capable of a noble death (14:31)]
Character Analysis	Complexity	complex; multiple (often contradictory) traits
	Development	much
	Inner Life	some
Character Classification	Degree of Characterization	individual
Character Evaluation	Response to Jesus	both adequate and inadequate
	Role in the Plot	partially fulfills Mark's purpose of revealing Jesus' identity; advances Jesus' passion by denying him
Character Significance	Representative Value	those who are loyal to Jesus and zealous about him, but sometimes fail miserably; those who love Jesus but are unstable and sometimes unable to keep their promises

JESUS' MOTHER

Character in Text and Context. Information about Jesus' mother in the Markan narrative is extremely sparse. In 3:31–35, she is simply identified as the mother of Jesus and only from 6:3 do we know that her name is "Mary."[20] By implication,

20. Malbon suggests that Jesus' mother (and brothers) do not appear by name in the Markan narrative in order to facilitate Jesus' defining who his mother and brothers are ("Fallible Followers," 35).

she hails from Nazareth (1:9), and has other children besides Jesus (3:32; 6:3). Since Jesus' father is mentioned nowhere, Jesus' mother may have been a widow. Within the Markan narrative, she never speaks, has no traits (except perhaps for implicit misunderstanding), does not show any development, and her inner life is absent. The only actions ascribed to her are that she comes to the house where Jesus is on that occasion and remains outside, while sending for her son and calling him (3:31).[21] In doing so, she gives Jesus an opportunity to define his true family. Thus in terms of her characterization, Jesus' mother is clearly an agent; her only role is to advance the Markan plot.

The setting of 3:31-35 is presumably Peter's house in Capernaum. First, in 1:29 and 2:1, the terms οἰκία/οἶκος ("house" or "home"), referring to Peter's house in Capernaum, are first used. Second, 3:7 and 4:1 indicate that Jesus is near the Sea of Galilee, where Capernaum is located. Hence, when 3:20 mentions that Jesus enters a house (οἶκος), this is presumably his home base in Capernaum—Peter's house.[22] For Mark, the house is a place of withdrawal and private teaching in Jesus' ministry.[23] After hearing rumors of her son being mentally unstable, Jesus' mother and her family go in search of him to control him (3:21, 31). She probably perceives that her son's assumed condition is jeopardizing the honor of the family.[24] While the indication that she stands "outside" may simply mean that she and her family could not enter the house where Jesus is because of the crowd (cf. 2:2), Mark certainly gives the term symbolic significance. In 3:31-35, Jesus' family "outside" is contrasted with those who sit "around" Jesus "inside," and the next chapter also stresses the contrast between "outsiders" and "insiders" (4:10-11).[25] Morna Hooker notes that there is no direct contact between Jesus and his family—their message is brought to him—which indicates Jesus' distance from his family.[26] George Aichele notes the irony: "His own people/his mother and his brothers, whom one might otherwise expect to be insiders, are *outside* of (*exō*) the house. And

---

21. Marcus notes that while Jesus called two brothers away from their family in 1:19-20, Jesus' natural family is trying to call him back to his blood relatives (*Mark 1–8*, 276).

22. It is unlikely that Jesus is at his home in Nazareth because it says that when his family heard he was in a house, they went over to restrain him (3:19-21).

23. Stephen C. Barton, *Discipleship and Family Ties in Mark and Matthew* (SNTSMS 80; Cambridge: Cambridge University Press, 1994), 69.

24. Cf. David M. May, "Mark 3:20-35 from the Perspective of Shame/Honor," *BTB* 17 (1987): 83–87; Barton, *Discipleship*, 85. Susan Miller's assessment of Jesus' family being concerned for his welfare (he has had no time to eat [3:20]) is probably too positive (*Women in Mark's Gospel*, 36–37).

25. Cf. Barton, *Discipleship*, 72.

26. Hooker, *Mark*, 118.

yet it is *they* who charge *Jesus* with being 'outside himself' (*existē*, 3.21)! The outsiders accuse the insider of being outside."[27]

The actions of Jesus' family provide Jesus an opportunity to identify his true family. As Tolbert states, "Jesus is no longer their son or brother, friend or relative, automatically by birth or custom. . . . Traditional relationships no longer apply. . . . Jesus uses the occasion to define the kind of family suitable to this new age."[28] Over against his natural or biological family, Jesus' true, spiritual family is defined in two ways: (i) implicitly, these are those who are "around" Jesus and pay attention to his teaching (3:32, 34; 4:10); (ii) explicitly, these are those who do God's will (3:35). Jesus' mother clearly has not understood Jesus' mission and presumes she can control him, and Mark firmly places her "outside" (Jesus' spiritual family).[29] The association of Jesus' family and the scribes, and their similar opinion of Jesus ("he is out of his mind" and "he is demon-possessed"), do not improve the characterization of Jesus' mother either. In the light of 4:10-13, 33-34, what distinguishes insiders from outsiders is *not* the ability to understand Jesus' teaching (clearly, no one understood it), but an apparent willingness to come to Jesus and ask for clarification. Instead, Jesus' mother comes to summon him, without an indication that she is willing to pay attention to her son's teaching. In view of Mark's evaluative point of view, her nonverbal response to Jesus of remaining "outside" is thus inadequate. It is remarkable that she makes no further appearance in the Markan narrative (at the cross, for example), implying that she does not change.[30] Her significance for today is that she may represent those who, based on certain privileges, assume they are insiders and have access to Jesus (e.g., those born in a Christian family) but who are actually outsiders because they misunderstand Jesus and presume they can control him.

---

27. George Aichele, "Jesus' Uncanny 'Family Scene,'" *JSNT* 74 (1999): 33–34 (original emphasis).

28. Tolbert, *Sowing the Gospel*, 148. Cf. James R. Edwards, who comments that there is "no proxy membership in God's kingdom" (*The Gospel according to Mark* [PNTC; Grand Rapids: Eerdmans, 2002], 125).

29. Cf. Barton, *Discipleship*, 75; Miller, *Women in Mark's Gospel*, 38.

30. Bas M. F. van Iersel's suggestion that 15:40-41 perhaps restores the present rift between Jesus and his biological family (*Mark: A Reader-Response Commentary* [JSNTS 164; Sheffield: Sheffield Academic Press, 1998], 174) has no value because the absence of Jesus' mother in these verses is rather conspicuous (in contrast to John 19:25-27). Even if Mary, the mother of James and Joses in 15:40, is the same as in 6:3 (so Gundry, *Mark*, 976–77, but contra Witherington, *Gospel of Mark*, 194), she is not called the mother of Jesus. Besides, if she can also be identified as the mother of James in 16:1, she shows fear rather than faith and remains silent rather than testifying (16:7-8).

Jesus' Mother		
Narrative Appearances	3:31-35; 6:3	
Origin	Birth, Gender, Ethnicity, Nation/City	female
	Family (Ancestors, Relatives)	son Jesus, other sons and daughters
Upbringing	Nurture, Education	
External Goods	Epithets, Reputation	
	Age, Marital Status	married (perhaps widowed)
	Socio-Economic Status, Wealth	
	Place of Residence/Operation	from Nazareth, appears in Capernaum
	Occupation, Positions Held	
	Group Affiliation, Friends	
Speech and Actions	In Interaction with Jesus	indirect: she sends for Jesus and calls him
	In Interaction with Other Characters	indirect: she listens to people's rumors about her son
Death	Manner of Death, Events after Death	
Character Analysis	Complexity	uncomplicated; no traits (except perhaps for misunderstanding)
	Development	none
	Inner Life	none
Character Classification	Degree of Characterization	agent
Character Evaluation	Response to Jesus	inadequate: misunderstanding, remaining on the outside
	Role in the Plot	triggers Jesus' defining his true family

Character Significance	Representative Value	those who, based on certain privileges, presume to have access to Jesus

THE WOMAN WITH HAEMORRHAGES

Character in Text and Context. Mark narrates the story of the woman with haemorrhages in 5:25-34, sandwiched into the story of Jairus and his dying daughter (5:21-24, 35-43). Mark does not provide any details about the woman's identity—no name, no indication of her family or socio-economic and marital status. Instead, in 5:25-26, Mark narrates her situation in great detail: she has been suffering from haemorrhages for twelve years, during which she has suffered much at the hands of many doctors and has spent all she had, but instead of getting better her condition has become worse. The effect of this is that Mark focuses on the immense suffering this woman has endured. Besides, her condition of chronic uterine bleeding has also made her ritually unclean according to the Jewish purity laws (Lev. 15:19-30). This means that she is not allowed to have contact with people lest they become unclean too. Hence, her medical condition has made her a socio-religious outcast.

Twelve years into her desperate situation, she hears about Jesus (5:27). Mark does not tell the reader what information she has acquired about Jesus; instead, he focuses on the woman's surprisingly bold move. Coming up behind Jesus in the crowd, she touches his garment, and power flows out from Jesus and she is healed immediately (5:27-30).[31] Knowing that someone has pulled power out of him, Jesus turns about in the crowd and demands to know who it is (5:30, 32). Candida Moss clarifies:

> The power that heals the woman does not come from the garments but from Jesus himself. In the words of Mark, the power goes out of him (ἐξ αὐτοῦ) not out of his garments. We cannot argue that Jesus' garments were already endowed with power by virtue of their proximity to his body because it is only at the moment that the woman grasps the hem of his garment that power leaves *the body of Jesus himself*. This is not an act of simple magical transference from garment to woman; the woman's touch pulls power out of Jesus himself.[32]

---

31. Candida R. Moss perceptively notes that the bodies of the woman and Jesus parallel each other in the sense that both are porous and leak uncontrollably ("The Man with the Flow of Power: Porous Bodies in Mark 5:25-34," *JBL* 129 [2010]: 508, 516).

Probably realizing that she can no longer go unnoticed, the woman comes forward with great trepidation and confesses all that has happened (5:33). The episode concludes by Jesus affirming her and her actions, indicating that her faith has healed (literally "saved") her (5:34).

Character Analysis and Classification. Mark reveals various traits of the woman. She is proactive and persistent in that she has apparently not resigned herself to her condition but has continually sought healing. Also on this occasion, after hearing about Jesus, she shows initiative and courage to get to Jesus amidst a large crowd—something not allowed by her unclean condition. She also exhibits deductive reasoning and calculated risk-taking: realizing that her unclean condition prevents her from approaching Jesus in public, she reasons that just touching his clothes discreetly or secretly may heal her (5:27-28). Even though her bold, intuitive, perceptive attitude and actions are probably fueled by desperation (perhaps even superstition), interestingly, Jesus labels it as "faith" (5:34).[33] The woman arguably shows little development. The reader may be surprised that after twelve years of suffering (not only from her condition but also from the failed treatments, the resultant economic demise, and the exclusion from social life), she has apparently not resigned herself to her fate. The reader may also be surprised by her bold desperation to mingle among the crowd in order to touch Jesus, thereby violating the purity laws. Both the narrator and the woman herself reveal some of her inner life. In 5:28, the woman reveals her inner thoughts, providing the rationale for her action in 5:27. The narrator reveals that she suffers (5:26), has an inner realization or sensation of her healing (5:29, 33; "she knew in her body"), and is afraid in coming forward (5:33). To sum up, this woman exhibits multiple traits, shows little development, and some aspects of her inner life are revealed. As such, I place her on the characterization continuum as one having personality.

Character Evaluation and Significance. Regarding our first criterion of evaluation, her response to Jesus, she initially shows a somewhat desperate, perhaps even superstitious, faith, although the reader should observe that Jesus

---

32. Moss, "Flow of Power," 510. Miller states that the woman risks her life in touching Jesus because she may be destroyed by coming into contact with the holy (Lev. 15:31)—Jesus is anointed by the Holy Spirit (1:10) (*Women in Mark's Gospel*, 58).

33. Cf. Marshall, *Faith*, 105; Williams, *Other Followers*, 116. Tolbert perceptively comments that in Mark, faith is the prerequisite for healing, not its result. Tolbert also sees a connection with the parable of the sower (which is actually a parable about hearing), and argues that the woman's faith was her response to hearing (about Jesus [5:27]), and it bore fruit (*Sowing the Gospel*, 169–70). Cf. Moss, who remarks that "[t]he emphasis on her faith as the agent of her healing is typical of Markan miracle stories in general" ("Flow of Power," 515).

nowhere condemns it. After Jesus demands to know who it is who touched him, she comes forward to testify publicly (she tells "the whole truth"), and even though she comes with great trepidation, Jesus again does not comment on this. The reader must note that Jesus speaks of her in familial ("daughter") and "salvific" language—"your faith has 'saved' you"—thus approving her actions.[34] Hence, Mark indicates that the woman's response to Jesus is adequate.[35] Regarding the second criterion of evaluation, she advances the plot in that her actions reveal the healing-salvific nature of Jesus' mission. In the Markan narrative, she is the first sick character who actively approaches Jesus with an attitude of faith (in 2:5, it is the faith of the ill man's friends that moves Jesus to action). She is an encouraging example for Jairus (if Jesus can heal her, he can also heal Jairus's daughter) and for others who also want to touch Jesus for their healing (6:56; cf. 3:10). She also functions as an example for the reader because if the reader reaches out to Jesus in faith, he too would be "healed" (saved).[36] Finally, the woman's significance is that she represents those who cautiously, desperately, secretly, but expectantly, approach Jesus to meet their needs.

Woman with Haemorrhages		
Narrative Appearances	5:25–34	
Origin	Birth, Gender, Ethnicity, Nation/City	female, presumably Galilean
	Family (Ancestors, Relatives)	
Upbringing	Nurture, Education	

34. The epithet "daughter" implies that she has acted according to the will of God (cf. 3:35) (Miller, *Women in Mark's Gospel*, 61). Graham H. Twelftree notes that since others also "touched" Jesus (5:31), it was her faith that healed the woman rather than the touching per se (*Jesus the Miracle Worker: A Historical and Theological Study* [Downers Grove, IL: InterVarsity, 1999], 74–75). For the adequacy of the woman's faith/response, see Marshall, *Faith*, 105–9. Frederick J. Gaiser observes that while the woman was merely "healed" when she touched Jesus (5:29), she is "saved" after she confesses the whole truth in a personal encounter with Jesus (5:34) ("In Touch with Jesus: Healing in Mark 5:21-43," *WW* 30 [2010]: 8).

35. Cf. Broadhead, *Mark*, 55–56.

36. Cf. Susan Haber, "A Woman's Touch: Feminist Encounters with the Hemorrhaging Woman in Mark 5.24-34," *JSNT* (2003): 192; Mary Healy, *The Gospel of Mark* (Grand Rapids: Baker Academic, 2008), 107.

External Goods	Epithets, Reputation	unclean
	Age, Marital Status	
	Socio-Economic Status, Wealth	socio-religious outcast; deteriorated (spent all on doctors)
	Place of Residence/Operation	near the Sea of Galilee, probably Capernaum
	Occupation, Positions Held	
	Group Affiliation, Friends	
Speech and Actions	In Interaction with Jesus	she touches Jesus and, at Jesus' challenge, comes forward to testify
	In Interaction with Other Characters	spent all she had on doctors
Death	Manner of Death, Events after Death	
Character Analysis	Complexity	little complex; multiple traits
	Development	little
	Inner Life	some
Character Classification	Degree of Characterization	personality
Character Evaluation	Response to Jesus	adequate: initial faith, public testimony
	Role in the Plot	advances the plot by encouraging others and also the reader to "touch" Jesus in faith
Character Significance	Representative Value	those who desperately, furtively, but expectantly approach Jesus to meet their needs

BARTIMAEUS

Character in Text and Context.[37] The Bartimaeus episode closes Mark's major section on discipleship (8:22–10:52) and, appropriately, epitomizes true discipleship. We learn that Jesus and his disciples are on the road to Jerusalem

37. This analysis of Bartimaeus is adapted from Bennema, "Figurenanalyse."

(10:32, 46), where Jesus is soon to be arrested and killed. The character and his ironic situation are immediately introduced: Bartimaeus or "son of honor" is a blind beggar seated by the roadside (10:46).[38] Although Bartimaeus is unable to follow Jesus at this stage, he is not passive. Hearing that Jesus the Nazarene is passing by, Bartimaeus cries out, addressing Jesus as "Son of David" (10:47). The text does not indicate how he infers that Jesus the Nazarene is the messianic Son of David, but sightless Bartimaeus certainly shows insight.[39] Understanding Jesus' true identity and mission is an important aspect of Markan discipleship and Bartimaeus is off to a good start. Besides, he is not easily deterred by the crowd's attempt to shut him up but persists in getting Jesus' attention (10:48). Bartimaeus succeeds: Jesus stops and asks the crowd to call him (10:49), echoing Jesus "calling" his first disciples (1:17, 20).[40] Bartimaeus follows his shouting with more dramatic actions—he throws away his garment and jumps up—showing his eagerness to meet Jesus (10:50).[41]

Jesus' question to Bartimaeus, "What do you want me to do for you?" (10:51), echoes his question to the sons of Zebedee in the previous episode (10:36). However, unlike James and John who request personal power (which is denied), Bartimaeus asks for sight (which will be granted to him). James and John have journeyed with Jesus for a while, but appear to have failed to grasp a key aspect of discipleship because Jesus has to repeat that whoever wants to be first/great must adopt a servant identity (cf. 9:33-35 and 10:43-44). In contrast, Bartimaeus shows he is ahead by asking for sight—in order to follow Jesus, as 10:52 will show. Jesus deems Bartimaeus's attitude and understanding of his identity and discipleship as "faith" (10:52). His faith probably consists of

---

38. Cf. Wendy J. Cotter, *The Christ of the Miracle Stories: Portrait through Encounter* (Grand Rapids: Baker Academic, 2010), 56.

39. Twelftree asserts that the cry for mercy is not simply a cry for healing but also has salvific connotations (*Jesus the Miracle Worker*, 90). In contrast, Webb contends that, at this stage, Bartimaeus is merely asking for alms and has an inadequate understanding of Jesus' identity (*Mark at the Threshold*, 175–76). Others, however, contend that Bartimaeus's address of Jesus is positive (Marshall, *Faith*, 127–28; Marcus, *Mark 8–16*, 759). For the possible relation between the messianic Son of David and healing, see Moloney, *Gospel of Mark*, 209. For a more critical discussion of Bartimaeus's use of the title "Son of David," see Gundry, *Mark*, 600–601; Elizabeth Struthers Malbon, "The Jesus of Mark and the 'Son of David,'" in *Between Author and Audience in Mark: Narration, Characterization, Interpretation*, ed. Elizabeth Struthers Malbon (NTM 23; Sheffield: Phoenix, 2009), 162–67; Cotter, *Christ*, 50–51, 62–63.

40. For the interpretation of the Bartimaeus episode as a "call story," see van Iersel, *Mark*, 342–43.

41. It is doubtful whether we should read anything more in Bartimaeus's actions (esp. the throwing away his garment), such as "the sign of starting a new life" (cf. R. T. France, *The Gospel of Mark* [NIGTC; Grand Rapids: Eerdmans, 2002], 424; Cotter, *Christ*, 54–55, 67–71; *pace* Marshall, *Faith*, 141–42).

seeking Jesus based on some understanding of who Jesus is and what he can do. As Telford states, "Faith for Mark . . . is connected with understanding, and understanding with the true significance of Jesus' person and mission."[42] Although Jesus' utterance, "your faith has healed/saved you" (ἡ πίστις σου σέσωκέν σε), to Bartimaeus (10:52), and earlier to the haemorrhaging woman (5:34), suggests that their trust in him facilitated their physical healing, it does not exclude a spiritual or soteriological dimension. Both characters display aspects of discipleship in that they persistently seek Jesus based on some understanding of who he is and what he can do; and this is considered faith.[43]

The episode peaks when Bartimaeus receives his sight and follows Jesus on the way (10:52). Most scholars have noted the dramatic contrast between Bartimaeus's starting position as a blind beggar who is sitting *beside* the way (ἐκάθητο παρὰ τὴν ὁδόν; 10:46), and his final position as a seeing disciple who follows Jesus *on* the way (ἠκολούθει τῷ Ἰησοῦ ἐν τῇ ὁδῷ; 10:52).[44] "On the way" (ἐν τῇ ὁδῷ) is a well-recognized Markan shorthand for "on the way of discipleship." Indeed, this phrase occurs five out of six times in 8:22–10:52, Mark's major section on discipleship (8:27; 9:33, 34; 10:32, 52). Four of these refer to the disciples accompanying Jesus on the road. In 8:27-29, Jesus asks his disciples "on the way" about their understanding of his identity, and although Peter's confession on behalf of the disciples is accurate, it soon becomes clear that their understanding does not include suffering, rejection, and death, or that the road of discipleship is the road of self-denial and the cross (8:31-35). The disciples continue to misunderstand what true discipleship is because "on the way" they argue about greatness and Jesus has to clarify what true greatness means (9:33-35). Finally, while "on the way" again (10:32), Jesus explains what the road of discipleship holds (10:33-34), but James and John misunderstand and Jesus provides correction yet again (10:35-45). This is why the contrast is so apparent when, following this episode and closing Mark's

42. Telford, *Theology*, 101. Cf. Marshall, who also stresses the relation between perception and faith (*Faith*, 126–29). As with the story of the woman with haemorrhages, Tolbert sees again a connection with the parable of the sower (indicating four types of hearing) in that Bartimaeus *hears* of Jesus' presence (10:47) and responds in faith—Bartimaeus typifies the good soil (*Sowing the Gospel*, 190). Differently, Cotter views Bartimaeus's "faith" more in terms of his determination to reach Jesus despite the attitude of people and cultural norms (*Christ*, 74).

43. Cf. Ludger Schenke, who states, "Daß der Glaube den Blinden gerettet hat, zeigt sich nämlich in seiner Nachfolge Jesu 'auf dem Wege' des Kreuzes" (*Die Wundererzählungen des Markusevangeliums* [SBB 5; Stuttgart: Katholisches Bibelwerk, 1974], 357).

44. E.g., Schenke, *Wundererzählungen*, 355; Marshall, *Faith*, 140; Gundry, *Mark*, 593; Twelftree, *Jesus the Miracle Worker*, 89; Broadhead, *Mark*, 88; Moloney, *Gospel of Mark*, 211; Peter Dschnulnigg, *Das Markusevangelium* (ThKNT 2; Stuttgart: Kohlhammer, 2007), 290; Cotter, *Christ*, 52.

major section on discipleship, we encounter blind, immobile Bartimaeus who, after his miraculous healing, immediately follows Jesus "on the way" (10:52). Bartimaeus outperforms the "professional" disciples in following Jesus on the way of discipleship.[45] The remarkable development in Bartimaeus's situation from being a blind beggar seated alongside the road to a healed man following Jesus on the road is probably the most explicit Markan picture of discipleship. In showing understanding, faith, and discipleship, Bartimaeus proves an exemplary disciple.[46]

Character Analysis and Classification. We have learned that Bartimaeus shows multiple traits: he is proactive, persistent, eager, responsive, and shows understanding, faith, and discipleship. Bartimaeus probably shows little development because the reader may be surprised that a blind, marginalized beggar shows profound wisdom in his response to Jesus' question by asking for something that enables him to follow Jesus as a disciple, whereas two of the "professional" disciples had just failed on the same issue in the previous episode. Finally, neither the narrator nor Bartimaeus reveals any aspects of Bartimaeus's inner life. In sum, Bartimaeus shows some complexity, little development, and no inner life, and therefore I place him on the character continuum as a type/personality.

Character Evaluation and Significance. Regarding the first criterion of character evaluation, I assess Bartimaeus's response to Jesus as adequate. Jesus himself evaluates Bartimaeus's attitude and responses as "faith," and in addition, Bartimaeus starts to follow Jesus as a disciple as soon as he receives his sight. Regarding the second criterion, Bartimaeus advances the plot in two ways. First, in contrast to the failure of James and John, Bartimaeus requests Jesus to enable him to become his follower, thereby exemplifying true discipleship for

45. For the contrast between the disciples and Bartimaeus, see also Cotter, *Christ*, 44–46. Tolbert argues that Bartimaeus exemplifies two Markan themes: (i) he epitomizes faith-empowered healings where the supplicant for healing initiates the action, and with Jesus responding; (ii) he epitomizes discipleship where Jesus initiates the call, with the person responding by following or not (*Sowing the Gospel*, 189–90).

46. Cf. Marshall, *Faith*, 124, 140, 143–44; Williams, *Other Followers*, 152–67; Twelftree, *Jesus the Miracle Worker*, 91; Dschnulnigg, *Markusevangelium*, 288; Marcus, *Mark 8–16*, 765. Broadhead claims that the healing of Bartimaeus shows that "true discipleship is the greatest miracle of all" (*Mark*, 144). Tolbert notes that "[a]s an example of the common folkloric strategy of end stress, the last one healed in the Gospel is the symbolic ideal" (*Sowing the Gospel*, 191). While Schenke surely attributes too much insight to Bartimaeus when he states that "Der Blinde glaubt, daß Jesu Leidensweg nach Jerusalem der Heilsweg ist" (*Wundererzählungen*, 360), Gundry seems to downplay Bartimaeus's discipleship in that his following is "a kind of following less than that required of disciples" (*Mark*, 595). Webb even denies that Bartimaeus is a model disciple because he is absent at Gethsemane and the cross (*Mark at the Threshold*, 177).

the reader. Second, soon after this episode, Jesus arrives in Jerusalem where he will be handed over to his opponents to be killed, and so Bartimaeus's following Jesus on the road of discipleship foreshadows Jesus' own "end of the road."[47] The representative value of Bartimaeus is that no matter how marginalized people are, if they call out to Jesus and respond to him wisely, they can become true and effective disciples.

47. Cf. Williams, who states that "[t]hrough the Bartimaeus story, Mark prepared the way for Jesus to enter Jerusalem as the Son of David (11.10) and to act as the authoritative king in that city" (*Other Followers*, 17).

Bartimaeus		
Narrative Appearances	10:46–52	
Origin	Birth, Gender, Ethnicity, Nation/City	male, presumably Judean
	Family (Ancestors, Relatives)	father Timaeus
Upbringing	Nurture, Education	
External Goods	Epithets, Reputation	
	Age, Marital Status	
	Socio-Economic Status, Wealth	socio-economic outcast
	Place of Residence/Operation	Jericho
	Occupation, Positions Held	beggar
	Group Affiliation, Friends	
Speech and Actions	In Interaction with Jesus	calls Jesus' attention, responsive to Jesus, follows Jesus
	In Interaction with Other Characters	he is not put off by people's attempt to quiet him
Death	Manner of Death, Events after Death	
Character Analysis	Complexity	multiple traits
	Development	little
	Inner Life	none
Character Classification	Degree of Characterization	type/personality
Character Evaluation	Response to Jesus	adequate: he shows faith and discipleship
	Role in the Plot	he models faith and discipleship to the reader, and foreshadows Jesus' road
Character Significance	Representative Value	marginalized people can become effective followers of Jesus if they call out to him and respond wisely

4.2. Characters in the Gospel of John

As I mentioned in the beginning of this chapter, I assume that the reader of John's Gospel was also familiar with the Markan narrative, and hence with the characters of Peter, Jesus' mother, and Pilate. This does not imply that we can read these Johannine characters through a Markan lens; rather, our reading of these Johannine characters is informed by a prior understanding of them from a Markan perspective. We will see that at times John's information concurs with what we know about these characters from the Markan narrative, but at other times, John's information complements or even deviates from that of Mark. In section 3.3, regarding character evaluation, I suggested that the criterion for evaluating the Johannine characters is their response to Jesus, and that the Johannine plot revolves around the revelation of the Father and Son (in terms of their identity, character, mission, and relationship), people's response to this revelation, and the conflict this causes.[48]

PETER

John provides various details about Peter's identity. First, he is from the town of Bethsaida (1:44), at the Sea of Galilee, and he was probably a fisherman before he joined Jesus (21:2-3; cf. Mark 1:16). Second, Peter has a brother Andrew and their father is called "John" (1:40-42). Third, his original name is "Simon" but Jesus renames him "Peter" (1:42). A change of name was a significant event since, in ancient thought, the name usually reflected aspects of the person's character. However, John does not explain the significance of Peter's change of name, perhaps because Peter's true significance will be revealed only in John 21—an account only preserved in this Gospel. Fourth, there are various indications that Peter has a leading position among the Twelve: he speaks on their behalf (6:68-69 uses plurals), he takes initiative (13:24; 18:10; 21:3), he is sometimes approached or named first (18:15; 20:2; 21:2), and he often responds first (6:68-69; 13:6, 36; 21:11). Although Peter is among the first of Jesus' disciples in John's Gospel, he does not immediately acquire the high profile that he receives in Mark.[49] First, Peter is introduced to Jesus by his brother rather than being called directly by Jesus (1:40-42). Then, Jesus' revelatory insight into Peter's life and his change of name do not elicit a faith-confession from him

---

48. The subsequent character studies of Peter, Jesus' mother, and Nicodemus in John's Gospel are briefer versions of those found in Bennema, *Encountering Jesus*, chs. 6, 8, and 9.

49. Cf. Arthur H. Maynard, "The Role of Peter in the Fourth Gospel," *NTS* 30 (1984): 543; Kevin Quast, *Peter and the Beloved Disciple: Figures for a Community in Crisis* (JSNTS 32; Sheffield: JSOT Press, 1989), 40–41.

(1:42), whereas Andrew, Philip, and Nathanael all display a true understanding of Jesus' identity (1:41, 45, 49). John delays Peter's confession until 6:68-69, where he functions as the spokesman of the Twelve. I will now examine Peter in text and context.

Peter's Understanding of Jesus. Peter's confession of Jesus comes at a crucial junction in Jesus' ministry because John 6 is a story of rejection and sifting. After the crowd has failed to become true followers (6:2, 26, 36) and the hostile "Jews" have rejected Jesus (6:41-59), even many of Jesus' disciples defect (6:60-66). Jesus then asks the Twelve whether they also want to leave. Peter's declaration on behalf of the Twelve affirms that they will stick to Jesus (6:68-69). Peter's rhetorical question, "Lord, to whom shall we go?," indicates that, for him, there is no alternative and hence defection is not an option. Peter's confession of Jesus as "the Holy One of God" differs from Peter's confession of Jesus as "the Christ" in Mark 8:29. Since the title "the Holy One of God" occurs in Mark only on the lips of the demon-possessed (Mark 1:24) and since Peter's confession in Mark is followed by Jesus' rebuke "Get behind me Satan," some scholars contend that Peter's declaration in 6:69 places him in the role of the devil and that Jesus' rebuke of Peter is transferred to Judas as a devil in 6:70b.[50] However, we should be careful about interpreting John through a Markan lens. "Holy" essentially is an attribute of God, and if "holy" qualifies objects, places, or people, it is to be understood in proximity or relationship to this holy God—set apart for God's use.[51] "The Holy One" is a frequent designation of God in the Old Testament (e.g., 2 Kgs. 19:22; Job 6:10; Pss. 71:22; 78:41; Prov. 9:10; Isa. 1:4; 5:19; Jer. 50:29; Ezek. 39:7), and Peter's assigning this title to Jesus probably implies his unity with God.[52] Thus Peter perceives Jesus as being closely related to the holy God, and perhaps even on a par with him.[53] Peter displays traits of perceptiveness, outspokenness, zeal, and loyalty.[54]

50. Arthur J. Droge, "The Status of Peter in the Fourth Gospel: A Note on John 18:10-11," *JBL* 109 (1990): 308 n. 7; Graydon F. Snyder, "John 13:16 and the Anti-Petrinism of the Johannine Tradition," *BR* 16 (1971): 11. John Painter briefly considers the possibility but then rejects it (*The Quest for the Messiah: The History, Literature and Theology of the Johannine Community*, 2nd ed. [Edinburgh: T. & T. Clark, 1993], 283–84; cf. Quast, *Peter and the Beloved Disciple*, 50–51).

51. Kent E. Brower, "Holiness," in *NBD*, 477; Herman N. Ridderbos, *The Gospel according to John: A Theological Commentary*, trans. J. Vriend (Grand Rapids: Eerdmans, 1997), 250.

52. Cf. Dongsu Kim, *An Exegesis of Apostasy Embedded in John's Narratives of Peter and Judas against the Synoptic Parallels* (SBEC 61; Lewiston, NY: Edwin Mellen, 2004), 85.

53. Cf. Bradford B. Blaine, *Peter in the Gospel of John: The Making of an Authentic Disciple* (SBLAB 27; Leiden: Brill, 2007), 45.

54. Timothy Wiarda, *Peter in the Gospels: Pattern, Personality and Relationship* (WUNT II/127; Tübingen: Mohr Siebeck, 2000), 115.

Peter's Misunderstandings. Peter frequently misunderstands the actions and mission of Jesus. First, when Jesus wants to wash Peter's feet during their final meal, his question regarding the propriety of Jesus' action (13:6), his reprimand of Jesus (13:8a), and his overreaction (13:9) show his misunderstanding of Jesus' action. While Peter reasons at an earthly/material level, Jesus is speaking of a spiritual cleansing that Peter (and the others) need in order to have a relationship with him (13:8b, 10). Second, shocked at the news of Jesus' departure, Peter interrupts him (13:33-36a). Jesus' reply that where he is going Peter can only follow later (13:36b) seems enigmatic, but the reader may observe that Jesus refers to the way of the cross, where Peter is not yet ready to follow. Only later—after the resurrection and Peter's reinstatement—Peter will follow Jesus on that same road (cf. 21:18-19). Peter, however, claims to be ready now to demonstrate the highest principle of loyalty and discipleship, namely, to lay down his life for Jesus (13:37; cf. 15:13). Jesus then painfully points out that Peter is not yet the disciple he thinks he is (13:38). Peter's third misunderstanding occurs at Jesus' arrest when he tries to take matters into his own hands and violently attacks Malchus, the servant of the high priest (18:10). Peter still cannot conceive the path Jesus has to take, and Jesus therefore rebukes him (18:11). Peter's last recorded misunderstanding is about Jesus' resurrection. When Mary reports that Jesus' body is missing, Peter and the Beloved Disciple run to the tomb to investigate the matter but they fail to understand that, according to the Scriptures, Jesus must rise from the dead (20:1-9).[55] Although Peter frequently misunderstands Jesus, we must note that he is not unique—many characters, including the Twelve, struggle to understand, misunderstand, or fail to understand Jesus.[56] Besides misunderstanding, Peter also displays traits of outspokenness, zeal, loyalty, and taking initiative.[57] In fact, Peter's misunderstandings are caused in part by his being too enthusiastic and impulsive, and overconfident of his loyalty to his master.

---

55. While it is ambiguous whether the Beloved Disciple's "belief" mentioned in 20:8 is a belief that Jesus had risen, the text certainly does not indicate that Peter reached resurrection faith (contra Krafft, "Personen," 25).

56. Barnabas Lindars's assessment of Peter as one who "represents faith without understanding" is too harsh (*The Gospel of John* [NCB; London: Oliphants, 1972], 450). Tom Thatcher's conclusion that "[b]efore Jesus' death, Peter was the pinnacle of ignorance" is also exaggerated ("Jesus, Judas and Peter: Character by Contrast in the Fourth Gospel," *BSac* 153 [1996]: 448). Craig S. Keener's evaluation of Peter as misunderstanding mitigated by his loyalty to Jesus seems more appropriate (*The Gospel of John: A Commentary* [Peabody, MA: Hendrickson, 2003], 909).

57. Cf. Wiarda, *Peter in the Gospels*, 107–10.

Peter's Failure. Peter's defection is narrated in 18:15-27. Peter and the Beloved Disciple follow Jesus to Annas's house—as loyal disciples (18:15a).[58] However, while the Beloved Disciple goes with Jesus into the courtyard, Peter must remain outside until the Beloved Disciple arranges for Peter to come in (18:15-16).[59] In 18:17-27, Peter is asked three times whether he is one of Jesus' followers, and every time Peter denies his association with Jesus.[60] This episode undoubtedly rates as the most tragic in Peter's life. First, he is unable to follow Jesus as closely as the Beloved Disciple, and worse, when the heat is on, he becomes disloyal—a defector or nondisciple. Peter's bravado in 13:37, sadly, amounts to nothing, as Jesus has foretold (13:38). By denying his association with Jesus, Peter essentially denies his discipleship.[61] Peter is not (yet) able to follow Jesus the whole way.

Peter's Restoration and Commission. Although there is considerable debate whether John 21 was part of the original Gospel, an important reason for accepting it—even if it was added at a later stage—is that it concludes the story of Peter. Peter's denial that he belongs to Jesus in John 18 has probably left the reader wondering how things will be resolved (for Mark's Gospel does not settle it).[62] John 21:2-3 tells us that seven of Jesus' disciples are in Galilee, where Peter resumes his old profession and is joined by the others. Why did they return to fishing after having met the risen Jesus and being commissioned (20:19-29)? The text does not provide answers. Perhaps Peter is still ashamed and feels inadequate to carry out the mission that Jesus has called him to, and, as the leader, he drags the others with him.[63] More likely, however, if a comparison with Mark 16:7 can be made, the disciples might have gone to Galilee in obedience to Jesus' command and their decision to go fishing is simply an

---

58. In the light of 20:2, the "other" disciple in 18:15a is probably the Beloved Disciple.

59. For the assumed rivalry between Peter and the Beloved Disciple, see the discussion in Bennema, *Encountering Jesus*, 60–61.

60. Brant remarks that Peter's denials are denials of identity—he is no longer a disciple—and his "I am not" is the antithesis to Jesus' "I am" (*Dialogue and Drama*, 197–98).

61. Contra Quast, who suggests that Peter's denials are more denials of his violence in the garden, afraid of retribution for cutting off Malchus's ear (*Peter and the Beloved Disciple*, 87). Kim also diminishes the significance of Peter's denials, claiming that he does not deny Jesus directly and publicly, and hence there is no need for repentance (and restoration) (*Apostasy*, 59–67). Others go too far, claiming that Peter's denial is his confession/testimony (Droge, "Status of Peter," 311; Beck, *Discipleship Paradigm*, 141).

62. Cf. Dorothy A. Lee, "Partnership in Easter Faith: The Role of Mary Magdalene and Thomas in John 20," *JSNT* 58 (1995): 40; Timothy Wiarda, "John 21.1-23: Narrative Unity and Its Implications," *JSNT* 46 (1992): 53–71; Richard Bauckham, "The Beloved Disciple as Ideal Author," *JSNT* 49 (1993): 27–28; Stibbe, *John*, 206.

63. Cf. Stibbe, *John*, 210.

effective use of their waiting period.[64] After the account of the miraculous catch of fish, Jesus is seen having breakfast with his disciples (21:4-14).[65] Only in John's Gospel do we learn that Peter's fellowship with Jesus is restored (21:15-17). We may safely interpret this encounter between Jesus and Peter as reconciliation when we observe the parallels between the accounts in John 18 and John 21: (i) the mention of a charcoal fire on both occasions (18:18; 21:9); (ii) both the denial and the restoration happen in the presence of others ("they" in 21:15 probably refers to all disciples present);[66] (iii) Peter's threefold denial is matched by Jesus' threefold repetition of a question in 21:15-17. The three verses follow the same pattern—Jesus asks Peter a question, Peter replies, Jesus gives Peter a commission.[67] Each time Jesus affirms Peter by giving him a commission. In the threefold repetition of Peter's commissioning—"Feed my lambs," "Tend my sheep," "Feed my sheep"—there is very little or no difference in meaning.[68] After commissioning him, Jesus prepares Peter for his future mission by warning him how he will die—probably on a cross (21:18-19a; cf. 2 Pet. 1:14). Next, Jesus encourages Peter to follow him (21:19b). Earlier, Peter pledged that he would follow Jesus and even lay down his life for him, but he was unable to stick by Jesus when it mattered. Now Jesus assures him that he is ready to follow him all the way—even unto death. Thus Peter's commission and his impending death are conceptually linked: *as a shepherd*, he will eventually lay down his life for the sheep—quite literally. In this, Peter's life is patterned on the life of the good shepherd himself as outlined in 10:1-18.[69]

Character Analysis and Classification. Peter is a complex character whose traits include outspokenness and zeal (6:68-69; 13:6, 36), impetuousness (13:6-9; 18:10; 21:7), loyalty (6:68-69; 13:37), love (21:15-17), perceptiveness (6:68-69), misunderstanding (13:8-9, 37; 18:10), ambition (cf. his rivalry with the Beloved

64. D. A. Carson, *The Gospel according to John* (Leicester, UK: InterVarsity, 1991), 669; George R. Beasley-Murray, *John* (WBC 36; Milton Keynes, UK: Word, 1991), 399; Andreas J. Köstenberger, *John* (BECNT; Grand Rapids: Baker Academic, 2004), 588.

65. Peter's act of jumping into the water (21:7) may make it evident that his affection, loyalty, and priority really lie with Jesus (Wiarda, "John 21.1-23," 59).

66. Cf. Wiarda, "John 21.1-23," 55. Contra Thatcher, "Jesus, Judas and Peter," 446.

67. The different uses of the verb "to love" in 21:15-17 do not reveal any substantial variation in meaning (Bennema, *Encountering Jesus*, 59-60).

68. It becomes evident in his first Epistle that Peter has understood and realized his mission, and that, in turn, he is able to exhort others to follow in his footsteps and humbly tend God's flock (1 Pet. 5:1-4).

69. Cf. Culpepper, *Anatomy of the Fourth Gospel*, 120; Andreas J. Köstenberger, *The Missions of Jesus and the Disciples according to the Fourth Gospel: With Implications for the Fourth Gospel's Purpose and the Mission of the Contemporary Church* (Grand Rapids: Eerdmans, 1998), 158-59; Bauckham, "Beloved Disciple," 35-36.

Disciple), failure/disloyalty (18:15-27), and the ability to take initiative (13:24; 21:3, 11). Peter is also unstable and presents conflicting traits, making room for considerable character development. While he displays profound insight into Jesus' identity he also frequently misunderstands him. He functions as spokesman and leader of the Twelve but fails surprisingly when he denies being Jesus' disciple. His initiative to go fishing after he had been commissioned in 20:21-23 may also be unexpected. He thus exhibits insight, confidence, discipleship, and leadership but also dullness, failure, and disloyalty. As Collins aptly states, "Simon Peter appears as a man of contradictions and ambivalence."[70] Regarding his inner life, Peter knows Jesus' identity (6:69) and asserts that he loves him (21:15-17); Jesus unmasks Peter's bravado (13:36-38); and the narrator mentions that Peter was saddened (21:17). I thus place Peter on the character continuum as an individual.

Character Evaluation and Significance. Regarding the first criterion of character evaluation, Peter produces various responses to Jesus: adequate responses but marked by frequent misunderstandings, and inadequate responses during Jesus' arrest and trial. Yet, Peter's restoration and commission probably tips the balance, indicating that Peter stays firmly on Jesus' side. The second criterion for Peter's character evaluation relates to his involvement in the plot of John's Gospel, which revolves around the revelation of the Father and Son in terms of their identity, character, mission, and relationship, and people's response to this revelation (cf. section 3.3). Peter advances the plot in various ways. First, at a crucial juncture in Jesus' ministry, Peter professes Jesus' true identity and his loyalty to him. Second, despite his failures, Peter also exemplifies discipleship in that his love for and devotion to Jesus will ultimately be demonstrated in his laying down his life for his master (cf. 15:13). In terms of his significance for today, Peter represents the Christian in the making: those who are zealous for Jesus but sometimes fail miserably; those who can see Jesus for who he is but who can also misunderstand profoundly. Peter also offers hope for those who have turned their backs on Jesus but wish to return. More specifically, Peter represents budding Christian leaders who must learn to give themselves up to Jesus and to those who are entrusted to them.

---

70. Collins, "John," 365. Cf. Wiarda, *Peter in the Gospels*, 116–17. Tolmie's evaluation of Peter's characterization as "not complex" and showing "no development" is rather surprising and probably due to not taking sufficiently into account 6:68-69 and John 18, 20, and 21 (*Jesus' Farewell*, 142). Davies also evaluates Peter as a flat character (*Rhetoric and Reference*, 332). Kim's evaluation of Peter as a rock-like character who remained loyal to Jesus throughout is at the other extreme (*Apostasy*, 74–76, 143–47). Similarly, Blaine's portrayal of Peter as consistently positive is overstated, minimizing his misunderstandings, failures, and instability (*Peter in the Gospel of John*, 78–79, 183–93).

Simon Peter		
Narrative Appearances	1:40-44; 6:8, 68; 13:6-9, 24-25, 36-37; 18:10-11, 15-18, 25-27; 20:2-6; 21:2-3, 7, 11, 15-17, 20-21	
Origin	Birth, Gender, Ethnicity, Nation/City	male, Galilean
	Family (Ancestors, Relatives)	brother Andrew, father John
Upbringing	Nurture, Education	fisherman
External Goods	Epithets, Reputation	Peter
	Age, Marital Status	
	Socio-Economic Status, Wealth	possibly lower middle class
	Place of Residence/Operation	from Bethsaida in Galilee; travels with Jesus
	Occupation, Positions Held	probably a fisherman, spokesperson of the Twelve
	Group Affiliation, Friends	the Twelve
Speech and Actions	In Interaction with Jesus	adequate belief, frequent misunderstanding, loyal to Jesus, temporary defection
	In Interaction with Other Characters	in rivalry with the Beloved Disciple
Death	Manner of Death, Events after Death	honorable death foretold
Character Analysis	Complexity	complex; multiple (often contradictory) traits
	Development	much
	Inner Life	some
Character Classification	Degree of Characterization	individual
Character Evaluation	Response to Jesus	adequate but marked by frequent misunderstandings; inadequate during Jesus' arrest and trial; eventually adequate

	Role in the Plot	confesses Jesus' true identity and loyalty to him; exemplifies the highest mark of discipleship in laying down his life for Jesus
Character Significance	Representative Value	those who are zealous for Jesus but sometimes fail miserably; those who can see Jesus for who he is but who can also misunderstand profoundly

JESUS' MOTHER

In the Gospel of John, Jesus' mother is an anonymous character, married to Joseph (6:42), and she has, besides Jesus, other sons (2:12; 7:3).[71] She has an unnamed sister, and probably knows Mary the wife of Clopas, Mary Magdalene, and the Beloved Disciple (19:25). Jesus' family lives in Nazareth (1:45; 18:5; 19:19) but Jesus' mother seems to accompany her son at various points during his ministry—in Cana (2:1-5), Capernaum (2:12), and Jerusalem (19:25-27). Jesus' mother has a noticeable presence only on two occasions—in Cana, at the beginning of Jesus' ministry (2:3-5), and at the foot of the cross toward the end of Jesus' ministry (19:25-27).

Jesus' Mother at the Wedding in Cana. While most scholars struggle with the enigmatic exchange between Jesus and his mother in 2:3-5, Ritva Williams provides an insightful social-scientific analysis of this conversation. She draws attention to three social conventions of first-century Mediterranean culture. First, a first-century Mediterranean wedding took place in the public realm since it formalized the union of two households and their honor rather than two individuals. Second, the bond between mother and son was the closest of Mediterranean relationships, and when the son grew up, he became her supporter and defender. Third, the male head of the family was responsible for representing, defending, and if possible enhancing the family's honor in the public space, sometimes by establishing a patron–client relationship through a broker.[72] Williams then suggests reading 2:1-12 as "a story about a widowed

---

71. Troy W. Martin finds that ancient authors most often use the epithet "mother of X" when the name of a mother is well known to the readers. Martin thus concludes that Jesus' mother is anonymous in John's Gospel *precisely* because the community was familiar with her name ("Assessing the Johannine Epithet 'the Mother of Jesus,'" *CBQ* 60 [1998]: 63–73).

72. Ritva H. Williams, "The Mother of Jesus at Cana: A Social-Science Interpretation of John 2:1-12," *CBQ* 59 (1997): 680–84.

mother at a wedding who brokers from her son a favor that preserves the honor of the groom's family and enhances her son's honor in an unexpected way."[73]

Jesus' mother's statement in 2:3, "they have no wine," reveals that she is observant and practical. Running out of wine would mean a loss of honor—not only does the groom's family lack an adequate supply of wine but also the necessary social connections to preserve the family's honor.[74] Jesus' mother probably sees the embarrassing situation as an opportunity to enhance the honor of her family and extend the family's web of reciprocal relationships. She thus takes on the role of a broker, providing the groom's family privileged access to her son as the patron.[75] The text provides no information on how much Jesus' mother understands about her son's identity and mission at this stage, but it would be unlikely that she expected him to perform a miracle.[76] Besides, within the Johannine story world, the first miracle is only about to happen now (2:11). Nevertheless, she believes her son can do something and her request may be an implicit reminder to him of his family obligations.[77]

Jesus' reply in 2:4 is puzzling and complex. First, in addressing his mother as "woman" (he does so again in 19:26), Jesus is not rude but seems to use an acceptable form of address—he speaks similarly to other women (4:21; 8:10; 20:15; cf. 20:13).[78] Nevertheless, Jesus' use of this impersonal address for his biological mother may suggest that he distances himself from her and rejects any claim she might make on him because of her family relationship.[79] Second, regarding Jesus' question, "What has this to do with us?," Williams explains that Jesus' mother acts as the broker on behalf of the groom's family (whether

73. Williams, "Mother of Jesus," 680. Cf. Fehribach, *Women*, ch. 2. While Williams does not explain why Jesus' mother is a widow, Fehribach contends that her request to Jesus (rather than her husband) to meet the need (2:3) suggests widowhood (*Women*, 38).

74. Williams, "Mother of Jesus," 684.

75. Williams, "Mother of Jesus," 685. Cf. Fehribach, *Women*, 28.

76. Cf. Williams, "Mother of Jesus," 686; Beverly Roberts Gaventa, *Mary: Glimpses of the Mother of Jesus* (Edinburgh: T. & T. Clark, 1999), 83. Contra Collins, "Representative Figures," 31; Maccini, *Her Testimony Is True*, 99–100.

77. Williams, "Mother of Jesus," 686.

78. Judith M. Lieu, "The Mother of the Son in the Fourth Gospel," *JBL* 117 (1998): 65; cf. Williams, "Mother of Jesus," 688.

79. Raymond E. Brown, Karl P. Donfried, Joseph A. Fitzmyer, and John Reumann, eds., *Mary in the New Testament: A Collaborative Assessment by Protestant and Roman Catholic Scholars* (Philadelphia: Fortress Press, 1978), 188–89. Cf. Schüssler Fiorenza, *In Memory of Her*, 327; Carson, *John*, 170; Beck, *Discipleship Paradigm*, 55; Martin Scott, *Sophia and the Johannine Jesus* (JSNTS 71; Sheffield: JSOT Press, 1992), 180; Gail R. O'Day, *The Gospel of John* (NIB 9; Nashville: Abingdon, 1995), 536; Maccini, *Her Testimony Is True*, 102; Lieu, "Mother of the Son," 65; Fehribach, *Women*, 29, 37; Keener, *Gospel of John*, 505.

they have asked her or not), which is in need of patronage—a share in someone else's honor. By doing so, however, she has made someone else's problem her own and intrudes on Jesus' social space. Jesus' question should read something like: What concern is that (the shortage of wine) to us? It is the groom's problem. Why should we get involved?[80] Jesus thus dissociates himself from his mother's interests.[81] Third, Jesus' statement that his "hour" has not yet come is also enigmatic.[82] I have suggested elsewhere that Jesus' hour has two separate referents in John's Gospel—the hour of Jesus' messianic ministry (2:4; 4:23; 5:25) and the hour of his passion or glorification (7:30; 8:20; 12:23; 13:1; 17:1).[83] Although Jesus indicates in 2:4b that the time of the messianic age, that is, the new age of justice and peace ("salvation") that God would initiate through his Messiah, has not yet begun, his subsequent action of turning water into wine serves to lift the "not yet" from the messianic hour. The events at the wedding at Cana thus mark Jesus' inauguration of the messianic age (cf. the phrase "an hour is coming, *and is now*" in 4:23 and 5:25).[84] Williams correctly observes that Jesus and his mother appear to be at cross-purposes. Jesus' mother uses her privileged access to her son, seeking to broker a favor from him and reminding him of his obligations as head of her family, thereby enhancing the family's honor and reciprocal networks. Jesus' answer in 2:4 shows that he realizes his mother is drawing him into the local game of honor and patronage, whereas his concern is the mission that God had given him.[85] Jesus' reply should thus be seen as a mild rebuke that his mother's "earthly" motivations do not correspond to his "heavenly" mandate.[86]

We can hardly assume that Jesus' mother grasped the significance of what her son was saying in 2:4, and hence her reaction in 2:5 should be evaluated with caution. According to Williams, she may have viewed her son's reply as typical male grumbling, while expecting him to do what was necessary

---

80. Williams, "Mother of Jesus," 687–88. Contra Conway, who argues that Jesus' mother pushes Jesus before his time, trying to force a miracle, and Jesus' sharp response complicates the characterization of his mother ("Ambiguity," 337–38).

81. Brown et al., *Mary*, 191. Cf. Köstenberger, *John*, 95.

82. It seems inappropriate to take 2:4b as a question, "Has not my time come?," as Williams suggests ("Mother of Jesus," 689).

83. Cornelis Bennema, *Excavating John's Gospel: A Commentary for Today* (Delhi: ISPCK, 2005 [repr. Eugene, OR: Wipf & Stock, 2008]), 38–39.

84. For an explanation how the miracle signifies the start of Jesus' messianic ministry, see Carson, *John*, 172–75; Stibbe, *John*, 43–46; Fehribach, *Women*, 29–30; Bennema, *Excavating John's Gospel*, 39–40.

85. Williams, "Mother of Jesus," 689. Cf. Fehribach, *Women*, 31–36; Scott, *Sophia*, 180.

86. Contra Williams, who contends that 2:4, rather than a rebuke or rebuff, is merely a signal that Jesus recognizes what his mother is asking of him ("Mother of Jesus," 689).

because it was a question of honor—a confidence that came from her privileged relationship with her son.[87] Beck, however, contends that her response shows that she has reevaluated her relationship with him, accepting the newly revealed hierarchy in which Jesus' role is defined exclusively in terms of his Father's sovereignty, with no place for human familial obligation.[88] Be that as it may, when she tells the servants to do whatever Jesus says, it is in fact a directive to obey Jesus' word, and it is possible that she has accepted (and perhaps understood something of) Jesus' correction.[89] In the Johannine narrative, people are encouraged to trust Jesus' word (above miraculous signs) (4:48-50; 6:68; cf. 20:29), as well as to adhere continually to his word (15:7). Thus while Jesus' mother may not have understood the mission of her son and hence the true meaning of his reply in 2:4, her directive in 2:5 is a true Johannine command.

In sum, at a wedding celebration, Jesus' mother witnesses the symbolic inauguration of her son's messianic ministry. In fact, she plays an active role in precipitating this important event because of her powers of observation, her implicit request to Jesus, and her instruction to the servants to obey Jesus' word.[90] Many scholars connect the wedding at Cana with the scene at the foot of the cross, and diminish the significance of the part of Jesus' mother in the former event. They argue that she had no role in Jesus' ministry because his hour had not yet come (2:4) and only gains significance when that hour comes (19:26-27).[91] However, that Jesus' mother makes only two appearances in the Johannine narrative does not mean that the two events interpret one another. Besides, the "hour" in 2:4 and 19:27 do not have the same referent. The "hour" in 2:4 denotes the messianic hour whose "not yet" aspect is removed in the subsequent miracle, whereas the "hour" in 19:27 lacks theological significance and simply means "from that moment" (cf. "hour" in 5:35; 16:2). Jesus' mother did not have to wait until 19:27 to experience the messianic blessings or be assigned a role; she was a catalyst for Jesus' messianic ministry in John 2. Jesus'

---

87. Williams, "Mother of Jesus," 689–90. Cf. Fehribach, *Women*, 31–32.

88. Beck, *Discipleship Paradigm*, 57. Cf. Raymond E. Brown, *The Gospel according to John XIII–XXI* (AB 29a; London: Chapman, 1971), 109; Rudolf Bultmann, *The Gospel of John*, trans. G. R. Beasley-Murray (Philadelphia: Westminster, 1971), 117.

89. Cf. Beck, *Discipleship Paradigm*, 61; Francis J. Moloney, *The Gospel of John* (SP 4; Collegeville, MN: Liturgical, 1998), 67–68; Beirne, *Women and Men*, 57.

90. Cf. Fehribach, *Women*, 37; Keener, *Gospel of John*, 501; Beirne, *Women and Men*, 52–53, 61; Howard, "Significance of Minor Characters," 66.

91. Brown, "Roles of Women," 697; Collins, "Representative Figures," 32–33; Culpepper, *Anatomy of the Fourth Gospel*, 133; Beck, *Discipleship Paradigm*, 62; Mary L. Coloe, *Dwelling in the Household of God: Johannine Ecclesiology and Spirituality* (Collegeville, MN: Liturgical, 2007), 54–55.

mother thus has a more positive role than in the Markan narrative. Besides, in the Johannine narrative she makes one further appearance.

Jesus' Mother at the Foot of the Cross. Standing at the foot of the cross were, among others, four women—Jesus' mother, her sister, Mary (the wife or mother) of Clopas, and Mary Magdalene—and the Beloved Disciple (19:25-26). When Jesus sees his mother and the Beloved Disciple standing together, he says to her, "Woman, see, your son," and to the Beloved Disciple, "See, your mother" (19:26-27a). From that "hour," the Beloved Disciple takes Jesus' mother into his own home (19:27b). How must we interpret this incident? Most Johannine scholars interpret 19:26-27 symbolically as the constitution of the church or the community of believers, in which Jesus' mother represents Judaism,[92] Jewish Christianity finding a home in Gentile Christianity,[93] faithful Israel finding a home in the Christian community,[94] or the spiritual mother or new Eve of all believers.[95] Brown later modified his position (see n. 95), arguing that Jesus reinterprets who his mother and his brothers are in terms of discipleship: Jesus' mother and the Beloved Disciple (who is now Jesus' brother) become models for Jesus' true family of disciples.[96] The obvious lack of consensus among scholars who interpret the scene at the foot of the cross symbolically makes us question the validity of this approach.[97] There are several problems with a symbolic understanding of 19:25-27 as the inception of the church or family of believers. First, such understanding would require the Beloved Disciple to be addressed as "man," and them to be given to each other as brother and sister, not as mother and son.[98] Second, Jesus dissociates himself from this new relationship—the woman is no longer *his* mother but the Beloved Disciple's. Third, the Beloved Disciple takes Jesus' mother into *his* home rather than together becoming part of *Jesus'* home (which would fit a symbolic interpretation). Fourth, Jesus has already begun to constitute a spiritual family during his ministry when people believed in and remained with him.[99]

---

92. Krafft, "Personen," 18–19.

93. Bultmann, *Gospel of John*, 673.

94. Rudolf Schnackenburg, *The Gospel according to St John*, 3 vols. (London: Burns & Oates, 1968–82), 3:278–79.

95. Brown, *John XIII–XXI*, 926–27. Cf. Lieu, "Mother of the Son," 71–76.

96. Brown, "Roles of Women," 698–99; idem, "The 'Mother of Jesus' in the Fourth Gospel," in *L'Évangile de Jean: Sources, rédaction, théologie*, ed. Marinus de Jonge (BETL 44; Leuven: Leuven University Press, 1987), 310. Cf. Culpepper, *Anatomy of the Fourth Gospel*, 134; Scott, *Sophia*, 219–20; Beirne, *Women and Men*, 170–94; Coloe, *Household of God*, 55–56, 112–13, 145.

97. Cf. Conway, *Men and Women*, 81.

98. Lieu, "Mother of the Son," 69–70.

This leads us to an alternative interpretation. I suggest that Jesus fulfills his filial obligations with a practical solution: he constitutes a new earthly family consisting of his mother and his most intimate disciple. Knowing that he will no longer be able to care for his mother, he provides a home for her with the disciple he was closest to.[100] Jesus' command suggests that his father Joseph had died—perhaps before the wedding at Cana took place (see n. 73, above)—and hence someone would have to provide for his mother. This incident illustrates how the community of believers that Jesus had already constituted during his lifetime (namely those who adequately responded to him and followed him) should function—with practical care for one another's needs. There is one more dimension: Jesus' address of his mother as "woman" is possibly meant to create some distance between them (cf. 2:4). Being in the process of returning to his Father (starting with the cross and culminating in the ascension), Jesus can no longer maintain links with this world or his biological family.[101] The connection between 2:3-5 and 19:25-27, then, is not the occurrence of the "hour" but the issue of filial obligations. Jesus' addressing his mother as "woman" on both occasions indicates that his loyalty lies primarily with his family "from above." At the wedding in Cana, Jesus distances himself from his mother's plans because his primary concern is his Father's mission—though he implicitly fulfills his filial obligations to his mother. At the cross, Jesus fulfills his filial obligations to his mother but once again distances himself from his family below in order to return to his Father above.[102]

Character Analysis and Classification. Jesus' mother is an uncomplicated character with various traits—she is practical, observant, caring, and shows initiative. She shows no development and no aspects of her inner life are revealed. Hence, I put her on the character continuum as an agent or type.

Character Evaluation and Significance. Regarding the first criterion of character evaluation, although John does not record an explicit belief-response from her, it would not be too wide of the mark to suggest that she was on Jesus' side (in contrast to her position in Mark's Gospel).[103] Regarding the second

---

99. More suitable Johannine pictures of the church or family of believers are the one flock (10:2-4, 16) or the vine with the branches (15:1-5). For a critical assessment of the symbolic interpretations, see Martin, "Johannine Epithet," 64–66; Lieu, "Mother of the Son," 71; Gaventa, *Mary*, 90–91.

100. Cf. Williams, "Mother of Jesus," 690; Edwards, *Discovering John*, 109. Jesus may have put his mother in the care of the Beloved Disciple rather than of his brothers because there was a distance between them (7:1-9) (Williams, "Mother of Jesus," 690–91; Keener, *Gospel of John*, 1145).

101. Gaventa, *Mary*, 91; Resseguie, *Strange Gospel*, 159. Cf. Lieu, "Mother of the Son," 69–70.

102. Cf. Jesus' emphasis on the family "from above" (3:3-5 [elaborating 1:12-13]; 8:39-47; 20:17; 21:23) over his family "from below" (in 7:1-9, Jesus distances himself from his disbelieving, biological brothers).

criterion, she plays (probably unknowingly) an important role in the plot. First, she precipitates the inauguration of Jesus' messianic ministry by her request in 2:3, and the resulting first sign elicits belief from the disciples. Besides, in keeping with the thrust of John's Gospel, she directs people to obey Jesus' word in 2:5. The mother of Jesus thus functions as a catalyst in leading people to an authentic belief-response in Jesus. At the end of his life, Jesus makes of his mother (and the Beloved Disciple) an example of how the community of believers should care for one another. Besides, the phrase "After this, when Jesus knew that everything was now finished" (19:28) indicates that, *inter alia*, 19:26-27 was vital or contributed to the completion of Jesus' mission.[104] She thus advances the plot in that she functions (largely unknowingly) as a catalyst for both the beginning and end of Jesus' ministry, and while she initially tries to draw her son into her plans, she is ultimately drawn into his.[105] In terms of her significance for today, Jesus' mother represents those who, with good intentions, try to use Jesus for their own ends but find themselves drawn into his plan; catalysts who can direct people to obey Jesus or bring about events that advance the cause of Jesus.

Jesus' Mother		
Narrative Appearances	2:1-5, 12; 6:42; 19:25-27	
Origin	Birth, Gender, Ethnicity, Nation/City	female
	Family (Ancestors, Relatives)	various sons, including Jesus
Upbringing	Nurture, Education	
External Goods	Epithets, Reputation	the mother of Jesus
	Age, Marital Status	married (perhaps widowed)
	Socio-Economic Status, Wealth	

103. Contra Maccini, who only attributes a miracle faith to Jesus' mother because she requests a miracle from Jesus in 2:3 (an interpretation we denied) (*Her Testimony Is True*, 113, 199).

104. Cf. Lieu, "Mother of the Son," 69; Conway, *Men and Women*, 84.

105. Scott's evaluation of Jesus' mother as "a symbol of true discipleship in her service and faithfulness" is overrated (*Sophia*, 220).

	Place of Residence/Operation	Nazareth (but traveled in Galilee), Jerusalem
	Occupation, Positions Held	
	Group Affiliation, Friends	her family, her sister, Mary of Clopas, Mary Magdalene, the Beloved Disciple
Speech and Actions	In Interaction with Jesus	she initially tries to rope Jesus into her plans but eventually finds herself part of his plan
	In Interaction with Other Characters	directs people to obey Jesus' word
Death	Manner of Death, Events after Death	
Character Analysis	Complexity	uncomplicated; multiple traits
	Development	none
	Inner Life	none
Character Classification	Degree of Characterization	agent/type
Character Evaluation	Response to Jesus	no belief-response is recorded, but her attitude and catalyzing role indicate that she is on Jesus' side
	Role in the Plot	she is a catalyst at the beginning and end of Jesus' ministry
Character Significance	Representative Value	represents those who, with good intentions, try to use Jesus for their own ends but find themselves drawn into his plan; catalysts who can direct people to obey Jesus or bring about events that advance the cause of Jesus

NICODEMUS

One of the most intriguing characters in John's Gospel is Nicodemus, not least because scholars have evaluated him in different and contrasting ways: from someone who becomes Jesus' disciple,[106] to "the true Israelite,"[107] "a well-intentioned representative of the ruling classes,"[108] a fearful "secret believer,"[109] a *tertium quid*,[110] a pathetic character lacking courage and conviction,[111] one who has come "to a dead end,"[112] or even the typical unbeliever.[113] There are a few clues to Nicodemus's identity. First, he was a Pharisee (3:1), that is, part of the laity and an expert on the Mosaic law. Second, the phrase "a ruler of the Jews" (3:1) indicates that Nicodemus was probably a member of the Sanhedrin—the Jewish Supreme Court in Jerusalem. In 7:45-52, Nicodemus is present at a meeting of the chief priests and Pharisees, and such a meeting is explicitly called συνέδριον ("council") in 11:47, most probably referring to the Sanhedrin. Third, in 3:10 Jesus calls Nicodemus "*the* teacher of Israel" (the Greek σύ ["you"] is emphatic), indicating that he is Israel's chief rabbi. Fourth, Nicodemus's reply to Jesus, "How can a man be born when he is an old man?" (3:4), seems to imply that he was advanced in age.[114] Nicodemus very likely resided in Jerusalem, since that is where he appears to be in John 3, 7, and 19. He was almost certainly wealthy, considering that the extraordinary amount of spices he brought for Jesus' burial was worth a fortune. Nicodemus therefore appears to be a wealthy, leading Pharisaic scholar in Jerusalem and a member of the Sanhedrin. As such he would have enjoyed a prominent social, economic, and religious status. Regarding the historical referent of Nicodemus, Richard Bauckham presents a convincing case that he may have been the uncle of

---

106. Lindars, *Gospel of John*, 149; Ridderbos, *Gospel according to John*, 285; Moloney, *Gospel of John*, 511; Richard Bauckham, "Nicodemus and the Gurion Family," *JTS* 47 (1996): 29–32; Keener, *Gospel of John*, 533.

107. Sandra M. Schneiders, "Born Anew," *ThTo* 44 (1987): 191.

108. Schnackenburg, *St John*, 1:363.

109. Brown, *John XIII–XXI*, 959–60; Culpepper, *Anatomy of the Fourth Gospel*, 136, 146.

110. Jouette M. Bassler, "Mixed Signals: Nicodemus in the Fourth Gospel," *JBL* 108 (1989): 646. Cf. Köstenberger, *John*, 119.

111. Conway, *Men and Women*, 103.

112. Marinus de Jonge, "Nicodemus and Jesus: Some Observations on Misunderstanding and Understanding in the Fourth Gospel," in *Jesus: Stranger from Heaven and Son of God. Jesus Christ and the Christians in Johannine Perspective*, ed. and trans. Jeffrey E. Steely (SBLSBS 11; Missoula, MT: Scholars, 1977), 32–34. Cf. Krafft, "Personen," 20.

113. Collins, "Representative Figures," 15.

114. Contra Schnackenburg, *St John*, 1:368.

Naqdimon ben Gurion, a wealthy Jerusalem aristocrat during the Jewish War in 66–70 CE.[115]

Nicodemus and Jesus. The Nicodemus pericope probably starts in 2:23 and ends at 3:15, with 2:23–3:1 setting the stage.[116] While Jesus was in Jerusalem during the Passover festival, he performed miracles ("signs") so many people believed (ἐπίστευσαν) in him (2:23). Jesus, however, distrusted their belief-response—he did not "believe" or entrust himself to them (οὐκ ἐπίστευεν) because he knew people and their motivations (2:24-25). Although the text does not clarify in what way the people's belief-response was defective or deficient, it was nevertheless inadequate. Jesus did not question their belief because it was based on signs, for on another occasion he commends such belief (10:38; cf. 20:30-31). What was lacking in the people's response to Jesus in 2:23 will be clarified in the story of Nicodemus because he is included in this group—not socially but in the way he was drawn to Jesus and responded to him.

Scholars frequently give the impression that Nicodemus comes to Jesus alone, secretly at night, which could lead to the idea that Nicodemus is an anonymous or secret disciple.[117] A more likely scenario, however, is that Nicodemus, accompanied by his disciples, comes one evening to have a discussion with Jesus and his disciples (cf. the use of plurals in 3:2, 11-12). Theological discussion between rabbis and their followers frequently occurred "at night," that is, in the evening, after dark.[118] Hence, at the level of story, Nicodemus may speak for himself and his disciples, while at the level of narrative, John casts him as the representative of a larger group with the same faith-stance. Nicodemus is thus attracted to and even "believes" in Jesus on the basis of his signs, but Jesus is critical of his response. His coming "at night" (3:2) may also symbolize Nicodemus's spiritual position—for John, Nicodemus is still in the dark.[119] This is most likely not Nicodemus's evaluation of himself,

---

115. Bauckham, "Nicodemus," 1–37.

116. The reason for viewing 2:23 as the start of the Nicodemus story is threefold: (i) ἄνθρωπος in 3:1 alludes to its double use in 2:25; (ii) the antecedent of "him" in the phrase "he came to him at night" in 3:2 is Jesus in 2:24; (iii) the phrase "the signs that he was doing" in 2:23 is repeated by Nicodemus in 3:2. The conversation seems to end at 3:15 (rather than at 3:12 or 3:21), and 3:16-21 is the narrator's comments because: (i) 3:12-13 is one sentence in Greek, so that 3:12 has no break; (ii) the phrase "Son of man" used in 3:13-14 is Jesus' self-designation, and the switch to "Son (of God)" in 3:16-18 may indicate that the narrator has started speaking.

117. Cf. Painter, *Quest for the Messiah*, 197; Koester, *Symbolism*, 45; Ridderbos, *Gospel according to John*, 123; Moloney, *Gospel of John*, 510.

118. F. Peter Cotterell, "The Nicodemus Conversation: A Fresh Appraisal," *ExpTim* 96 (1984–85): 238; Bauckham, "Nicodemus," 31; Beirne, *Women and Men*, 73. The Qumran community also knew a similar practice (1QS 6:6-7). Carson, however, rejects this view (*John*, 187, 198).

since he comes with his disciples to establish who Jesus is—his assertion in 3:2 is in essence a question about Jesus' identity and authority (cf. 1:19, 22, 25). Nicodemus accepts that Jesus is a teacher and miracle worker from God but his identity eludes him.

Jesus, instead of satisfying his curiosity, talks about entry into the kingdom of God through a new birth "from above" (3:3). Nicodemus accepts this topic but misunderstands what Jesus is saying (3:4). Nicodemus thinks "from below"—he understands the new birth literally but misses its metaphorical meaning (cf. 3:6, 31). To clear up this misunderstanding, Jesus provides further revelation (3:5-8).[120] Nicodemus, however, is unable to keep pace with Jesus, as his question "How can these things be?" (3:9) shows. Jesus' rebuke in 3:10 reveals that he expected Nicodemus to understand at least some of what he is saying (cf. 3:11-12). Nicodemus has a cognitive problem—he fails to understand or think "from above" and therefore cannot become part of this saving realm. Although he recognizes that Jesus is "from God" on the basis of his signs, Nicodemus is unable to grasp the real significance of these signs. He fails to see the realm "from above" that the signs point to and to which Jesus belongs. Consequently, he remains "from below." So, in spite of a promising start, Nicodemus fades out of the conversation and disappears into the darkness from which he came (cf. the rapid decrease in the number of words from 3:2 to 3:4 to 3:9). He remains ambiguous, and we must look at his two later appearances to determine whether he is able to progress in his understanding.

Nicodemus and His Colleagues. Nicodemus reappears in 7:45-52, where we read about a gathering of the chief priests and the Pharisees—probably a meeting of the Sanhedrin. During the feast of Tabernacles, a discussion arises among the crowds regarding Jesus' identity and origin, provoking the chief priests and Pharisees to send temple guards to arrest Jesus (7:25-32). However, this delegation fails to arrest him and their excuse angers the Sanhedrin (7:44-49). At this point, Nicodemus throws himself into the debate (7:50-51). We learned from 2:23—3:1 that Nicodemus's initial "belief" was deficient, but now it also appears anonymous or secret. The same could not be inferred from John 3—we rejected a scenario in which Nicodemus came to Jesus secretly, alone, and in the middle of the night—but is suggested here in John 7. The question, "None of the authorities or Pharisees have believed in him, have they?" (7:48),[121] reveals that the Sanhedrin is unaware that one of them,

---

119. Cf. Beirne, *Women and Men*, 73.

120. For an elaborate explanation of the birth of water-and-Spirit, see Bennema, *Power of Saving Wisdom*, 169–72.

121. In the Greek, the question expects a negative answer.

Nicodemus, "believes" in, or is sympathetic to Jesus. Nicodemus shows courage when he defends Jesus by confronting his colleagues on judicial procedure, but his challenge is rudely suppressed (7:51-52).[122] Although Nicodemus has apparently remained sympathetic to Jesus, he seems hesitant to associate himself openly with him. He does not answer the Sanhedrin's question in 7:48, and the ferocious response of his colleagues in 7:52 may have robbed him of any courage to ally himself publicly with Jesus. Once again, Nicodemus starts well but fails to follow through and vanishes.[123] Hence, Nicodemus remains ambiguous. On the one hand, he remains sympathetic to Jesus, to the point of defending him and triggering an angry reaction from his colleagues. On the other hand, he appears unwilling to associate himself openly with Jesus and take the kind of stand that John would recommend. In John 3, we were uncertain about Nicodemus's attitude and what he had grasped of Jesus' identity, and this incident only adds to his ambiguity.

Nicodemus and Joseph of Arimathea. Nicodemus's final appearance is at Jesus' burial in 19:38-42. Narratologically, Joseph and Nicodemus are clubbed together—even though Joseph makes the request to Pilate and Nicodemus brings the spices, there is unity in their actions. Nicodemus's association with Joseph of Arimathea, who is described as a secret disciple of Jesus because of his fear of the Jews, may confirm the secrecy of Nicodemus's "belief" or convictions that we noted earlier. When one considers that bodies of crucified people are normally not buried but left on the cross to decay or thrown into a common grave, it is especially unusual to bestow honor on a "criminal" as Joseph and Nicodemus did.[124] The significance of Nicodemus's involvement in Jesus' burial is a debated issue. Some argue that Nicodemus is preoccupied with death or does not find life in Jesus' death and hence remains in the darkness.[125] Others, however, view Nicodemus positively, considering that such an extraordinary amount of expensive spices (weighing approximately 32.5 kilograms) is only used for a royal burial (cf. 2 Chron. 16:14; Josephus, *Antiquities* 15:61; 17:199; *b.*

122. The description of Nicodemus as being "one of them" (7:50) may indicate that he has not sided with Jesus. Alternatively, it may be a challenge to the Pharisees' claim in 7:48 that *not one of them* had believed in Jesus (so Moloney, *Gospel of John*, 255). Brant remarks that Nicodemus identifies himself with the authorities in 7:51 ("our law"), but that by their question in 7:52 they distance themselves from him (*Dialogue and Drama*, 191).

123. Beirne (*Women and Men*, 95) and Edwards (*Rediscovering John*, 105) conclude too much, contending that Nicodemus here reaches mature faith.

124. Carson, *John*, 629; Beasley-Murray, *John*, 358.

125. Krafft, "Personen," 20; de Jonge, "Nicodemus and Jesus," 32–34; Dennis D. Sylva, "Nicodemus and His Spices (John 19.39)," *NTS* 34 (1988): 148–51. In addition, Nicodemus and Joseph's burying Jesus according to the custom of "the Jews" (19:40) may also indicate that they are still siding with "the Jews."

Semaḥoth 47a).[126] Perhaps Nicodemus does recognize Jesus' kingship—a theme that incidentally comes to the fore in John 18–19. But does the text give enough indication that Nicodemus openly takes Jesus' side and has grasped who Jesus really is? Nicodemus shows a curious mix of boldness and fear, in both John 7 and John 19. He is bold enough to speak up for Jesus in the Sanhedrin and to take a risk in burying Jesus, but at the same time he is afraid to ally himself openly with Jesus and he is seen associating with another fearful disciple. I conclude that John does not provide sufficient evidence that Nicodemus's actions or understanding of Jesus is adequate for salvation. Although Nicodemus remains sympathetic to Jesus, it is uncertain what he understands of Jesus and his mission.[127] Nicodemus ultimately remains who he is—sympathetic but ambiguous.[128]

Character Analysis and Classification. Nicodemus displays a complex set of traits. Although he shows initiative and remains sympathetic to Jesus throughout, he also continues to be ambiguous and indecisive—there is no evidence of adequate belief or open commitment. It is unclear whether he was able or willing to profess allegiance to Jesus, whether a lack of understanding or fear of his colleagues in the Sanhedrin prevented him from arriving at or expressing an adequate belief in Jesus. He shows courage and risks being associated with Jesus, but he displays secrecy and fear at the same time. Nicodemus reveals a glimpse of his inner thoughts in 3:2, when he claims knowledge of Jesus. There is some development in Nicodemus's character. The reader is probably surprised that the intellectual Nicodemus, steeped in Israel's religious tradition, is a bit slow when it comes to understanding spiritual realities and does not seem to progress. After each initiative (3:2; 7:50-51), Nicodemus is reprimanded and quietly leaves the stage (3:10; 7:52), but returns unexpectedly (7:50; 19:39). Besides, Nicodemus's traits of showing initiative and courage are in tension with his secrecy, possible fear, and silent exit from each scene when he is reprimanded. Surprisingly, Nicodemus's intellect and courage do not take him all the way to a public confession of Jesus (in contrast

---

126. E.g., Schnackenburg, *St John*, 3:295; O'Day, *Gospel of John*, 836; Beirne, *Women and Men*, 85–86, 96–97; Koester, *Symbolism*, 229–30; Bauckham, "Nicodemus," 32.

127. Cf. Gabi Renz, "Nicodemus: An Ambiguous Disciple? A Narrative Sensitive Investigation," in *Challenging Perspectives on the Gospel of John*, ed. John Lierman (WUNT II/219; Tübingen: Mohr Siebeck, 2006), 274–79. Contra Bauckham ("Nicodemus," 31–32), who argues that Nicodemus's acknowledgment of Jesus' kingship became full Christian faith after the resurrection, and Beirne (*Women and Men*, 97–98), who contends that Nicodemus's act reflects his growth in faith and discipleship.

128. See especially Bassler, "Mixed Signals," 635–46.

to the Samaritan woman and the man born blind). In sum, I place Nicodemus on the character continuum as one having personality.

Character Evaluation and Significance. John implicitly gives a negative evaluation of Nicodemus's ambiguity—to stay in the twilight zone is not acceptable. First, Nicodemus makes little or no cognitive progress in any of his appearances, and hence John's evaluation of Nicodemus's starting position (which is inadequate) remains valid. Second, Nicodemus remains ambiguous and secretive regarding his beliefs about Jesus. If fear of his colleagues keeps Nicodemus from a public allegiance to Jesus, then, in the light of Jesus' command to his disciples when faced with persecution, "You must also testify" (15:27), Nicodemus's stance would be inadequate.[129] Elsewhere John is also implicitly critical of such an attitude when he contrasts the bold testimony of the man born blind in the face of persecution with his fearful parents' failure to testify (9:13-34; cf. 12:42). To testify is an expression of discipleship, and discipleship is essential to remain in a life-giving relationship with Jesus. It thus remains unclear whether Nicodemus experienced the new birth that would have brought him into the kingdom of God. Besides, there is no evidence of any form of confession or discipleship. John's implicit message to the reader is that anonymous discipleship or secret Christianity will not suffice.[130] A public confession of some kind that Jesus is the Christ seems appropriate and necessary. For John, remaining in the twilight zone, that is, continual ambiguity, anonymity, or secrecy, is not a valid option. Nicodemus is attracted to the light but does not remain in the light; he keeps moving in and out of the shadows, and within John's dualism, there is no place for a twilight zone. People often feel compelled to put Nicodemus on one or the other side of John's dualistic world, but John does not redeem Nicodemus of his ambiguity. The point John wants to make is that continual ambiguity is not an acceptable attitude. Nicodemus thus represents those who are religious, sympathetic, and attracted to Jesus ("seekers") but whose allegiance to Jesus remains ambiguous. Nicodemus advances the plot in that his initiating a conversation with Jesus gives Jesus an opportunity to clarify an important aspect of his mission, namely how people can enter the divine, saving realm.

129. Even if Nicodemus's speech in 7:50 can be called "testimony," he did not sustain it after his colleagues attacked him in 7:52.

130. Cf. Culpepper, *Anatomy of the Fourth Gospel*, 136, 146; Bassler, "Mixed Signals," 645–46; Beck, *Discipleship Paradigm*, 69. Contra some overly positive conclusions of Nicodemus's being a believer, disciple, and example to follow (Lindars, *Gospel of John*, 149, 304; Schnackenburg, *St John*, 1:364–65; Moloney, *Gospel of John*, 511; Edwards, *Rediscovering John*, 105). Collins's analysis that Nicodemus is the type of an unbeliever, however, seems too negative ("Representative Figures," 15–16; "John," 363).

Nicodemus		
Narrative Appearances	3:1-9; 7:50-51; 19:39	
Origin	Birth, Gender, Ethnicity, Nation/City	male, Judean
	Family (Ancestors, Relatives)	possibly part of the Gurion family
Upbringing	Nurture, Education	rabbinic training
External Goods	Epithets, Reputation	the leading rabbi in Israel
	Age, Marital Status	advanced in age
	Socio-Economic Status, Wealth	high social status (respected, highly educated), wealthy
	Place of Residence/Operation	Jerusalem
	Occupation, Positions Held	Pharisaic scholar, member of the Sanhedrin
	Group Affiliation, Friends	Pharisees, Sanhedrin, Joseph of Arimathea
Speech and Actions	In Interaction with Jesus	shows initiative but lacks understanding; sympathetic but no open commitment; ambiguous
	In Interaction with Other Characters	ambiguous, secretive, boldness combined with fear
Death	Manner of Death, Events after Death	
Character Analysis	Complexity	complex; multiple traits
	Development	some
	Inner Life	little
Character Classification	Degree of Characterization	personality
Character Evaluation	Response to Jesus	inadequate: sympathetic but ambiguous; attracted to Jesus but no open commitment

	Role in the Plot	he gives Jesus an opportunity to explain entrance into the kingdom of God
Character Significance	Representative Value	those who are religious, sympathetic, and attracted to Jesus ("seekers") but whose allegiance to Jesus remains ambiguous

PILATE

Pilate has been variously characterized:[131] from being weak, indecisive, and accommodating in the Gospels to being tough, cruel, and prone to flaunting his authority in Josephus and Philo.[132] I will examine whether the Johannine Pilate is indeed weak, indecisive, and accommodating or more in keeping with the Pilate portrayed in Philo and Josephus. Having clarified earlier that I assume that John was familiar with Mark's Gospel, I will also look at the Markan Pilate. I will start, however, with an analysis of the Johannine text.

Character in Text and Context. Pilate occurs only in the passion narratives (John 18–19), where he interacts with Jesus and "the Jews," who bring Jesus to trial. Although John's Gospel does not provide any details about Pilate (e.g., he is given no title), the text seems to imply that he was Rome's representative in Judea with full jurisdiction. Regarding Jesus' trial in 18:28–19:16a, John has organized the exchanges between Pilate and "the Jews," and between Pilate and Jesus such that they alternate with each other. As many scholars have observed, structurally, this episode consists of seven rounds, with Pilate moving in and out of the palace with each round. In rounds one, three, five, and seven, Pilate comes *out of* the palace to interact with "the Jews" (18:29; 18:38b; 19:4; 19:13); in rounds two, four, and six, he goes *into* the palace to interact with Jesus (18:33; 19:1; 19:9).

Round One (18:28-32). While presenting Jesus to Pilate, "the Jews" do not enter the palace since that would render them ritually unclean and disqualify them from participating in the Passover meal (18:28). Ironically, their actions concerning Jesus make them spiritually "unclean" and prevent them from partaking in the real Passover meal on the cross (cf. 1:29; 6:51-55). When Pilate comes out to inquire about the charges (18:29), his question is surprising since he must have known why "the Jews" brought Jesus to him.[133] The Roman

131. This analysis is based on Bennema, "Character of Pilate," 238–51.

132. Brian Charles McGing, "Pontius Pilate and the Sources," *CBQ* 53 (1991): 416–17; Bond, *Pontius Pilate*, 174–75; Conway, "Ambiguity," 333; Neyrey, *Gospel of John*, 305.

cohort could only have been present at Jesus' arrest (18:3) with Pilate's consent, implying that "the Jews" had contacted Pilate earlier and probably informed him about their scheme to kill Jesus (cf. 11:47-53).[134] The reply of "the Jews" that Jesus is an evildoer is not a legal charge and reveals some of their perplexity about Pilate's question (18:30). Pilate does not, however, humor "the Jews" and, knowing that they want Jesus' death, he taunts them, flaunting his authority (18:31).

Round Two (18:33-38a). Entering the palace, Pilate asks Jesus whether he is the king of the Jews (18:33). Pilate's question reveals that he has had contact with "the Jews" prior to Jesus' arrest, when they had probably told him that Jesus claimed to be a king—a political charge of insurrection against Rome (cf. 19:12). This explains Jesus' counterquestion in 18:34, but Pilate is quick to distance himself from "the Jews" (18:35). Pilate may have assisted "the Jews" in arresting Jesus—any potential insurrection needed to be investigated—but he does not side with them and probably wants to examine the case for himself.[135] Going back to Pilate's earlier question about kingship, Jesus asserts that his kingdom is not from this world (18:36). Nevertheless, although Jesus' kingdom is "from above," it exists and operates *in* this world, and one cannot be loyal to both Jesus and his kingdom, and to the Roman emperor and his empire. Although in Greek, Pilate's question in 18:37 expects the answer "yes," he has probably concluded that Jesus' kingdom is not a threat to Rome. Hence, his statement seems condescending—"You are a king then!"[136] Perhaps knowing that Pilate is searching for truth, Jesus extends an implicit invitation to discover truth—liberating truth about the divine reality present in his teaching (cf. 8:31-32; 17:17). Pilate's "What is truth?" is not an earnest question (for he leaves immediately) but a dismissive remark. This indicates that he does not take Jesus seriously and is probably irritated with Jesus' responses and his own lack of success in cracking the case. Not understanding Jesus, Pilate implicitly rejects him and his invitation.

Round Three (18:38b-40). Coming out of the palace, Pilate informs "the Jews" that the charges against Jesus are baseless (18:38b). Although Pilate

---

133. It is unclear whether Pilate's coming out indicates that he is forced from the beginning to comply with the demands of "the Jews" (Culpepper, *Anatomy of the Fourth Gospel*, 142) or whether he shows tact and courtesy (Bond, *Pontius Pilate*, 175).

134. Cf. Bond, *Pontius Pilate*, 167.

135. Contra Warren Carter who contends that Pilate had allied himself with "the Jews" to remove Jesus (*Pontius Pilate: Portraits of a Roman Governor* [Collegeville, MN: Liturgical, 2003], 141–42).

136. Cf. Bart D. Ehrman, "Jesus' Trial before Pilate: John 18.28–19.16," *BTB* 13 (1983): 128; Thomas W. Gillespie, "The Trial of Politics and Religion: John 18.28–19.16," *ExAud* 2 (1986): 71.

appears honest, he is also taunting "the Jews." This becomes more evident in 18:39 where Pilate, by referring to Jesus as "the king of the Jews," is most likely mocking "the Jews" about their nationalistic hopes. He does not seriously seek Jesus' release. If he had seriously considered Jesus a king, he would never have offered to release him.[137] Pilate has known since before Jesus' arrest that "the Jews" wanted Jesus' death (cf. 18:31)—and he uses this knowledge to taunt "the Jews" and flaunt his authority. In desperation and frustration, "the Jews" shout out not to release Jesus (18:40).

Round Four (19:1-3). Pilate, though not convinced that Jesus poses a threat to Rome, resorts to cruel and calculated measures to extract truth from Jesus (19:1). Jennifer Glancy makes a good case for understanding the scourging as an act of judicial rather than punitive torture, a means of interrogation to extract truth.[138] Pilate may not know the truth (cf. 18:38a), but he thinks he can get it out of Jesus: Pilate has Jesus tortured with a *mastix*, a whip studded with lumps of bone or metal, in order to extract a confession.[139]

Round Five (19:4-7). Pilate is now convinced that there is no real case and that Jesus is innocent (19:4; cf. 18:38), but he also knows that "the Jews" are determined to have Jesus killed.[140] For those who view the scourging as a punishment, the phrase "to let you know that I find no case against him" is problematic. However, Pilate's statement makes perfect sense when the flogging is seen as judicial torture to extract truth. Pilate demonstrates to "the Jews" that despite having Jesus whipped he gets no admission of guilt, and hence Jesus' flogged body testifies to guiltlessness.[141] With his exclamation—"See the man!"—Pilate scoffs at "the Jews" about this pathetic figure whom he considers innocent and harmless (19:5).[142] Aggravated, "the Jews" demand Jesus' crucifixion but Pilate continues to taunt them (19:6). For the first time, "the Jews" level a (religious) charge: Jesus has blasphemed by

---

137. Cf. Bond, *Pontius Pilate*, 181–82.

138. Glancy, "Torture," 107–36. Most scholars perceive the scourging to be punitive torture, aimed to inflict pain as punishment (e.g., Culpepper, *Anatomy of the Fourth Gospel*, 142; David K. Rensberger, *Overcoming the World: Politics and Community in the Gospel of John* [London: SPCK, 1988], 93; Neyrey, *Gospel of John*, 300; cf. the scholars mentioned by Glancy, "Torture," 121–22 n. 48), but this is unlikely in the *middle* of an interrogation.

139. Glancy, "Torture," 121–22.

140. Neyrey comments that instead of the verdict and sentence, Jesus' trial goes through a completely new cycle in 19:5-16 (*Gospel of John*, 300).

141. Glancy, "Torture," 125.

142. The author may be alluding to Jesus' humanity or to his title "Son of Man" (cf. Bond, *Pontius Pilate*, 185–86). Dieter Böhler understands the phrase as a royal proclamation, echoing 1 Sam. 9:17 ("'Ecce Homo!' (Joh 19,5) ein Zitat aus dem Alten Testament," *BZ* 39 [1995]: 104–8).

equating himself with God (19:7; cf. 5:18; 10:33)—a capital offense according to the Mosaic law (Lev. 24:16).

Round Six (19:8-11). Pilate becomes rather afraid, perhaps driven by a superstitious belief about divine matters, and wants to know Jesus' origin (19:8-9).[143] Annoyed by Jesus' silence, Pilate tries to assert his authority and fails; instead, Jesus points out that Pilate's authority is God-given (literally, "given from above") (19:10-11).[144] Jesus' remark that the one who handed him over to Pilate (either Judas or Caiaphas/"the Jews") is guilty of a greater sin does not mean Pilate himself is guiltless—he rejects Jesus, does not use his God-given authority to do justice, and will hand Jesus over to "the Jews" (19:16a).[145]

Round Seven (19:12-16a). A mixture of belief in Jesus' innocence, superstitious fear, and Jesus' words in 19:11 drives Pilate to make his first real attempt to release Jesus. It comes too late, however, for "the Jews" play their trump card. They skillfully manipulate Pilate by modifying their allegation from a religious (19:7) to a political one (19:12). By questioning Pilate's loyalty to the emperor, they corner him, leaving him no option but to release Jesus. Hearing their words, Pilate sits on the judge's bench to demonstrate his authority over "the Jews."[146] Pilate knows what "the Jews" want and while he realizes they have forced his hand, he too has a card up his sleeve. He taunts them saying, "See your king!," causing the exasperated "Jews" to demand Jesus' crucifixion (19:14b-15a). Pilate now plays *his* trump card. With his "Shall I crucify your king?," Pilate shrewdly manipulates "the Jews" into admitting their allegiance to Rome and denying their religious loyalties (19:15).[147] Having

143. Cf. Bultmann, *Gospel of John*, 661; Stibbe, *John as Storyteller*, 108; Bond, *Pontius Pilate*, 187. "Rather afraid" makes more sense than "even more afraid" (niv) or "more afraid than ever" (nrsv) since Pilate has not shown fear previously. Moloney observes that Pilate asks "the fundamental question of Johannine Christology: 'Where are you from?'" (*Gospel of John*, 495).

144. Jesus probably refers to the power God has given Pilate for this particular moment (Bultmann, *Gospel of John*, 662; Brown, *John XIII–XXI*, 892–93) rather than to a possible God-given authority of the state (cf. Rom. 13:1). Ironically, Pilate presumes to have authority whereas in reality it is Jesus who does (1:12; 5:27; 10:18; 17:2).

145. Judas is most often the subject of the verb "to hand over" in John, including in 18:2, 5. Here, the reference could be to "the Jews" who hand Jesus over to Pilate (18:30, 35) (Jesus' use of the singular is perhaps generic) and/or to Caiaphas as the leader of "the Jews" (although never related to the verb "to hand over," he is the leading voice in 11:47-53). Whoever the subject, his/their sin is greater because while Pilate has God-given authority, his/theirs comes from the devil (8:44; 13:2, 27).

146. The translation "and he [Pilate] seated him [Jesus] on the judge's seat" (19:13b) is unlikely (cf. Bond, *Pontius Pilate*, 190; Conway, *Men and Women*, 161; contra O'Day, *Gospel of John*, 822).

147. Cf. Culpepper, *Anatomy of the Fourth Gospel*, 143; Bond, *Pontius Pilate*, 191–93; Conway, *Men and Women*, 162; Carter, *Pontius Pilate*, 150–51. As Schnackenburg observes, both "the Jews" and Pilate

secured this victory, Pilate hands Jesus over to "the Jews" to be crucified (19:16a).

Beyond the Trial. After Jesus' trial, Pilate's power play continues. In 19:19-22, Pilate mocks the nationalistic, messianic hopes of "the Jews" with the inscription "Jesus the Nazarene, the king of the Jews" on the cross. He then flaunts his authority by refusing the alteration "the Jews" suggest. Pilate's power over the Jewish people is also apparent in 19:31 and 19:38 when they need his consent on a religious matter.[148]

Character Analysis and Classification. Pilate is probably the most complex character in the Johannine narrative. In his dealing with Jesus, Pilate seeks to uncover the truth in his own cruel and efficient way. He misunderstands and disparages Jesus' kingship and rejects the (saving) truth he has to offer, but he is also convinced that Jesus is innocent, and tries to release him. At the same time, he uses Jesus to manipulate and taunt "the Jews." In his politically motivated game of mocking and manipulating "the Jews" to admit their allegiance to Rome, he chooses to sacrifice the truth/Jesus. Pilate does not use his God-given authority to mete out justice; instead he rejects the truth/Jesus and thus condemns himself.[149] He knows what is true and just—Jesus is innocent and should be released—but does not act accordingly. In the final evaluation, Pilate does not come to the light (cf. 3:20-21) and his response to Jesus falters.[150] Regarding "the Jews," Pilate is cruel, taunting, condescending, and manipulative. Knowing that they want to kill Jesus but need his approval, Pilate repeatedly taunts them and flaunts his authority. In return, "the Jews" manage to manipulate Pilate when they realize he wants to release Jesus. Knowing he is cornered and must concede, Pilate extracts a high price—a declaration of their allegiance to Rome and a denial of their religious loyalties. A seemingly victorious Pilate becomes a victim of his own political game because he too pays a price for his victory—denying and perverting truth and justice. Indeed, it is a hollow victory.[151] Yet, on hearing the charge of "the Jews" that Jesus claimed to be the Son of God, Pilate also shows (superstitious) fear. In sum, Pilate

---

sacrifice their convictions—"the Jews" their theological convictions and Pilate his conviction of justice (*St John*, 3:266).

148. Contra Culpepper, who contends that these are all Pilate's efforts to atone for his concession to "the Jews" (*Anatomy of the Fourth Gospel*, 143).

149. In fact, Pilate is on trial and condemns himself (Ehrman, "Jesus' Trial," 128; Raymond E. Brown, "The Passion according to John: Chapters 18 and 19," *Worship* 49 [1975]: 129-30).

150. Culpepper concludes that "although he [Pilate] seems to glimpse the truth, a decision in Jesus' favor proves too costly for him" (*Anatomy of the Fourth Gospel*, 143). Cf. O'Day, *Gospel of John*, 825-26.

151. Culpepper, *Anatomy of the Fourth Gospel*, 143.

is a complex character with multiple traits including being cruel, calculating, taunting, manipulative, provocative, and afraid.

In my reading of the Johannine Pilate, I differ from the majority of scholars who portray Pilate as weak and indecisive.[152] While I tend to agree with scholars who view Pilate as a strong character, they seem to overrate Pilate's control over the situation at the trial by downplaying the force of 19:12, where "the Jews" finally get a grip on Pilate.[153] Pilate is a competent, calculating politician who wants to show "the Jews" he is in charge while also trying to be professional in handling Jesus' case. But he is unable to achieve either aim because he underestimates the determination and shrewdness of "the Jews." He might have released the innocent Jesus had he not been manipulated into sacrificing the truth/Jesus to ensure his own political survival and triumph. He knows Jesus is innocent but does not use his God-given authority to bring justice for fear of losing the political game. Pilate ultimately chooses Caesar and the empire "from below" instead of Jesus and his kingdom "from above."

There are three indications of development in Pilate. First, although Pilate is convinced early on about Jesus' innocence, he does not attempt to release him, but surprisingly he tries fervently to release him later. Second, it is rather unexpected that Pilate, the calculating politician, is outwitted by "the Jews" and is forced to yield. Third, it may surprise the reader that the strong Pilate shows fear on one occasion. Regarding Pilate's inner life, the narrator reveals that he is afraid (19:8) and he wants to release Jesus (19:12). Some scholars contend that the structure of the passage, in which Pilate alternately goes in and out of the palace, reflects his inner conflict—he goes back and forth in his mind, unable to take sides.[154] This picture seems incorrect. Pilate despises "the Jews" and is clear about his strategy, but he is also in search of the truth about

---

152. E.g., Brown, *John XIII–XXI*, 864 (the honest, well-disposed man who adopts a middle position); Culpepper, *Anatomy of the Fourth Gospel*, 143 (Pilate avoids making a decision); Stibbe, *John as Storyteller*, 109 (Pilate is indecisive, representing the "impossibility of neutrality"). Although Martinus C. de Boer seeks to avoid the weak/strong dichotomy, he nevertheless characterizes Pilate as a reluctant participant in the drama who, seeking to release Jesus, is manipulated by "the Jews" from beginning to end ("The Narrative Function of Pilate in John," in *Narrativity in Biblical and Related Texts*, ed. G. J. Brooke and J.-D. Kaestli [BETL 149; Leuven: Leuven University Press, 2000], 143–44, 146 n. 24).

153. Rensberger, *Overcoming the World*, 94–95; Bond, *Pontius Pilate*, 190–192; Conway, *Men and Women*, 161; Carter, *Pontius Pilate*, 127, 150. While Christopher M. Tuckett also views Pilate as a strong, pigheaded man, surprisingly he does not deal with 19:12 ("Pilate in John 18–19: A Narrative-Critical Approach," in *Narrativity in Biblical and Related Texts*, ed. G. J. Brooke and J.-D. Kaestli [BETL 149; Leuven: Leuven University Press, 2000], 138). O'Day presents a more balanced view (*Gospel of John*, 813–26).

154. E.g., Stibbe, *John as Storyteller*, 106, 109.

Jesus. Although he tries to play both sides and fails, he is not indecisive: he ultimately opts for the emperor and his own political survival at the expense of truth and justice. Nevertheless, Pilate does go back and forth in his mind, constantly weighing his political options, and this is what the structure of the passage probably emphasizes.[155] Considering his location on the axes of complexity (complex, multiple traits), development (some), and inner life (little/some), I suggest classifying the character of Pilate as one having personality but bordering on being an individual.[156]

Character Evaluation and Significance. I use two criteria to evaluate Pilate's character: (i) his response to Jesus in relation to the author's evaluative point of view, purpose, and worldview; (ii) his role in the plot. I consider first Pilate's response to Jesus. In view of Pilate's misunderstanding, rejection, compromise of truth and justice, and choosing Caesar rather than Jesus, I conclude that Pilate's response to Jesus is inadequate. He searches for truth, is convinced of Jesus' innocence, and tries to release him, but he eventually sacrifices his convictions and Jesus.[157] I now turn to Pilate's role in the plot. Pilate significantly advances the plot in two ways. First, God's salvific plan for the world involves "giving" his Son (3:16), which he does at the cross. Jesus is constantly aware of this salvific mission: he says he will give his life for the life of the world (6:51) and lay down his life for the sheep (10:15). In his consent to have Jesus crucified, Pilate propels the Johannine plot to its climax. Second, since Pilate was Rome's representative in Judea, Jesus' trial is acted out before the Roman authorities, the greatest power of the then-known "civilized" world. In line with the universal scope of John's Gospel, Jesus' trial must unfold on the world stage because he is sent into the world and his saving act on the cross will have cosmic consequences. Even Pilate's words affixed on the cross assist the cosmic scope of Jesus' salvific mission since the phrase "Jesus, the king of 'the Jews,'" written in Greek, Latin, and Aramaic, the major languages of the then-known world, was for everyone to read. Regarding his representative value for today, I suggest that Pilate represents those in positions of authority who compromise truth and justice to safeguard their career and ensure survival; those who start well on a quest for truth but abandon it because other things (career, image, and so on) take precedence.

---

155. Cf. Lincoln, *Saint John*, 458.

156. We must not understand the character of Pilate in a modern individualistic sense but as a "collectivist identity" or "group-oriented personality," where Pilate's identity is embedded in a larger group (e.g., the Romans) (cf. sections 2.4 and 3.2).

157. Cf. de Boer's observation that for Pilate Jesus is not *his* king but remains the king *of "the Jews"* ("Narrative Function," 150).

Pilate		
Narrative Appearances	18:29–19:15, 19-22, 31, 38	
Origin	Birth, Gender, Ethnicity, Nation/City	male, Roman
	Family (Ancestors, Relatives)	
Upbringing	Nurture, Education	trained as an administrator
External Goods	Epithets, Reputation	
	Age, Marital Status	
	Socio-Economic Status, Wealth	high social status
	Place of Residence/Operation	Herod's palace in Jerusalem
	Occupation, Positions Held	Rome's representative in Judea
	Group Affiliation, Friends	Rome
Speech and Actions	In Interaction with Jesus	searches for truth, is cruel/ efficient, willing to release him but in the end hands him over to be crucified
	In Interaction with Other Characters	taunts "the Jews," flaunts his authority, eventually gives in to their pressure but manipulates them
Death	Manner of Death, Events after Death	
Character Analysis	Complexity	complex; multiple traits
	Development	some
	Inner Life	little/some
Character Classification	Degree of Characterization	personality/individual

Character Evaluation	Response to Jesus	inadequate: misunderstanding, rejection, compromising truth and justice, choosing Caesar rather than Jesus
	Role in the Plot	brings the Johannine plot to its climax
Character Significance	Representative Value	represents those in positions of authority who compromise truth and justice to safeguard their career and ensure survival; those who start well on a quest for truth but eventually abandon it because other things (career, image, and so on) take precedence

Characterization of Pilate in Other Sources. In Mark's Gospel, I do not see a radically different picture from that in John's Gospel. Realizing that the chief priests had handed Jesus over out of envy, Pilate's remark concerning whether he should release the king of the Jews appears an intentional mockery, sneering at their nationalistic hopes (15:9-10). Although his handing Jesus over to be crucified because he "considered to satisfy the crowd" (15:15) may indicate weakness, it could equally point to Pilate's ability to be calculating. Perceiving the potential for a riot (15:11; cf. Matt. 27:24), Pilate may well have decided to give in on this occasion.[158] Thus while John significantly expands on Mark's account of Pilate, he essentially agrees with Mark's characterization of Pilate.

When we turn to the writings of Josephus and Philo, we observe that Pontius Pilate, the Roman governor or procurator of Judea from 26 to 36/37 CE, did not like or understand the Jews. From the work of Brian McGing and Helen Bond, we learn that although Pilate appears to have been a relatively competent governor, he provoked the Jews on various occasions. However, he may have done so unintentionally, being ignorant about and insensitive to the rigorous Jewish customs and laws. In his conflicts with the Jews, Pilate could stubbornly and willfully resist the Jews but also give in—especially when his loyalty to the emperor was questioned. He could be decisive but also be noncommittal, use brute force or show restraint.[159] This implies that the Johannine portrait of

158. Cf. Bond's analysis of Pilate in Mark's Gospel as skillful, manipulative, and loyal to the emperor (*Pontius Pilate*, 103–17).

159. McGing, "Pontius Pilate," 416–38; Bond, *Pontius Pilate*, chs. 2–3.

Pilate does not differ greatly from those of Josephus and Philo. In John's Gospel, Pilate refuses to give in to the demands of "the Jews" and mocks them, but they find a way to compel Pilate into yielding. Similarly, Josephus and Philo record incidents where Pilate provokes the Jews and refuses to give in to their wishes but eventually has to concede. Whether in John, Mark, Josephus, or Philo, Pilate appears cruel, decisive, calculating, and provocative. He appears to choose the course of action that is to his advantage and ensures his political survival.

4.3. Characters in the Acts of the Apostles

Most scholars have recognized that 1:8 is programmatic for the book of Acts, that is, Luke describes the growth of the church in Jerusalem (Acts 2–7), in Judea and Samaria (Acts 8–12), and to the ends of the earth (Acts 13–28). Luke's account of the church's growth is not neutral but intentionally follows the spread of Christianity, initially through the experiences of Peter and then westward through those of the apostle Paul (indicated by the thick line below).

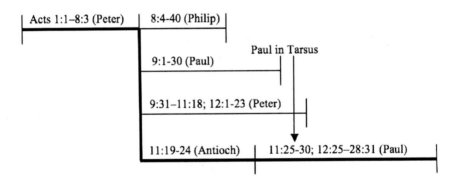

Many scholars, however, contend that Luke's purpose for writing Acts was more than just to recount the spread of Christianity. Jacob Jervell, for example, argues that Luke strives to remove misconceptions among Jewish Christians about Paul, regarding his teaching about Israel and the law, his alleged apostasy from Judaism, and his mission to the Gentiles.[160] Differently, Max Turner contends that Luke "attempts to explain and so to legitimate the Church in the light of her founding moments" in order to show how "she [the church] is

---

160. Jacob Jervell, *The Theology of the Acts of the Apostles* (Cambridge: Cambridge University Press, 1996), 16–17. Jervell also argues that the church is primarily a Jewish church, the restored Israel, with the Gentile believers incorporated into it (*Theology*, 34–43). For a critique of viewing Acts as an apology for Paul, see Peterson, "Luke's Theological Enterprise," 533.

the fulfilment of the promises to Israel."[161] David Peterson draws attention to a growing consensus among scholars to see Acts as a work of edification for Christians, although questions remain about the precise nature and purpose of the edification. Peterson's own position is that Luke aims to encourage believers about the progress or triumph of God's word through opposition, conflict, and suffering.[162] Taking a different view, Darr argues that the Acts narrative focuses attention on whether or not the (secondary) characters recognize and respond correctly to the divine will as it is manifested through the protagonists.[163] Similarly, Beverly Gaventa states, "Luke presents and assesses these human characters in relationship to their place in and reception of the larger story of God. What makes human characters interesting or important for Luke pertains to their response or resistance to God."[164] In the Gospels, it is crucial how characters respond to the protagonist, Jesus. In Acts, Peter and Paul have become the primary spokespersons of the divine, although Stephen, Philip, Barnabas, and James cannot be discounted.

This brief discussion helps to define the two criteria for character evaluation in the Acts of the Apostles. First, I suggest that we evaluate the characters in Acts by how they respond to the various protagonists (especially Peter and Paul) regarding the divine message, and how they perform as witnesses for Jesus and contribute to the growth of the church. Those who are specifically chosen as Jesus' witnesses are the apostles or "sent ones"—the twelve disciples who had been with Jesus from the beginning (Luke 24:48; Acts 1:2, 8, 21-22) and Paul (Acts 22:14–15; 26:16). However, it would be simplistic to assert that the early church's mission is solely the responsibility of the apostles when the first expansion of the church occurs through *non-apostles* (8:1-4; 11:19-21). Hence, I suggest that Luke views *all* believers as potential witnesses for Jesus in this world and as being able to contribute to the growth of the church.[165] Second, the plot of the Acts of the Apostles revolves around

161. Max Turner, "The 'Spirit of Prophecy' as the Power of Israel's Restoration and Witness," in *Witness to the Gospel: The Theology of Acts*, ed. I. Howard Marshall and David Peterson (Grand Rapids: Eerdmans, 1998), 348.

162. Peterson, "Luke's Theological Enterprise," 534–44.

163. Darr, *On Character Building*, 55–57. Cf. Perkins, who states that "the message of the apostles parallels that of Jesus himself" (*Peter*, 88).

164. Gaventa, *Acts of the Apostles*, 27.

165. Cf. Eckhard J. Schnabel, *Early Christian Mission*, 2 vols. (Downers Grove, IL: InterVarsity, 2004), 1:734. Contra Peter G. Bolt, who argues that only the twelve apostles and Paul are witnesses of Jesus, with the reader simply "listening" to their testimony ("Mission and Witness," in *Witness to the Gospel: The Theology of Acts*, ed. I. Howard Marshall and David Peterson [Grand Rapids: Eerdmans, 1998], 191–214).

proclamation and conflict, namely the conflict caused by the proclamation and spread of the gospel that the crucified Jesus is God's Messiah and Lord, and the fulfillment of Israel's (and the entire world's) hopes; in view of this, we will consider the characters' role in the plot.

PETER

Peter is a dominant presence in Acts 1–12, which describes the church's expansion in Judea and Samaria, but appears only once after that, in 15:7. In keeping with his programmatic statement in 1:8, Luke seems to follow the expansion of the church westward and so, from Acts 13 onwards, the camera swings from Peter and the Jerusalem church to Paul and his missionary activities in Asia Minor, Greece, and Rome. Nevertheless, Peter plays a major role in the first half of Acts as the spokesperson of the apostles and leader of the Jerusalem church.[166] Luke provides no information about Peter's identity (barring the mention of his original name "Simon" in 10:18 [cf. 15:14]), which is unsurprising because readers will already know Peter from Luke's Gospel.

Peter and the Jerusalem Church (Acts 1–5). Acts 1–5 describes Jesus' ascension, the election of Matthias, the outpouring of the Spirit at Pentecost, and the first few months in the life of the early church. From the outset, Peter takes a leading role—he stands up to address the group of believers regarding the replacement of Judas (1:15), stands up to address the crowd regarding the enigmatic events at Pentecost (2:14), and answers the crowd's burning question when they are deeply affected by his speech (2:37-38). Besides showing initiative (a trait the reader recognizes from the Synoptic accounts), Peter also exhibits other traits in Acts 1–2, such as insight (in relating Scripture to the various events), being purposeful/decisive (1:16, 22; 2:38-40), and eloquent (2:14-36). Compared to his Synoptic portrayal, Peter seems to have changed—from being outspoken to well spoken. Besides, while it might seem that Peter's leading role in Acts is simply a continuation of his role in Luke's Gospel, the reader should actually be surprised because Peter denied belonging to Jesus during Jesus' trial and none of the Synoptic Gospels resolve the issue (although Luke 22:32 may hint at a restoration).[167]

Acts 3–5 describes how Peter and the other apostles come to be at odds with the Sanhedrin authorities over the proclamation of the crucified Jesus as God's messianic agent of Israel's renewal. Peter continues to lead—he initiates

---

166. In Acts 1–12, Peter is the unquestioned leader in the Jerusalem church (Simon J. Kistemaker, *Acts* [NTC; Grand Rapids: Baker, 1990], 61).

167. Cf. Ben Witherington, *The Acts of the Apostles: A Socio-Rhetorical Commentary* (Grand Rapids: Eerdmans, 1998), 116.

the conversation with the crippled beggar (3:4-6), explains to the crowd what has happened (3:12), addresses the Jewish authorities (4:8), and exposes the lies of Ananias and Sapphira (5:3, 8). During these events, Peter displays various traits: piety (3:1), insight (3:6, 12-26; 4:8-12; 5:3-4, 9), faith (in Jesus) (3:6-7; 16),[168] resourceful (he exploits every opportunity to proclaim Jesus and God's purposes [3:12-26; 4:8-12; cf. 2:14-36]), determination (3:4-7), boldness (3:14-15; 4:13), being filled with the Spirit (4:8; cf. 2:4), and steadfastness (4:18-20). Acts 1–5 also reveals aspects of Peter's inner life: he expresses his confidence (2:29), he is aware of his compatriots' ignorance (3:17), and the authorities recognize that Peter is bold (4:13).

Peter's Missionary Activities in Samaria and Judea (Acts 8–11). After the stoning of Stephen, a severe persecution of the Jerusalem church begins and believers scatter throughout Judea and Samaria (8:1). Peter gets involved in the Samaritan mission when, as representatives of the Jerusalem church, he and John go to Samaria to check up on Philip's evangelistic success in Samaria (8:5-14).[169] Peter and John are instrumental in confirming and completing the salvation experience of the Samaritans because, at variance with the Acts 2:38 paradigm (conversion, baptism, the gift of the Holy Spirit), the Samaritans had not yet received the Holy Spirit (8:15-17).[170] Regarding Peter's traits, his leading role continues, revealed in the clause "Peter and John" (8:14), and he is the one to confront Simon the magician (8:20). In addition, Peter has insight into Simon's motives (8:20-23), and is involved in proclaiming the good news (8:25; cf. 5:42).

After Paul's conversion, the church throughout Judea, Galilee, and Samaria had peace and grew in numbers, and Peter went to the Judean coast to visit the believers (9:31-43). Peter's healing the paralyzed Aeneas is instrumental in the conversion of numerous people in the area (8:35). Something similar happens when Peter travels to nearby Joppa. Peter's raising Tabitha from the dead causes many people to believe in Jesus (8:40-42).[171] In the light of the healings of the crippled beggar (3:7), Aeneas, and Tabitha, it is reasonable to add the ability to

---

168. Regarding Peter and John's encounter with the crippled beggar, Gaventa remarks that "the faith that is active must be that of Peter and John, since the man himself shows no sign of expecting a healing" (*Acts of the Apostles*, 87).

169. Differently, Gaventa contends that the purpose of Peter and John's journey is not to inspect but to connect Samaria to Jerusalem (*Acts of the Apostles*, 137-38). I think that both elements are in view. They came to oversee Philip's work and to carry out a repair action to conform to the Acts 2:38 paradigm.

170. Cf. Perkins, *Peter*, 90-91.

171. Carsten Peter Thiede notes that "[t]he trust of Tabitha's friends in Peter's powers was so great that they did not bury her" (*Simon Peter: From Galilee to Rome* [Exeter, UK: Paternoster, 1986], 139).

heal as another of Peter's traits (cf. also 5:12-16). From the accounts thus far, it is clear that Peter plays a crucial role in the life of the early church. James Dunn observes how Peter and the Jerusalem church oversee various missionary efforts. After bringing Philip's initial efforts in Samaria under the supervision of the Jerusalem church, Peter and John carry on the Samaritan mission (8:14-25). Similarly, Philip later evangelizes the Judean coastal plain (8:26, 40), after which Peter revisits the area (9:32-43).[172] Yet, Peter's most momentous encounter is with Cornelius.

The most significant dispute in early Christianity runs along ethnic lines—the inclusion of Gentile believers into the Jewish church. The seeds are sown by Philip in his mission to the Samaritans and then to the Ethiopian eunuch (8:5-13, 26-40), and by Greek-speaking Jewish believers in Antioch, resulting in a mixed Jewish-Gentile church (11:19-21). However, it is Paul's programmatic mission to the Gentiles that abolishes the Jewish ethnic boundary. Nevertheless, Luke credits Peter with the decisive breakthrough to the Gentiles when he narrates Peter's encounter with the God-fearer Cornelius in Acts 10.[173] Chronologically, the first Gentile conversions happen at Antioch (and in substantial numbers) because the phrase "those who were scattered" in 11:19 goes back directly to 8:1.[174] Narratologically, however, Cornelius and his household are the first Gentile converts. According to Thiede, Peter's speech in 10:34-43 establishes his authority regarding the issue of admitting Gentiles into the church:

> This speech, then, is a turning point in the history of the church. Indeed it is possibly the single most important speech in the entire book of Acts. It is the fullest summary of the gospel message: all later exposition, as indeed all later NT theology, is inherent in Peter's speeches with this one as their peak. It opens the door to the Gentiles, to "all nations," as commanded by Jesus (Mk. 13:10; Mt. 28:19). And it prepares the way for a comprehensive redefinition of the people of God.[175]

---

172. James D. G. Dunn, *Beginning from Jerusalem*, vol. 2 of *Christianity in the Making* (Grand Rapids: Eerdmans, 2009), 278–92, 380–83.

173. Cf. Dunn, *Beginning from Jerusalem*, 301–8. Thiede argues that prior to his encounter with Cornelius, in 9:32-43, Peter has already been involved in a Gentile mission (*Simon Peter*, 138). Nevertheless, Peter has not been "converted" because, as Gaventa observes, Peter's rejection of the animals in the vision indicates his rejection of the Gentiles (*Acts of the Apostles*, 165).

174. Cf. Ben Witherington, *The Acts of the Apostles: A Socio-Rhetorical Commentary* (Grand Rapids: Eerdmans, 1998), 368. Contra Thiede, who contends that these Jewish believers followed the precedent set by Peter (*Simon Peter*, 150).

In a sense, Acts 10 is not simply the story of Cornelius's conversion but also of Peter's conversion in that he has come to realize that God also intends the Gentiles to be part of his people.[176] While Peter's encounter with the God-fearer Cornelius causes conservative Jewish believers ("those of the circumcision") to criticize him for his table fellowship with Gentiles, his explanation is readily accepted (11:1-18).[177] Nevertheless, the issue of admitting Gentiles into the people of God resurfaces in Acts 15.[178] In these pivotal events, we notice more of Peter's traits: he is devout (10:10, 14), obedient (10:19-20, 23, 29), and shows insight (10:34-35, 46-48). Regarding his inner life, Peter is hungry and desires to eat something (10:1), he is perplexed (10:17), ponders the vision (10:19), admits that he has learned (10:34), and remembers Jesus' words (11:16).

Peter's Imprisonment and Disappearance (Acts 12). Following the killing of James, Herod imprisons Peter (12:1-4), but Peter is miraculously released by an angel (12:6-11). During this event Peter shows obedience (12:7-9), and, in terms of his inner life, he quickly goes from bafflement to understanding (12:11). Peter's miraculous escape causes great commotion, and he flees to Caesarea (12:19). After 12:19, Peter disappears from the scene and the focus shifts to Paul for the remainder of Acts. [Although Acts does not mention it, Peter may soon have moved to Antioch to seek refuge. During Paul's trip to southern Galatia (Acts 13–14), Peter probably arrived in Antioch and began participating in mixed table fellowship regularly (Gal. 2:11-12). This would also explain why Peter turns up at the Jerusalem council in Acts 15; he may have traveled with Paul and Barnabas from Antioch to Jerusalem.[179]]

175. Thiede, *Simon Peter*, 146–47 (quotation from p. 146). Yet, Peter's speech does not include the promise of the gift of the Spirit, and ironically, Peter is interrupted by the Spirit in 10:44 (Gaventa, *Acts of the Apostles*, 171).

176. Cf. Witherington, *Acts of the Apostles*, 360–61.

177. Peter's equating the outpouring of the Spirit on Cornelius and his household with the first outpouring at Pentecost safeguards equality of the Gentiles with the Jewish believers both before God and within the church (Thiede, *Simon Peter*, 149).

178. While Schnabel calls the agreement in 11:18 "paradigmatic for all conversions of Gentiles" (*Early Christian Mission*, 2:992), Dunn is more cautious, stating that the Jerusalem church might have accepted Cornelius as an exception (*Beginning from Jerusalem*, 401–2, 446). For Peter's successful pioneering role in the ethnic debate in Acts 10, 11, 15, see Richard Bauckham, "James, Peter, and the Gentiles," in *The Missions of James, Peter, and Paul: Tensions in Early Christianity*, ed. Bruce Chilton and Craig Evans (NovTSup 115; Leiden: Brill, 2005), 103–42.

179. Regarding Luke's mention of Peter's disappearance to "another [unnamed] place" in 12:17, Thiede remarks, "Writing during Peter's lifetime and to a high-ranking Roman official, Luke wants to avoid anything that might compromise the activities of Peter, legally a fugitive from state authority, within the Roman empire. Luke knew where Peter went and where he was at the time of writing, but he

Peter's Reappearance at the Jerusalem Council (Acts 15). Peter makes his final appearance at the Jerusalem council in Acts 15. While we know of Peter's move to Caesarea after the persecution by King Herod (and probably further north to Antioch), his reappearance in Jerusalem may have to do with his earlier pioneering role in the inclusion of Gentiles into the people of God, which is the issue here too. Apparently, some conservative believers in the Jerusalem church had traveled to Antioch to demand that Gentile believers be circumcised (15:1), even though, as James clarifies later, they were not acting on behalf of the Jerusalem leadership (15:24). After a heated dispute with the circumcision faction, the Antioch church sends Paul and Barnabas to Jerusalem to discuss the issue (15:2). While the conservative Jewish faction, now identified as Pharisaic believers, advocates a Jewish Torah–observing Christianity (15:5), Peter defends Paul's position by recalling his Cornelius experience (15:7-11).[180] Under the leadership of James, the Jerusalem council then formally settles the ethnic dispute of how Gentile believers should be admitted into the people of God. Just as in Acts 11, Peter is the persuasive one and James bases his decision on Peter's argument (15:14).[181] Peter's awareness of his calling as an apostle to the Gentiles (cf. Paul's calling in 9:15) shows an aspect of his inner life (15:7).

Character Analysis and Classification. We have seen that Peter's portrayal in Acts is characterized by many traits and aspects of his inner life. In terms of development, Peter is a changed man when compared to his portrayal in Luke's Gospel (and the other Synoptics): from being an impulsive, outspoken, unstable character, he has become stable, eloquent, bold, insightful, and persuasive. As Pheme Perkins states, "Any failures shown by the apostle during Jesus' lifetime have been eradicated by his post–Resurrection transformation."[182] Thus I place him as an individual on the resulting characterization continuum.

Character Evaluation and Significance. In terms of character evaluation, Peter has a leading role in the early church, characterized by a profound understanding of events in the light of Scripture, successful proclamation of the good news about Jesus, and being a bold, eloquent witness for Jesus, thus contributing significantly to the ethnic and numerical expansion of the

---

remained silent" (*Simon Peter*, 154). However, while Thiede assumes that Luke refers to Rome, I contend that it is Antioch (without denying that Peter could have moved to Rome after the Antioch incident in Galatians 2 and the subsequent Jerusalem council in Acts 15).

180. While Paul's contact with Peter is assumed in Acts 9:26-27, it is more explicit in Galatians 1–2.

181. Perkins observes that the Jerusalem leadership has shifted from Peter to James (*Peter*, 94). Similarly, Thiede contends that, with the singling out of James in 12:17, Peter shows that he sees James as his successor (*Simon Peter*, 152–53).

182. Perkins, *Peter*, 89.

church. Peter thus is an exemplary witness for Jesus.[183] In relation to the second criterion of character evaluation, Peter advances the plot in significant ways. First, he takes initiative to complete the number of apostolic witnesses. Second, he explains crucial events to each audience in the light of Scripture—whether perplexed crowds, hostile Sanhedrin authorities, or a conservative faction of the Jerusalem church. Third, he represents the Jerusalem church in overseeing important missionary activities in Judea and Samaria. Fourth, he has a pioneering role in the salvation of Gentiles and their incorporation into the church.[184] In terms of his significance for today, Peter represents those who aspire to be insightful, bold, eloquent, pioneering leaders in the church.

Peter		
Narrative Appearances	1:13, 15; 2:14, 37-38; 3:1, 3-4, 6, 11-12; 4:8, 13, 19; 5:3, 8-9, 15, 29; 8:14, 20; 9:32, 34, 38-40; 10:5, 9, 13-14, 17-19, 21, 25-26, 32, 34, 44-46; 11:2, 4, 7, 13; 12:3, 5-7, 11, 14, 16, 18; 15:7	
Origin	Birth, Gender, Ethnicity, Nation/City	male
	Family (Ancestors, Relatives)	
Upbringing	Nurture, Education	uneducated (4:13)
External Goods	Epithets, Reputation	reputation for being able to heal (5:15)
	Age, Marital Status	
	Socio-Economic Status, Wealth	
	Place of Residence/Operation	Jerusalem, Samaria, Judea
	Occupation, Positions Held	apostle, a leader in the Jerusalem church, a leading witness for Jesus
	Group Affiliation, Friends	apostles, Jesus believers

183. Perkins even claims that "Peter comes closer to stepping into the place of Jesus than any of the apostles" (*Peter*, 89).

184. For an account of Peter's significance beyond the narrative of Acts, see Martin Hengel, *Saint Peter: The Underestimated Apostle*, trans. Thomas H. Trapp (Grand Rapids: Eerdmans, 2010).

Speech and Actions	In Interaction with Protagonists	follows up the missionary work of Philip, defends Paul in the Jerusalem council and influences James
	In Interaction with Other Characters	argues with hostile opponents, interprets events scripturally, heals people
Death	Manner of Death, Events after Death	
Character Analysis	Complexity	complex; multiple traits
	Development	some
	Inner Life	much
Character Classification	Degree of Characterization	individual
Character Evaluation	Response to Protagonists, Witness to Jesus	adequate
	Role in the Plot	advances the plot in significant ways
Character Significance	Representative Value	those who seek to be influential and pioneering leaders in the church

PILATE

Pilate figures three times in Acts: once in Peter's speech (3:13), once in the believers' prayer (4:27), and finally in Paul's speech (13:28). From sources outside Acts we know that Pilate was the governor of Judea until 36/37 CE, which means that he was still Rome's representative in Judea during the first few years after the church's inception. Yet, Pilate has no active role in Acts—he is merely remembered for his part in the death of Jesus. As for his identity, only his name, "Pontius Pilate," is mentioned (4:27) and from the context we infer that he must have been a high-ranking Roman official because he was instrumental in Jesus' death (3:13; 4:27; 13:28). This lack of information about Pilate is not surprising since Luke would assume that his readers are familiar with the events surrounding Jesus' trial narrated in his Gospel (Luke 23:1-5, 11-25).

Character Analysis and Classification. The information about Pilate may be minimal, but there is something to be gleaned. The text hints at Pilate being outmaneuvered by the Jewish authorities: (i) Pilate was unsuccessful in his attempt to release Jesus (3:13); (ii) without a basis for the death penalty, the Jewish authorities manipulated Pilate into having Jesus killed (13:28-29). There is perhaps a little development in Pilate's characterization because the information in 3:13 that Pilate tried to release Jesus seems at odds with the information in 4:26-27 that Pilate and others had assembled in order to kill Jesus. Helen Bond remarks that although Luke "clearly wants to lay the bulk of the blame on the Jewish chief priests, Pilate's lack of interest and weakness inevitably lead him to a place in this evil alliance. The Roman governor has not been whitewashed."[185] The narrator reveals one aspect of Pilate's inner life—he had decided (literally, "judged") that Jesus should be released (3:13). In terms of his character classification, Pilate is an agent or plot functionary who was used by the Jewish authorities to bring about Jesus' death, but he borders on being a type.

Character Evaluation and Significance. Pilate clearly does not fare well as a witness for Jesus. On the one hand, in his capacity as Rome's representative, Pilate "judged" that Jesus should be released, but from the context and Luke's Gospel it is clear that Pilate failed to go through with it because the Jewish authorities managed to outmaneuver him. Thus while Pilate had the opportunity to be just to Jesus and hence be a true witness for him, he fails to do so. In terms of his role in the plot, Pilate does not have one in the plot of Acts—he is merely remembered for his role in the plot of Luke's Gospel. Pilate's significance for today is that he represents those who failed to be a witness for Jesus when they had the opportunity.

---

185. Bond, *Pontius Pilate*, 160. Luke clarifies in 4:28 that both Pilate and his allies operated within the boundaries God had set for them (cf. John 19:11).

Pontius Pilate		
Narrative Appearances	3:13; 4:27; 13:28	
Origin	Birth, Gender, Ethnicity, Nation/City	male, Roman
	Family (Ancestors, Relatives)	
Upbringing	Nurture, Education	presumably well educated
External Goods	Epithets, Reputation	
	Age, Marital Status	
	Socio-Economic Status, Wealth	
	Place of Residence/Operation	Jerusalem (4:27)
	Occupation, Positions Held	high-ranked Roman official
	Group Affiliation, Friends	Herod, Jesus
Speech and Actions	In Interaction with Protagonists	instrumental in Jesus' death
	In Interaction with Other Characters	outmaneuvered by the Jewish authorities
Death	Manner of Death, Events after Death	
Character Analysis	Complexity	uncomplicated
	Development	perhaps a little
	Inner Life	very little
Character Classification	Degree of Characterization	agent/type
Character Evaluation	Response to Protagonists, Witness to Jesus	inadequate
	Role in the Plot	none
Character Significance	Representative Value	those who have the opportunity to be a witness for Jesus but fail

BARNABAS

Barnabas appears twenty-three times in Acts, primarily in chapters 13–15 where he is Paul's co-worker during the first missionary journey and accompanies him to the Jerusalem council. The narrative reveals a lot about Barnabas's identity: (i) he is a Levite from Cyprus (4:36); (ii) his original name is Joseph but the apostles rename him Barnabas, which means "son of encouragement" (4:36);[186] (iii) he is a small landowner, but sells his land and gives the proceeds of the sale to the church (4:37);[187] (iv) he is a good man, full of the Holy Spirit and of faith (11:24); (v) he is either a prophet or a teacher in the Antioch church (13:1; cf. 11:26). It appears that Barnabas is a somewhat affluent man who sacrificially donates his wealth to the church. He probably became a prominent and influential member (even leader) in both the Jerusalem church and the Antioch church.[188]

It must be noted that while Luke first refers to them as "Barnabas and Paul" (11:30; 12:25; 13:2, 7), the order is reversed to "Paul and Barnabas" and becomes the norm (13:42–43, 46, 50; etc.). This reflects that Paul quickly rose to prominence (from 13:9 onwards), most likely because Barnabas promotes Paul, recognizes his gifts and calling, and helps him to succeed. The only exceptions are 14:14 and 15:12, 25 where, once again, it is "Barnabas and Paul," but this can be explained. In 14:14, the audience in Lystra likens Barnabas to Zeus, the chief god in the Greek pantheon, and Paul as Hermes, son of Zeus—perhaps they perceive Barnabas as a father figure and hence he is named first. In 15:12, 25,

---

186. Etymologically, this is incorrect because "Barnabas" does not mean "son of encouragement" (Gaventa, *Acts of the Apostles*, 101). Witherington, however, argues that παράκλησις refers to a kind of speech activity and thus favors the meaning "son of exhortation" (= preacher) since *nabas* may be derived from *nabi*, "prophet/preacher" (*Acts of the Apostles*, 209). See also the discussion in Sebastian Brock, "ΒΑΡΝΑΒΑΣ: ΥΙΟΕ ΠΑΡΑΚΛΗΣΕΩΣ," *JTS* 25 (1974): 93–98. Markus Öhler notes the linguistic connection between "son of encouragement (παράκλησις)" and his ability to exhort/encourage (παρακαλεῖν) others (11:23; 14:22; 15:31) (*Barnabas: Die historische Person und ihre Rezeption in der Apostelgeschichte* [WUNT 156; Tübingen: Mohr Siebeck, 2003], 459).

187. According to Old Testament law, Levites were not permitted to own land (Num. 18:21-24; Deut. 10:9; 18:1-4; Josh. 13:14), but by New Testament times this was no longer adhered to (Witherington, *Acts of the Apostles*, 209).

188. Murphy notes that Barnabas being sent to Antioch as a representative of the Jerusalem church (11:22) parallels the assignment for Peter and John in 8:14 and probably indicates Barnabas's leadership position in the Jerusalem church. Barnabas probably also held a position of leadership in the Antioch church since he is named in 13:1 at the head of the list ("Role of Barnabas," 326, 331). Besides, Barnabas's successful introduction of Paul to the Jerusalem apostles in 9:27 indicates that Barnabas enjoyed a high level of respect and trust (Öhler, *Barnabas*, 460).

Luke's reference to "Barnabas and Paul" at the Jerusalem council might reflect Barnabas's original Jerusalem connection and prominence.[189]

Character Analysis and Classification. While Barnabas is an uncomplicated character, he shows many traits: (i) he is generous in that he sells his property and gives the proceeds from the sale to the Jerusalem church (4:37);[190] (ii) he is courageous, willing to risk introducing the newly converted Paul to the Jerusalem apostles who were wary of Paul (9:27), and to speak boldly in front of a hostile Jewish crowd (13:46; 14:3); (iii) as his name indicates, he is an encourager (9:27; 11:23); (iv) he is good, tending toward excellence;[191] (v) he is trusting in that he believes in Paul and promotes him in the Jerusalem and Antioch church (9:27; 11:25-26);[192] (vi) he is persuasive (13:46-49; 14:1); (vii) he appears selfless because from being "Barnabas and Paul" (11:30; 12:25; 13:2, 7), it becomes "Paul and Barnabas" (13:42-43, 46, 50; etc.), implying that he moves from a mentoring to a supporting role; (viii) he is trustworthy in that he is first sent as a representative of the Jerusalem church to Antioch (11:22) and later as a representative of the Antioch church to Jerusalem (15:2). There is a small degree of development in the characterization of Barnabas in that it probably surprises the reader when Barnabas gets involved in a heated dispute with Paul that leads to a parting of ways (15:36-41). Considering that Barnabas selflessly promotes Paul in the Jerusalem church and the Antioch church, and accompanies Paul on the first missionary journey and at the Jerusalem council, this unpleasant breakdown of a successful missionary association is surprising. Yet, Barnabas acts consistently with his earlier characterization, risking association with untested people—notably Paul himself (9:27).[193] The text does not clarify whether Barnabas is perhaps showing favoritism toward John Mark (Col. 4:10 reveals that John Mark was his cousin) or if Paul is too harsh. Some details of Barnabas's inner life are revealed: he rejoices when he sees what God has been doing in the Antioch church (11:23); he is full of the Holy Spirit (11:24); and

189. Cf. Öhler, who sketches three phases in the relationship: (i) Barnabas as Paul's mentor (till 13:1); (ii) Barnabas as Paul's supporter (from 13:9 till 15:35); (iii) Barnabas's separation from Paul (*Barnabas,* 461–62).

190. Later, in 11:29-30, Barnabas once again brings relief to the Jerusalem church (Murphy, "Role of Barnabas," 326).

191. According to Kistemaker, Barnabas is good in the sense that he is "of sterling character, wholesome, capable, and helpful" (*Acts,* 421). Witherington notes that Barnabas is the only character in Acts called good (*Acts of the Apostles,* 370).

192. Barnabas's choice of Paul as his righthand man in Antioch is based on his earlier contact with Paul and his knowledge of Paul's calling (Kistemaker, *Acts,* 422; Witherington, *Acts of the Apostles,* 370).

193. Murphy, "Role of Barnabas," 340. Murphy adds that Barnabas focuses on people's potential rather than their limitations.

he tears his clothes when he learns of the intentions of the Lystrans, revealing extreme distress (14:14). Considering the degree of complexity (multiple traits though uncomplicated), development (little), and inner life (some), I categorize Barnabas on the character continuum as one who has personality.[194]

Character Evaluation and Significance. Barnabas functions well as a witness for Jesus, the first criterion of character evaluation. He sells the land he owns and gives all the proceeds to the Jerusalem church, exemplifying that which Jesus asked of the rich ruler (Luke 18:18-23). He supports and mentors Paul. He approves of the mixed Jewish-Gentile church in Antioch and is instrumental in its continued growth (11:24) and mission (13:1-3). As a Greek-speaking Jewish Christian from Cyprus, the bilingual and multicultural Barnabas is "the right man in the right place."[195] He faithfully testifies about Jesus on his missionary journey with Paul. In relation to the second criterion for character evaluation, Barnabas advances the plot in two ways. First, he introduces and recommends Paul in the Jerusalem church and Antioch church. Second, he partakes in and advances the mission of proclaiming God's word and Jesus (13:5; 14:3). In terms of his significance for today, Barnabas represents those with influence in the church, who selflessly promote others and give them opportunities to succeed.

Barnabas		
Narrative Appearances	4:36; 9:27; 11:22, 30; 12:25; 13:1-2, 7, 43, 46, 50; 14:12, 14, 20; 15:2, 12, 22, 25, 35-37, 39	
Origin	Birth, Gender, Ethnicity, Nation/City	male, Jewish, Cypriot
	Family (Ancestors, Relatives)	Levite
Upbringing	Nurture, Education	
External Goods	Epithets, Reputation	Barnabas, a good man, full of the Holy Spirit and faith
	Age, Marital Status	
	Socio-Economic Status, Wealth	as a Levite, he has a high status among the Jewish people; he has considerable means but gives it to the church

194. Using the categories of flat and round characters, Öhler classifies Barnabas as a round character (*Barnabas*, 473 n. 36).

195. Kistemaker, *Acts*, 421. Cf. Öhler, *Barnabas*, 465–67.

	Place of Residence/Operation	Jerusalem, Antioch, Asia Minor
	Occupation, Positions Held	first a landowner, then a church worker/leader and missionary
	Group Affiliation, Friends	Jerusalem and Antioch church, Paul, John Mark
Speech and Actions	In Interaction with Protagonists	introduces Paul to the Jerusalem church and Antioch church; promotes Paul
	In Interaction with Other Characters	proclaims the gospel; promotes John Mark
Death	Manner of Death, Events after Death	
Character Analysis	Complexity	uncomplicated; multiple traits
	Development	little
	Inner Life	some
Character Classification	Degree of Characterization	personality
Character Evaluation	Response to Protagonists, Witness to Jesus	adequate
	Role in the Plot	he promotes Paul and advances the church's Gentile mission
Character Significance	Representative Value	those who have influence in the church and selflessly promote others and give them opportunities to succeed

LYDIA

Lydia finds mention in just three verses (16:14–15, 40), but they present a surprisingly rich characterization of her. Acts 16:14–15 provides various clues about her identity.[196] First, she is a merchant, dealing in purple cloth. Second, she is from Thyatira in the Roman province of Asia, but has apparently settled in

---

196. See also Richard S. Ascough, *Lydia: Paul's Cosmopolitan Hostess* (Collegeville, MN: Liturgical, 2009), 5.

Philippi, which according to 1:12 is "a leading city of the district of Macedonia and a Roman colony." Richard Ascough describes her as a "cosmopolitan woman" because she has links to two urban centers (Thyatira and Philippi) and functions in two dominant cultures (Greek and Roman).[197] Her business was probably arranging the sales of dyed woolen goods in Philippi, which, from a socio-economic perspective, puts her in the "middle class."[198] Third, she is a God-fearer, that is, a quasi-official sympathizer of Judaism, shown through acts of piety (e.g., almsgiving and synagogue participation) (cf. Paul's meeting on the Sabbath in a place of prayer in 16:13).[199] Fourth, she owns a house and probably is the head of the household—the basic social unit in first-century cultures, comprising the nuclear family, dependents (parents, relatives), slaves, freedmen and freedwomen, and sometimes even honored guests.[200]

Character Analysis and Classification. Although Lydia is not a complex character, she exhibits multiple traits. From 16:14-15, we learn that she is enterprising, attentive, responsive, pious, influential (she prevails upon her entire household to be baptized), persuasive (she persuades Paul and Silas to stay in her home), faithful, and hospitable.[201] There is very little development in her characterization in that the reader may be surprised that she seems to be the head of the household (there is no mention of her husband as the *paterfamilias*)—she

197. Ascough, *Lydia*, 12.

198. James D. G. Dunn identifies her as "a woman with a substantial business in luxury goods" (*The Acts of the Apostles* [Valley Forge, PA: Trinity, 1996], 219). Cf. Kistemaker, *Acts*, 590; Witherington, *Acts of the Apostles*, 492. F. Scott Spencer, however, presents a case for a lower social status of Lydia ("Women of 'the Cloth' in Acts: Sewing the Word," in *A Feminist Companion to the Acts of the Apostles*, ed. Amy-Jill Levine [with Marianne Blickenstaff] [New York: T. & T. Clark, 2004], 148–49). For more detailed discussions of Lydia's profession and social status, see Jean-Pierre Sterck-Degueldre, *Eine Frau namens Lydia: Zu Geschichte und Komposition in Apostelgeschichte 16,11–15.40* (WUNT II/176; Tübingen: Mohr Siebeck, 2004), 213–38; Friedrich Gustav Lang, "Neues über Lydia? Zur Deutung von 'Purpurhändlerin' in Apg 16,14," *ZNW* 100 (2009): 29–44.

199. Scott McKnight, "Proselytism and Godfearers," in *DNTB*, 846. Cf. Witherington, *Acts of the Apostles*, 493.

200. Suzanne Dixon, *The Roman Family* (Baltimore: Johns Hopkins University Press, 1992), 1–8; Carolyn Osiek, "The Family in Early Christianity: 'Family Values' Revisited," *CBQ* 58 (1996): 10–12. See also the discussions in Margaret M. Mitchell, "Why Family Matters for Early Christian Literature," in *Early Christian Families in Context: An Interdisciplinary Dialogue*, ed. David L. Balch and Carolyn Osiek (Grand Rapids: Eerdmans, 2003), 345–58; Ascough, *Lydia*, 29–35; Margaret Y. MacDonald, "Kinship and Family in the New Testament World," in *Understanding the Social World of the New Testament*, ed. Dietmar Neufeld and Richard E. DeMaris (New York: Routledge, 2010), 29–43.

201. Hospitality is an important motif in both Luke's Gospel and Acts. In Acts, new converts regularly extend hospitality to the visiting missionary (10:48; 18:20; 21:4, 7, 17; 28:14), which is naturally connected with the house church motif (Sterck-Degueldre, *Eine Frau namens Lydia*, 246).

may have been widowed or unmarried.[202] Regarding her inner life, the narrator reveals that God "opened her heart," that is, made her open-minded (16:14), and she considers herself faithful (16:15). Considering her character complexity (multiple traits), development (none/little), and inner life (little/some), I place her on the character continuum as a type but moving toward personality.

Character Evaluation and Significance. On the matter of character evaluation, Lydia does well. She responds positively to the good news proclaimed by the protagonist Paul and in turn becomes a positive witness for Jesus, managing to influence her entire household to be baptized (16:14-15). Sterck-Degueldre notes that the baptism of her household gives Lydia's conversion a collective character, which may reflect Luke's *Hausmotiv* (cf. 11:14; 16:31).[203] In addition, the "Christian" language of "brothers (and sisters)" in 16:40 may suggest that a house church has begun to meet in Lydia's home.[204] Regarding the second criterion, she advances the plot significantly, becoming Paul's first Greek convert after his "Macedonian call."[205] In addition, she provides Paul and Silas with a home base from which they can advance the Christian mission in Philippi (cf. 16:16-40). Witherington remarks that "[i]t was vital for Paul to find a venue where Christians could meet in this Roman colony, for he was promulgating a foreign religion, and not clearly licit, especially if it was distinguished from Judaism. Lydia's providing of a meeting place was thus crucial to the existence and growth of Christianity in this place."[206] Lydia's significance for today is that she represents those who are quick to respond to the gospel and to open their homes for its sake.[207]

---

202. Cf. Dunn, *Acts of the Apostles*, 219; Witherington, *Acts of the Apostles*, 493; Gaventa, *Acts of the Apostles*, 237. See also the discussion in Ascough, *Lydia*, 45–51.

203. Sterck-Degueldre, *Eine Frau namens Lydia*, 244.

204. Cf. Dunn, *Acts of the Apostles*, 219; Witherington, *Acts of the Apostles*, 499; Sterck-Degueldre, *Eine Frau namens Lydia*, 247–48. Ascough speculates that Lydia may be the patron of the Jesus group in Philippi (*Lydia*, 98). Kistemaker even calls Lydia's household "the core of the emerging church of Philippi" (*Acts*, 590).

205. Sterck-Degueldre also recognizes the strategic significance of Lydia's conversion: "Mit dem vom Geist bewirkten Übergang nach Makedonien verwirklicht sich die im Jerusalemer Konzil beschlossene Öffnung zu den Heiden in einer *römischen Kolonie* und zwar an einer *Frau*" (*Eine Frau namens Lydia*, 239).

206. Witherington, *Acts of the Apostles*, 487.

207. Cf. Sterck-Degueldre's remark about Lydia's exemplary behavior: "Lydia . . . wird zum Paradigma für die Aufnahme der Botschaft und die Unterstützung der Missionare" (*Eine Frau namens Lydia*, 248).

Lydia		
Narrative Appearances	16:14–15, 40	
Origin	Birth, Gender, Ethnicity, Nation/City	female, Greek
	Family (Ancestors, Relatives)	
Upbringing	Nurture, Education	perhaps some commercial training
External Goods	Epithets, Reputation	a God-fearer
	Age, Marital Status	
	Socio-Economic Status, Wealth	middle class, good social standing
	Place of Residence/Operation	from Thyatira but settled in Philippi
	Occupation, Positions Held	merchant in purple cloth; perhaps a house church leader
	Group Affiliation, Friends	Greeks, Romans, God-fearing women in Philippi
Speech and Actions	In Interaction with Protagonists	responsive and hospitable to Paul
	In Interaction with Other Characters	got her whole household baptized
Death	Manner of Death, Events after Death	
Character Analysis	Complexity	uncomplicated; multiple traits
	Development	perhaps a little
	Inner Life	little/some
Character Classification	Degree of Characterization	type/personality
Character Evaluation	Response to Protagonists, Witness to Jesus	adequate
	Role in the Plot	first convert in Greece; facilitates Paul and Silas's mission by providing them a home base

Character Significance	Representative Value	those who are quick to respond to the gospel and to open their homes for the sake of the gospel

4.4. Conclusion

One advantage of examining characters consistently using the same model is that it provides a basis for comparing characters—both within a narrative and across narratives. The following table presents the results of our character analysis and classification:

Narrative	Character	Complex-ity	Develop-ment	Inner Life	Degree of Character-ization
Mark	Peter	++	++	+	individual
	Jesus' Mother	0	0	0	agent
	Haemorrhaging Woman	+	−	+	personality
	Bartimaeus	+	−	0	type/personality
John	Peter	++	++	+	individual
	Jesus' Mother	−	0	0	agent/type
	Nicodemus	++	+	−	personality
	Pilate	++	+	−/+	personality/ individual
Acts	Peter	++	+	++	individual
	Pilate	0/−	0/−	0/−	agent/type
	Barnabas	++	−	+	personality
	Lydia	++	0/−	−/+	type/personality

Key: 0 = none, − = little, + = some, ++ = much

The following diagram visualizes the relative degree of characterization of the various characters across the narratives under investigation without explicit labels:

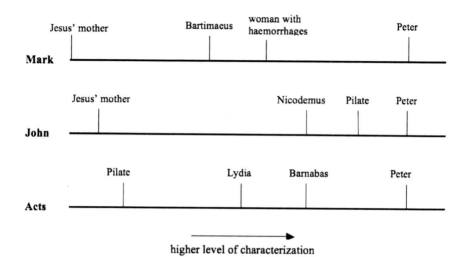

higher level of characterization

Continuum of Degree of Characterization

I will now make a few concluding observations about the characters that feature in more than one narrative. Although Jesus' mother features in both Mark's Gospel and John's Gospel with a low degree of characterization, there is a striking difference. Whereas Jesus' mother is firmly on Jesus' side in the Johannine narrative and functions as a catalyst for his ministry, in Mark she is placed outside Jesus' circle of followers and seems to oppose his ministry. Not surprisingly, Jesus' mother does not figure at the cross in Mark, while she does in John, with Jesus even addressing her. In short, while Mark's characterization of Jesus' mother is limited and negative, John depicts Jesus' mother more elaborately and positively. Peter, meanwhile, is consistently the most complex character in all three narratives. Yet, there are remarkable differences in Peter's characterization: only John records the "rivalry" between Peter and the Beloved Disciple, and Peter's restoration after his denial of Jesus. If John indeed wrote for readers who were familiar with Mark's Gospel, he certainly rescues the characters of Jesus' mother and Peter. Compared to his instability and failures in Mark and John, Peter is shown as stable and successful in Acts. Finally, while Pilate has a high degree of characterization in the Gospel of John, he is merely an agent in Acts. In keeping with the focus of the Gospels on Jesus' passion and resurrection, it is understandable that Pilate features more in these narratives, especially in John's Gospel, which seeks to stress the cosmic scope of Jesus' mission. In Acts where Jesus' trial is no longer an issue, Pilate features only occasionally, and mostly to fill in some details of the story's setting.

5

Conclusion

At the outset, the stated aim of the study was to develop a comprehensive theory of character in New Testament narrative. Having arrived at the end, we must reflect on what we have done and whether this goal has been achieved. Put simply, we carried out the process of identifying, deconstructing, constructing, and validating a paradigm for studying character in New Testament narrative. To elaborate, in Chapter 1, we reviewed the contributions of various scholars to the theory of character study in the New Testament, focusing on the Gospel of Mark, the Gospel of John, and the Acts of the Apostles as representative narrative material. We observed that many scholars seem to use or assume a pattern or paradigm of character reconstruction in the New Testament, while acknowledging that some might take issue with this analysis. Nevertheless, whether one sees a pattern, a paradigm, or just an array of approaches, the inevitable conclusion was that there is no robust, comprehensive theory of character in New Testament narrative. The surge in interest in New Testament characters in the last decade has not led to a consensus on how to study character in biblical narrative. This defined the task for our study.

In Chapter 2, we examined character in ancient Hebrew and Greco-Roman literature as well as modern literature. We observed that both the nature of character and the method of reconstructing character in ancient and modern literature are more alike than different, and therefore ancient and modern characterization should be viewed on a continuum. Using caution, it is thus legitimate and inevitable to apply aspects of modern literary methods to ancient narrative. In doing so, we deconstructed a dominant pattern or paradigm of character reconstruction in New Testament studies. While some might disagree that such a pattern or paradigm exists, they must admit that there is currently no comprehensive theory of character or agreed practice on how to reconstruct character from New Testament narrative. Therefore, our examination provided the basis and necessary parameters for constructing a (new) paradigm for the study of New Testament character.

In Chapter 3, then, we introduced our theory, consisting of a three-dimensional approach to understanding character in New Testament narrative. First, we studied character in text and context, using information in the text and other sources. In this process, we used the concept of a plausible historically informed modern reader, that is, a modern reader who has sound knowledge of the first-century Jewish and Greco-Roman world and who can give a plausible explanation for the ancient sources that are employed. Second, we analyzed and classified the characters along three continua (complexity, development, inner life), and plotted the resulting character on a continuum of degree of characterization (from agent to type to personality to individuality). Third, we evaluated the characters in relation to the narrative's point of view and their role in the plot, and then sought to determine the characters' representative value for today.

Finally, in Chapter 4, we sought to validate our proposed theory by applying it to select characters in the Gospel of Mark, the Gospel of John, and the Acts of the Apostles. The results of each character reconstruction were presented in a table, containing both character descriptors that correspond to ancient rhetorical *topoi* and aggregate information about the character in terms of their complexity, development, inner life, degree of characterization, evaluation, and significance. This latter meta-information about a character facilitates further analysis, such as how characters relate to each other within a narrative or across narratives.

I do not claim that this model is complete or exhaustive—some aspects may need clarification; other aspects may need to be built upon. Nevertheless, I contend that it is thorough enough to enable a comprehensive, nonreductionist study of New Testament characters. I would like to add that since this study was an attempt to develop a theory of *character*, I have not dealt at length with related, but vital aspects such as characterization, plot, and point of view. At this juncture, I am launching my theory of character into the public domain to be tested, evaluated, and undoubtedly improved upon.

An important by-product of our study is the idea that *character evaluation inevitably leads to self-evaluation*. Although I touched on this in section 3.3, I did not build on the idea because, strictly speaking, this pertains to the study of reader rather than character. Nevertheless, I raise it here because it is a direct consequence of character reconstruction. Scholars have recognized that the biblical authors are not neutral but aim at persuading their audiences about a particular perspective or point of view through the way they present their characters. Using the characters and their choices, the author thus urges the reader to choose too. For example, Tannehill explains how the author of Mark's Gospel uses characterization to influence the reader:

> The purpose of the author and the response which he anticipates from the reader begin to come clear when we consider the author's shaping of the disciples' role as indirect communication with the reader. The author assumes that there are essential similarities between the disciples and his anticipated readers, so that what he reveals about the disciples may become a revelation about the readers and so enable them to change.[1]

Building on Tannehill's observations, Williams asserts that Mark evaluates his characters by showing how they measure up to the teaching and example of Jesus, and calls on the reader to identify with some characters and dissociate from others, and in so doing to evaluate her own response to Jesus.[2] Similarly, I have argued that in order to accomplish his stated purpose in John 20:30-31, the evangelist puts various characters on the stage who interact with Jesus, producing an array of belief-responses in order to challenge his readers to evaluate their own stance regarding Jesus.[3] Regarding Luke–Acts, Darr stresses the rhetorical force of the text and the reader's involvement, where the reader witnesses what the characters witness and is forced to reflect on his own response.[4] Darr draws the following conclusion about Luke's dialogical quality of characterization:

> The process of constructing character is neither neutral nor unidirectional. Even as we fashion *dramatis personae*, we are being positioned and manoeuvred—indeed, shaped—by the rhetoric of the text. While building Luke's characters, the audience experiences a certain character building of its own![5]

---

1. Tannehill, "Disciples in Mark," 405.

2. Williams, *Other Followers*, 87–88.

3. Bennema, *Encountering Jesus*, 1, 212. Cf. Culpepper, *Anatomy of the Fourth Gospel*, 148; Conway, "Ambiguity," 324.

4. Darr, *On Character Building*, 56–57.

5. Darr, *On Character Building*, 59.

The study of New Testament characters, therefore, is not merely a cognitive exercise but also involves the volitional and affective aspects of the reader's personality.

This study is the first attempt at developing a comprehensive theory of character in New Testament narrative and will hopefully stimulate fruitful dialogue within the academy. I can think of three areas for further research to test, enhance, and expand my theory. The first and obvious suggestion is to test my theory on other New Testament writings, such as the Gospel of Matthew, the Gospel of Luke, and the narrative material in Revelation, and I presume that Old Testament narratives could also be examined using this theory. We could test how beneficial it is to analyze characters in these narratives according to the various ancient *topoi*, or seek to determine the impact of Hebraic characterization on New Testament narratives. In addition, further research must demonstrate the extent to which the meta-level of character information that we collect facilitates analysis of how the various characters relate to each other in and across narratives.

A second suggestion for further research is to study how a particular character appears across narratives and to clarify the differences in characterization in the light of the author's purpose and the rhetoric of the narrative. While I have made an attempt with the characters of Peter, Jesus' mother, and Pilate, more must be done. For example, we can examine in detail the character of the crowd (ὄχλος) in the four Gospels and the Acts of the Apostles. The crowd embodies, of course, the largest number of people and occurs frequently (fifty times in Matthew; thirty-eight times in Mark; sixty-three times in Luke–Acts; and twenty times in John), yet it is not an obvious character and has received virtually no attention from New Testament scholarship. We must examine whether the crowd is characterized differently in these writings, and if it is the case, explain why. In addition, we must ascertain whether the New Testament portraits of the crowd differ from the largely negative portrayal of the crowd that we find in both Josephus and Philo.

The third area of further research is the aretological aspect of characterization, that is, the concept of characters as moral agents of transformation. We noted that the author communicates his particular perspective or point of view through the characters in the story, implicitly leading the reader to evaluate the characters, thus creating various degrees of affinity or distance with these characters. Additionally, the reader's evaluation of the characters also leads to the reader's self-evaluation. This implies that the characters are potential change agents—they have the ability to effect transformation in the reader. An examination of characters as moral agents in an ethical reading of the biblical narratives will enhance the discipline of virtue ethics.[6]

6. Elsewhere, I made an attempt to explore this idea: Bennema, "Virtue Ethics," 167–81. Jonathan T. Pennington also stresses the aretological dimension of the Gospels in his *Reading the Gospels Wisely: A Narrative and Theological Introduction* (Grand Rapids: Baker Academic, 2012).

Bibliography

ANCIENT LITERATURE

Unless indicated otherwise, I have accessed the ancient literature via the Perseus Digital Library, ed. Gregory R. Crane, http://www.perseus.tufts.edu/hopper, and The Internet Classics Archive by Daniel C. Stevenson, http://classics.mit.edu.

Aeschylus. *Agamemnon.*

Apuleius. *The Golden Ass.*

Aristotle. *The Poetics.* Translated by W. Hamilton Fyfe. Loeb Classical Library 199. Cambridge, MA: Harvard University Press, 1982.

Chariton. *Chaereas and Callirhoe.*

Euripides. *Antiope.*

Euripides. *Electra.*

Euripides. *Ion.*

Euripides. *Medea.*

Euripides. *Orestes.*

Heliodorus. *Aethiopica.*

Plutarch. *Antony.*

Plutarch. *Lives.*

Sophocles. *Ajax.*

Sophocles. *Antigone.*

Sophocles. *Oedipus at Colonus.*

Sophocles. *Oedipus Tyrannus.*

Suetonius. *Lives of the Caesars.*

Tacitus. *Annals.*

Tatius. *Leucippe and Clitophon.*

Theophrastus. *Characters.* Edited and translated by J. Rusten. Loeb Classical Library 225. Cambridge, MA: Harvard University Press, 2002.

MODERN LITERATURE

Aichele, George. "Jesus' Uncanny 'Family Scene.'" *Journal for the Study of the New Testament* 74 (1999): 29–49.

Alter, Robert. *The Art of Biblical Narrative*. London: George Allen & Unwin, 1981.

Anderson, Paul N. *The Riddles of the Fourth Gospel: An Introduction to John*. Minneapolis: Fortress Press, 2011.

Ascough, Richard S. *Lydia: Paul's Cosmopolitan Hostess*. Collegeville, MN: Liturgical, 2009.

Aune, David E. "Greco-Roman Biography." Pages 107–26 in *Greco-Roman Literature and the New Testament: Selected Forms and Genres*. Edited by David E. Aune. Society of Biblical Literature Sources for Biblical Study 21. Atlanta: Scholars, 1988.

Bal, Mieke. *Narratology: Introduction to the Theory of Narrative*. Translated by C. van Boheemen. Toronto: University of Toronto Press, 1985.

Ball, David. Review of Cornelis Bennema, *Encountering Jesus: Character Studies in the Gospel of John*. *Journal for the Study of the New Testament* 33 (2011): 70.

Bar-Efrat, Shimon. *Narrative Art in the Bible*. Journal for the Study of the Old Testament Supplement Series 70. Sheffield: Almond Press, 1989.

Barton, Stephen C. *Discipleship and Family Ties in Mark and Matthew*. Society for New Testament Studies Monograph Series 80. Cambridge: Cambridge University Press, 1994.

Bassler, Jouette M. "Mixed Signals: Nicodemus in the Fourth Gospel." *Journal of Biblical Literature* 108 (1989): 635–46.

Bauckham, Richard. *Bible and Mission: Christian Witness in a Postmodern World*. Grand Rapids: Baker Academic, 2003.

———. "James, Peter, and the Gentiles." Pages 91–142 in *The Missions of James, Peter, and Paul: Tensions in Early Christianity*. Edited by Bruce Chilton and Craig Evans. Novum Testamentum Supplement Series 115. Leiden: Brill, 2005.

———. *Jesus and the Eyewitnesses: The Gospels as Eyewitness Testimony*. Grand Rapids: Eerdmans, 2006.

———. "John for Readers of Mark." Pages 147–71 in *The Gospels for All Christians: Rethinking the Gospel Audiences*. Edited by Richard Bauckham. Grand Rapids: Eerdmans, 1998.

———. "Nicodemus and the Gurion Family." *Journal of Theological Studies* 47 (1996): 1–37.

———. "The Beloved Disciple as Ideal Author." *Journal for the Study of the New Testament* 49 (1993): 21–44.

Beasley-Murray, George R. *John*. Word Biblical Commentary 36. Milton Keynes, UK: Word, 1991.

Beck, David R. *The Discipleship Paradigm: Readers and Anonymous Characters in the Fourth Gospel.* Biblical Interpretation Series 27. Leiden: Brill, 1997.

————. "The Narrative Function of Anonymity in Fourth Gospel Characterization." *Semeia* 63 (1993): 143–58.

————. "'Whom Jesus Loved': Anonymity and Identity. Belief and Witness in the Fourth Gospel." Pages 221–39 in *Characters and Characterization in the Gospel of John.* Edited by Christopher W. Skinner. Library of New Testament Studies 461. New York: T. & T. Clark, 2013.

Beck, Robert R. *Nonviolent Story: Narrative Conflict Resolution in the Gospel of Mark.* Maryknoll, NY: Orbis, 1996.

Beirne, Margaret M. *Women and Men in the Fourth Gospel: A Genuine Discipleship of Equals.* Journal for the Study of the New Testament Supplement Series 242. London: Sheffield Academic Press, 2003.

Bennema, Cornelis. "A Comprehensive Approach to Understanding Character in the Gospel of John." Pages 36–58 in *Characters and Characterization in the Gospel of John.* Edited by Christopher W. Skinner. Library of New Testament Studies 461. New York: T. & T. Clark, 2013.

————. "A Theory of Character in the Fourth Gospel with Reference to Ancient and Modern Literature." *Biblical Interpretation* 17 (2009): 375–421.

————. "Christ, the Spirit and the Knowledge of God: A Study in Johannine Epistemology." Pages 107–33 in *The Bible and Epistemology: Biblical Soundings on the Knowledge of God.* Edited by Mary Healy and Robin Parry. Milton Keynes, UK: Paternoster, 2007.

————. *Encountering Jesus: Character Studies in the Gospel of John.* Milton Keynes, UK: Paternoster, 2009.

————. *Excavating John's Gospel: A Commentary for Today.* Delhi: ISPCK, 2005. Repr., Eugene, OR: Wipf & Stock, 2008.

————. "Figurenanalyse und Wundererzählungen im Markusevangelium." In *Hermeneutik der frühchristlichen Wundererzählungen.* Edited by Bernd Kollmann and Ruben Zimmermann. Wissenschaftliche Untersuchungen zum Neuen Testament. Tübingen: Mohr Siebeck, forthcoming 2014.

————. "Gentile Characters and the Motif of Proclamation in the Gospel of Mark." In *Character Studies and the Gospel of Mark.* Edited by Christopher W. Skinner and Matthew Ryan Hauge. Library of New Testament Studies. New York: T. & T. Clark, forthcoming 2014.

————. "Judas the Betrayer: The Black Sheep of the Family." Pages 360–72 in *Character Studies in the Fourth Gospel: Narrative Approaches to Seventy Figures in John.* Edited by Steven A. Hunt, D. Francois Tolmie, and Ruben

Zimmermann. Wissenschaftliche Untersuchungen zum Neuen Testament 314. Tübingen: Mohr Siebeck, 2013.

———. "The Character of John in the Fourth Gospel." *Journal of the Evangelical Theological Society* 52 (2009): 271–84.

———. "The Character of Pilate in the Gospel of John." Pages 240–53 in *Characters and Characterization in the Gospel of John.* Edited by Christopher W. Skinner. Library of New Testament Studies 461. New York: T. & T. Clark, 2013.

———. "The Chief Priests: Masterminds of Jesus' Death." Pages 382–87 in *Character Studies in the Fourth Gospel: Narrative Approaches to Seventy Figures in John.* Steven A. Hunt, D. Francois Tolmie, and Ruben Zimmermann. Wissenschaftliche Untersuchungen zum Neuen Testament 314. Tübingen: Mohr Siebeck, 2013.

———. "The Identity and Composition of οἱ Ἰουδαῖοι in the Gospel of John." *Tyndale Bulletin* 60 (2009): 239–63.

———. "The Johannine Crowd: A Faceless, Divided Mass." Pages 347–55 in *Character Studies in the Fourth Gospel: Narrative Approaches to Seventy Figures in John.* Edited by Steven A. Hunt, D. Francois Tolmie, and Ruben Zimmermann. Wissenschaftliche Untersuchungen zum Neuen Testament 314. Tübingen: Mohr Siebeck, 2013.

———. *The Power of Saving Wisdom: An Investigation of Spirit and Wisdom in Relation to the Soteriology of the Fourth Gospel.* Wissenschaftliche Untersuchungen zum Neuen Testament II/148. Tübingen: Mohr Siebeck, 2002. Repr., Eugene, OR: Wipf & Stock, 2007.

———. "The Sword of the Messiah and the Concept of Liberation in the Fourth Gospel." *Biblica* 86 (2005): 37–49.

———. "Virtue Ethics in the Gospel of John: The Johannine Characters as Moral Agents." Pages 167–81 in *Rediscovering John: Essays on the Fourth Gospel in Honour of Frédéric Manns.* Edited by L. Daniel Chrupcała. Studium Biblicum Franciscanum 80. Milan: Edizioni Terra Santa, 2013.

Berlin, Adele. *Poetics and Interpretation of Biblical Narrative.* Sheffield: Almond Press, 1983.

Best, Ernest. *Mark: The Gospel as Story.* Edinburgh: T. & T. Clark, 1983.

———. "Peter in the Gospel according to Mark." *Catholic Biblical Quarterly* 40 (1978): 547–58.

Billault, Alain. "Characterization in the Ancient Novel." Pages 115–29 in *The Novel in the Ancient World.* Edited by G. Schmeling. Leiden: Brill, 1996.

Black, C. Clifton. "The Presentation of John Mark in the Acts of the Apostles." *Perspectives in Religious Studies* 20 (1993): 235–54.

Blaine, Bradford B. *Peter in the Gospel of John: The Making of an Authentic Disciple.* Society of Biblical Literature Academia Biblica 27. Leiden: Brill, 2007.

Boer, Martinus C. de. "Narrative Criticism, Historical Criticism, and the Gospel of John." *Journal for the Study of the New Testament* 47 (1992): 35–48.

———. "The Narrative Function of Pilate in John." Pages 141–58 in *Narrativity in Biblical and Related Texts.* Edited by G. J. Brooke and J.-D. Kaestli. Bibliotheca Ephemeridum Theologicarum Lovaniensium 149. Leuven: Leuven University Press, 2000.

Böhler, Dieter. "'Ecce Homo!' (Joh 19,5) ein Zität aus dem Alten Testament." *Biblische Zeitschrift* 39 (1995): 104–8.

Bolt, Peter G. "Mission and Witness." Pages 191–214 in *Witness to the Gospel: The Theology of Acts.* Edited by I. Howard Marshall and David Peterson. Grand Rapids: Eerdmans, 1998.

Bond, Helen K. *Pontius Pilate in History and Interpretation.* Society for New Testament Studies Monograph Series 100. Cambridge: Cambridge University Press, 1998.

Booth, Wayne. *The Rhetoric of Fiction.* 2nd ed. Chicago: University of Chicago Press, 1983.

Brady, David. "The Alarm to Peter in Mark's Gospel." *Journal for the Study of the New Testament* 4 (1979): 42–57.

Brant, Jo-Ann A. *Dialogue and Drama: Elements of Greek Tragedy in the Fourth Gospel.* Peabody, MA: Hendrickson, 2004.

Broadhead, Edwin K. *Mark.* Sheffield: Sheffield Academic Press, 2001.

Brock, Sebastian. "ΒΑΡΝΑΒΑΣ: ΥΙΟΕ ΠΑΡΑΚΛΗΣΕΩΣ." *Journal of Theological Studies* 25 (1974): 93–98.

Brower, Kent E. "Holiness." Pages 477–78 in *New Bible Dictionary.* Edited by D. R. W. Wood. 3rd ed. Leicester, UK: InterVarsity, 1996.

Brown, Raymond E. "Roles of Women in the Fourth Gospel." *Theological Studies* 36 (1975): 688–99.

———. *The Community of the Beloved Disciple.* New York: Paulist, 1979.

———. *The Gospel according to John XIII–XXI.* Anchor Bible 29a. London: Chapman, 1971.

———. "The 'Mother of Jesus' in the Fourth Gospel." Pages 307–10 in *L'Évangile de Jean: Sources, rédaction, théologie.* Edited by Marinus de Jonge. Bibliotheca

Ephemeridum Theologicarum Lovaniensium 44. Leuven: Leuven University Press, 1987.

———. "The Passion according to John: Chapters 18 and 19." *Worship* 49 (1975): 126–34.

———, Karl P. Donfried, Joseph A. Fitzmyer, and John Reumann, eds. *Mary in the New Testament: A Collaborative Assessment by Protestant and Roman Catholic Scholars.* Philadelphia: Fortress Press, 1978.

Bultmann, Rudolf. *The Gospel of John.* Translated by George R. Beasley-Murray. Philadelphia: Westminster, 1971.

Burnett, Fred W. "Characterization and Reader Construction of Characters in the Gospels." *Semeia* 63 (1993): 3–28.

Burridge, Richard A. *What Are the Gospels? A Comparison with Graeco-Roman Biography.* 2nd ed. Grand Rapids: Eerdmans, 2004.

Carson, D. A. *The Gospel according to John.* Leicester, UK: InterVarsity, 1991.

Carter, Warren. *Pontius Pilate: Portraits of a Roman Governor.* Collegeville, MN: Liturgical, 2003.

Chatman, Seymour. *Story and Discourse: Narrative Structure in Fiction and Film.* Ithaca, NY/London: Cornell University Press, 1978.

Cheng, Ling. *The Characterisation of God in Acts: The Indirect Portrayal of an Invisible Character.* Paternoster Biblical Monographs. Milton Keynes, UK: Paternoster, 2011.

Collins, Raymond F. "From John to the Beloved Disciple: An Essay on Johannine Characters." *Interpretation* 49 (1995): 359–69.

———. "Representative Figures." Pages 1–45 in *These Things Have Been Written: Studies on the Fourth Gospel.* Louvain Theological & Pastoral Monographs 2. Louvain/Grand Rapids: Peeters/Eerdmans, 1990. Originally in *Downside Review* 94 (1976): 26–46; 95 (1976): 118–32.

Coloe, Mary L. *Dwelling in the Household of God: Johannine Ecclesiology and Spirituality.* Collegeville, MN: Liturgical, 2007.

Conway, Colleen M. *Men and Women in the Fourth Gospel: Gender and Johannine Characterization.* Society of Biblical Literature Dissertation Series 167. Atlanta: Society of Biblical Literature, 1999.

———. "Speaking through Ambiguity: Minor Characters in the Fourth Gospel." *Biblical Interpretation* 10 (2002): 324–41.

Cotter, Wendy J. *The Christ of the Miracle Stories: Portrait through Encounter.* Grand Rapids: Baker Academic, 2010.

Cotterell, F. Peter. "The Nicodemus Conversation: A Fresh Appraisal." *Expository Times* 96 (1984–85): 237–42.

Culpeper, Jonathan. "Reflections on a Cognitive Stylistic Approach to Characterisation." Pages 139–49 in *Cognitive Poetics: Goals, Gains and Gaps*. Edited by G. Brône and J. Vandaele. Applications of Cognitive Linguistics 10. Berlin/New York: De Gruyter, 2009.

Culpepper, R. Alan. *Anatomy of the Fourth Gospel: A Study in Literary Design*. Philadelphia: Fortress Press, 1983.

———. "The Weave of the Tapestry: Character and Theme in John." Pages 18–35 in *Characters and Characterization in the Gospel of John*. Edited by Christopher W. Skinner. Library of New Testament Studies 461. New York: T. & T. Clark, 2013.

Darr, John A. *Herod the Fox: Audience Criticism and Lukan Characterization*. Journal for the Study of the New Testament Supplement Series 163. Sheffield: Sheffield Academic Press, 1998.

———. "Narrator as Character: Mapping a Reader-Oriented Approach to Narration in Luke–Acts." *Semeia* 65 (1993): 43–60.

———. *On Character Building: The Reader and the Rhetoric of Characterization in Luke–Acts*. Louisville: Westminster John Knox, 1992.

Davies, Margaret. *Rhetoric and Reference in the Fourth Gospel*. Journal for the Study of the New Testament Supplement Series 69. Sheffield: JSOT Press, 1992.

De Romilly, Jacqueline. *A Short History of Greek Literature*. Chicago: University of Chicago Press, 1985.

Dewey, Joanna. "Point of View and the Disciples in Mark." Pages 97–106 in *Society of Biblical Literature 1982 Seminar Papers*. Edited by Kent Harold Richards. Chico, CA: Scholars, 1982.

Dixon, Suzanne. *The Roman Family*. Baltimore: Johns Hopkins University Press, 1992.

Droge, Arthur J. "The Status of Peter in the Fourth Gospel: A Note on John 18:10-11." *Journal of Biblical Literature* 109 (1990): 307–11.

Dschnulnigg, Peter. *Das Markusevangelium*. Theologischer Kommentar zum Neuen Testament 2; Stuttgart: Kohlhammer, 2007.

Dunn, James D. G. *Beginning from Jerusalem*. Vol. 2 of *Christianity in the Making*. Grand Rapids: Eerdmans, 2009.

———. *Jesus Remembered*. Vol. 1 of *Christianity in the Making*. Grand Rapids: Eerdmans, 2003.

———. *The Acts of the Apostles*. Valley Forge, PA: Trinity, 1996.

Easterling, Patricia E. "Character in Sophocles." *Greece and Rome* 24 (1977): 121–29.

——. "Constructing Character in Greek Tragedy." Pages 83–99 in *Characterization and Individuality in Greek Literature*. Edited by Christopher B. R. Pelling. Oxford: Clarendon, 1990.

Eder, Jens, Fotis Jannidis, and Ralf Schneider, eds. *Characters in Fictional Worlds: Understanding Imaginary Beings in Literature, Film, and Other Media*. Revisionen 3. Berlin/New York: De Gruyter 2010.

Edwards, James R. *The Gospel according to Mark*. Pillar New Testament Commentary. Grand Rapids: Eerdmans, 2002.

Edwards, Ruth. *Discovering John*. London: SPCK, 2003.

Egan, Kieran. "What Is a Plot?" *New Literary History* 9 (1978): 455–73.

Ehrman, Bart D. "Jesus' Trial before Pilate: John 18.28–19.16." *Biblical Theology Bulletin* 13 (1983): 124–31.

Ewen, Yosef. *Character in Narrative*. Tel Aviv: Sifriyat Hapoalim, 1980 (in Hebrew).

——. "The Theory of Character in Narrative Fiction." *Hasifrut* 3 (1971): 1–30 (in Hebrew).

Farelly, Nicolas. *The Disciples in the Fourth Gospel: A Narrative Analysis of Their Faith and Understanding*. Wissenschaftliche Untersuchungen zum Neuen Testament II/290. Tübingen: Mohr Siebeck, 2010.

Fehribach, Adeline. *The Women in the Life of the Bridegroom: A Feminist Historical-Literary Analysis of the Female Characters in the Fourth Gospel*. Collegeville, MN: Liturgical, 1998.

Finnern, Sönke. *Narratologie und biblische Exegese: Eine integrative Methode der Erzählanalyse und ihr Ertrag am Beispiel von Matthäus 28*. Wissenschaftliche Untersuchungen zum Neuen Testament II/285. Tübingen: Mohr Siebeck, 2010.

Forster, E. M. *Aspects of the Novel*. New York: Penguin, 1976 (orig. 1927).

France, R. T. *The Gospel of Mark*. New International Greek Testament Commentary. Grand Rapids: Eerdmans, 2002.

Gaiser, Frederick J. "In Touch with Jesus: Healing in Mark 5:21–43." *Word and World* 30 (2010): 5–15.

Garton, Charles. "Characterisation in Greek Tragedy." *Journal of Hellenic Studies* 77 (1957): 247–54.

Gaventa, Beverly Roberts. *Mary: Glimpses of the Mother of Jesus*. Edinburgh: T. & T. Clark, 1999.

——. *The Acts of the Apostles*. Abingdon New Testament Commentaries. Nashville: Abingdon, 2003.

Gench, Frances Taylor. *Encounters with Jesus: Studies in the Gospel of John.* Louisville: Westminster John Knox, 2007.

Gill, Christopher. "The Character-Personality Distinction." Pages 1–31 in *Characterization and Individuality in Greek Literature.* Edited by Christopher B. R. Pelling. Oxford: Clarendon, 1990.

———. "The Question of Character-Development: Plutarch and Tacitus." *Classical Quarterly* 33 (1983): 469–87.

Gillespie, Thomas W. "The Trial of Politics and Religion: John 18.28–19.16." *Ex Auditu* 2 (1986): 69–73.

Glancy, Jennifer A. "Torture: Flesh, Truth, and the Fourth Gospel." *Biblical Interpretation* 13 (2005): 107–36.

Goldhill, Simon. "Character and Action, Representation and Reading: Greek Tragedy and Its Critics." Pages 100–127 in *Characterization and Individuality in Greek Literature.* Edited by Christopher B. R. Pelling. Oxford: Clarendon, 1990.

———. "Modern Critical Approaches to Greek Tragedy." Pages 324–47 in *The Cambridge Companion to Greek Tragedy.* Edited by Patricia E. Easterling. Cambridge: Cambridge University Press, 1997.

———. *Reading Greek Tragedy.* Cambridge: Cambridge University Press, 1986.

Goodacre, Mark. *The Synoptic Problem: A Way through the Maze.* New York: T. & T. Clark, 2001.

Gowler, David B. *Host, Guest, Enemy and Friend: Portraits of the Pharisees in Luke and Acts.* Emory Studies in Early Christianity 2. New York: Peter Lang, 1991.

Graham, Susan Lochrie. "Silent Voices: Women in the Gospel of Mark." *Semeia* 54 (1991): 145–58.

Greimas, Algirdas J. *Sémantique structurale: Recherche de méthode.* Paris: Larousse, 1966.

Griffin, Jasper. "Characterization in Euripides: *Hippolytus* and *Iphigeneia in Aulis.*" Pages 128–49 in *Characterization and Individuality in Greek Literature.* Edited by Christopher B. R. Pelling. Oxford: Clarendon, 1990.

Gundry, Robert H. *Mark: A Commentary on His Apology for the Cross.* Grand Rapids: Eerdmans, 1993.

Haber, Susan. "A Woman's Touch: Feminist Encounters with the Hemorrhaging Woman in Mark 5.24-34." *Journal for the Study of the New Testament* 26 (2003): 171–92.

Hägg, Tomas. *The Novel in Antiquity.* Berkeley: University of California Press, 1983.

Hanson, Kenneth C., and Douglas E. Oakman. *Palestine in the Time of Jesus.* Minneapolis: Fortress Press, 1998.

Harstine, Stan. *Moses as a Character in the Fourth Gospel: A Study of Ancient Reading Techniques.* Journal for the Study of the New Testament Supplement Series 229. London: Sheffield Academic Press, 2002.

Harvey, W. J. *Character and the Novel.* London: Chatto & Windus, 1965.

Healy, Mary. *The Gospel of Mark.* Grand Rapids: Baker Academic, 2008.

Hengel, Martin. *Judaism and Hellenism: Studies in Their Encounter in Palestine during the Early Hellenistic Period.* 2 vols. London: SCM, 1974.

———. *Saint Peter: The Underestimated Apostle.* Translated by Thomas H. Trapp. Grand Rapids: Eerdmans, 2010.

Hochman, Baruch. *Character in Literature.* Ithaca, NY/London: Cornell University Press, 1985.

Hooker, Morna D. *The Gospel according to St Mark.* Black's New Testament Commentaries. London: Black, 1991.

Horsley, Richard A., and John S. Hanson. *Bandits, Prophets & Messiahs: Popular Movements in the Time of Jesus.* Harrisburg, PA: Trinity, 1999.

Howard, James M. "The Significance of Minor Characters in the Gospel of John." *Bibliotheca Sacra* 163 (2006): 63–78.

Hunt, Steven A., D. Francois Tolmie, and Ruben Zimmermann, eds. *Character Studies in the Fourth Gospel: Narrative Approaches to Seventy Figures in John.* Wissenschaftliche Untersuchungen zum Neuen Testament 314. Tübingen: Mohr Siebeck, 2013.

Hunt, Steven A., D. Francois Tolmie, and Ruben Zimmermann. "An Introduction to Character and Characterization in John and Related New Testament Literature." Pages 1–33 in *Character Studies in the Fourth Gospel: Narrative Approaches to Seventy Figures in John.* Edited by Steven A. Hunt, D. Francois Tolmie, and Ruben Zimmermann. Wissenschaftliche Untersuchungen zum Neuen Testament 314. Tübingen: Mohr Siebeck, 2013.

Hurtado, Larry W. *Mark.* New International Biblical Commentary 2. Peabody, MA: Hendrickson, 1989.

Hylen, Susan E. *Imperfect Believers: Ambiguous Characters in the Gospel of John.* Louisville: Westminster John Knox, 2009.

Iersel, Bas M. van. *Mark: A Reader-Response Commentary.* Journal for the Study of the New Testament Supplement Series 164. Sheffield: Sheffield Academic Press, 1998.

Iser, Wolfgang. "The Reading Process: A Phenomenological Approach." *New Literary History* 3 (1972): 279–99.

Iverson, Kelly R. *Gentiles in the Gospel of Mark: "Even the Dogs Under the Table Eat the Children's Crumbs."* Library of New Testament Studies 339. London: T. & T. Clark, 2007.

Jervell, Jacob. *The Theology of the Acts of the Apostles.* Cambridge: Cambridge University Press, 1996.

Jonge, Marinus de. "Nicodemus and Jesus: Some Observations on Misunderstanding and Understanding in the Fourth Gospel." Pages 29–47 in *Jesus: Stranger from Heaven and Son of God. Jesus Christ and the Christians in Johannine Perspective.* Edited and translated by Jeffrey E. Steely. Society of Biblical Literature Sources for Biblical Study 11. Missoula, MT: Scholars, 1977.

Keener, Craig S. *The Gospel of John: A Commentary.* Peabody, MA: Hendrickson, 2003.

Kennedy, George A., trans. *Progymnasmata: Greek Textbooks of Prose Composition and Rhetoric.* Writings from the Greco-Roman World 10. Leiden: Brill, 2003.

Kermode, Frank. *The Genesis of Secrecy: On the Interpretation of Narrative.* Cambridge, MA: Harvard University Press, 1979.

Kern, Philip H. "Paul's Conversion and Luke's Portrayal of Character in Acts 8–10." *Tyndale Bulletin* 54 (2003): 63–80.

Kim, Dongsu. *An Exegesis of Apostasy Embedded in John's Narratives of Peter and Judas against the Synoptic Parallels.* Studies in Bible and Early Christianity 61. Lewiston, NY: Edwin Mellen, 2004.

Kim, Jean K. *Woman and Nation: An Intercontextual Reading of the Gospel of John from a Postcolonial Feminist Perspective.* Biblical Interpretation Series 69. Leiden: Brill, 2004.

Kingsbury, Jack Dean. *Conflict in Mark: Jesus, Authorities, Disciples.* Minneapolis: Augsburg Fortress Press, 1989.

———. *Matthew as Story.* Minneapolis: Augsburg Fortress Press, 1988.

Kistemaker, Simon J. *Acts.* New Testament Commentary. Grand Rapids: Baker, 1990.

Kitto, H. D. F. *Greek Tragedy: A Literary Study.* 2nd ed. London: Methuen, 1950.

Kitzberger, Ingrid Rosa. "Synoptic Women in John: Interfigural Readings." Pages 77–111 in *Transformative Encounters: Jesus and Women Re-viewed.* Edited by Ingrid Rosa Kitzberger. Biblical Interpretation Series 43. Leiden: Brill, 2000.

Koester, Craig R. *Symbolism in the Fourth Gospel: Meaning, Mystery, Community.* 2nd ed. Minneapolis: Fortress Press, 2003.

Köstenberger, Andreas J. *John.* Baker Exegetical Commentary on the New Testament. Grand Rapids: Baker Academic, 2004.

———. *The Missions of Jesus and the Disciples according to the Fourth Gospel: With Implications for the Fourth Gospel's Purpose and the Mission of the Contemporary Church.* Grand Rapids: Eerdmans, 1998.

Krafft, Eva. "Die Personen des Johannesevangeliums." *Evangelische Theologie* 16 (1956): 18–32.

Lai, Barbara M. Leung. *Through the "I"-Window: The Inner Life of Characters in the Hebrew Bible.* Hebrew Bible Monographs 34. Sheffield: Sheffield Phoenix, 2011.

Lang, Friedrich Gustav. "Neues über Lydia? Zur Deutung von 'Purpurhändlerin' in Apg 16,14." *Zeitschrift für die Neutestamentliche Wissenschaft* 100 (2009): 29–44.

Lawrence, Louise J. *An Ethnography of the Gospel of Matthew: A Critical Assessment of the Use of the Honour and Shame Model in New Testament Studies.* Wissenschaftliche Untersuchungen zum Neuen Testament II/165; Tübingen: Mohr Siebeck, 2003.

Lee, Dorothy A. "Martha and Mary: Levels of Characterization in Luke and John." Pages 197–220 in *Characters and Characterization in the Gospel of John.* Edited by Christopher W. Skinner. Library of New Testament Studies 461. New York: T. & T. Clark, 2013.

———. "Partnership in Easter Faith: The Role of Mary Magdalene and Thomas in John 20." *Journal for the Study of the New Testament* 58 (1995): 37–49.

Lehtipuu, Outi. "Characterization and Persuasion: The Rich Man and the Poor Man in Luke 16.19-31." Pages 73–105 in *Characterization in the Gospels: Reconceiving Narrative Criticism.* Edited by David Rhoads and Kari Syreeni. Journal for the Study of the New Testament Supplement Series 184. Sheffield: Sheffield Academic Press, 1999.

Lesky, Albin. *Greek Tragedy.* 2nd ed. London: Ernest Benn, 1967.

Lieu, Judith M. "The Mother of the Son in the Fourth Gospel." *Journal of Biblical Literature* 117 (1998): 61–77.

Lincoln, Andrew T. *The Gospel according to Saint John.* Black's New Testament Commentaries 4. London: Continuum, 2005.

————. *Truth on Trial: The Lawsuit Motif in the Fourth Gospel*. Peabody, MA: Hendrickson, 2000.

Lindars, Barnabas. *The Gospel of John*. NCB; London: Oliphants, 1972.

Lyons, William John. "Joseph of Arimathea: One of 'the Jews,' But with a Fearful Secret!" Pages 646–57 in *Character Studies in the Fourth Gospel: Narrative Approaches to Seventy Figures in John*. Edited by Steven A. Hunt, D. Francois Tolmie, and Ruben Zimmermann. Wissenschaftliche Untersuchungen zum Neuen Testament 314; Tübingen: Mohr Siebeck, 2013.

Maccini, Robert G. *Her Testimony Is True: Women as Witnesses according to John*. Journal for the Study of the New Testament Supplement Series 125. Sheffield: Sheffield Academic Press, 1996.

MacDonald, Margaret Y. "Kinship and Family in the New Testament World." Pages 29–43 in *Understanding the Social World of the New Testament*. Edited by Dietmar Neufeld and Richard E. DeMaris. New York: Routledge, 2010.

Malbon, Elizabeth Struthers. "Characters in Mark's Story: Changing Perspectives on the Narrative Process." Pages 45–69 in *Mark as Story: Retrospect and Prospect*. Edited by Kelly R. Iverson and Christopher W. Skinner. Society of Biblical Literature Resources for Biblical Study 65. Atlanta: Society of Biblical Literature, 2011.

————. "Fallible Followers: Women and Men in the Gospel of Mark." *Semeia* 28 (1983): 29–48.

————. *In the Company of Jesus: Characters in Mark's Gospel*. Louisville: Westminster John Knox, 2000.

————. *Mark's Jesus: Characterization as Narrative Christology*. Waco, TX: Baylor University Press, 2009.

————. "The Jesus of Mark and the 'Son of David.'" Pages 162–85 in *Between Author and Audience in Mark: Narration, Characterization, Interpretation*. Edited by Elizabeth Struthers Malbon. New Testament Monographs 23. Sheffield: Phoenix, 2009.

————. "The Jewish Leaders in the Gospel of Mark: A Literary Study of Markan Characterization." *Journal of Biblical Literature* 108 (1989): 259–81.

————. "The Major Importance of the Minor Characters in Mark." Pages 58–86 in *The New Literary Criticism and the New Testament*. Edited by Elizabeth Struthers Malbon and Edgar V. McKnight. Journal for the Study of the New Testament Supplement Series 109. Sheffield: Sheffield Academic Press, 1994.

Malina, Bruce J. *The New Testament World: Insights from Cultural Anthropology*. 3rd ed. Louisville: Westminster John Knox, 2001.

——, and Richard L. Rohrbaugh. *Social-Science Commentary on the Gospel of John*. Minneapolis: Fortress Press, 1998.

Marcus, Joel. *Mark 1–8*. Anchor Bible 27. New York: Doubleday, 2000.

——. *Mark 8–16*. Anchor Yale Bible 27a. New Haven: Yale University Press, 2009.

Margolin, Uri. "Character." Pages 66–79 in *Cambridge Companion to Narrative*. Edited by D. Herman. Cambridge: Cambridge University Press, 2007.

——. "Individuals in Narrative Worlds: An Ontological Perspective." *Poetics Today* 11 (1990): 843–71.

Marguerat, Daniel, and Yvan Bourquin. *How to Read Bible Stories: An Introduction to Narrative Criticism*. London: SCM, 1999.

Marshall, Christopher D. *Faith as Theme in Mark's Narrative*. Society for New Testament Studies Monograph Series 64. Cambridge: Cambridge University Press, 1989.

Martin, Michael W. "Progymnastic Topic Lists: A Compositional Template for Luke and Other Bioi?" *New Testament Studies* 54 (2008): 18–41.

Martin, Troy W. "Assessing the Johannine Epithet 'the Mother of Jesus.'" *Catholic Biblical Quarterly* 60 (1998): 63–73.

May, David M. "Mark 3:20-35 from the Perspective of Shame/Honor." *Biblical Theology Bulletin* 17 (1987): 83–87.

Maynard, Arthur H. "The Role of Peter in the Fourth Gospel." *New Testament Studies* 30 (1984): 531–48.

McGing, Brian Charles. "Pontius Pilate and the Sources." *Catholic Biblical Quarterly* 53 (1991): 416–38.

McKnight, Scott. "Proselytism and Godfearers." Pages 835–47 in *Dictionary of New Testament Background*. Edited by Stanley E. Porter and Craig A. Evans. Downers Grove, IL: InterVarsity, 2000.

Merenlahti, Petri. "Characters in the Making: Individuality and Ideology in the Gospels." Pages 49–72 in *Characterization in the Gospels: Reconceiving Narrative Criticism*. Edited by David Rhoads and Kari Syreeni. Journal for the Study of the New Testament Supplement Series 184. Sheffield: Sheffield Academic Press, 1999.

——, and Raimo Hakola. "Reconceiving Narrative Criticism." Pages 13–48 in *Characterization in the Gospels: Reconceiving Narrative Criticism*. Edited by David Rhoads and Kari Syreeni. Journal for the Study of the New Testament Supplement Series 184. Sheffield: Sheffield Academic Press, 1999.

Miller, Susan. *Women in Mark's Gospel*. Library of New Testament Studies 259. London: T. & T. Clark, 2004.

Mitchell, Margaret M. "Why Family Matters for Early Christian Literature." Pages 345–58 in *Early Christian Families in Context: An Interdisciplinary Dialogue*. Edited by David L. Balch and Carolyn Osiek. Grand Rapids: Eerdmans, 2003.

Moloney, Francis J. *Mark: Storyteller, Interpreter, Evangelist*. Peabody, MA: Hendrickson, 2004.

———. *The Gospel of John*. Sacra Pagina 4. Collegeville, MN: Liturgical, 1998.

———. *The Gospel of Mark: A Commentary*. Peabody, MA: Hendrickson, 2002.

Moore, Stephen D. *Literary Criticism and the Gospels: The Theoretical Challenge*. New Haven: Yale University Press, 1989.

Moss, Candida R. "The Man with the Flow of Power: Porous Bodies in Mark 5:25-34." *Journal of Biblical Literature* 129 (2010): 507–19.

Murphy, S. Jonathan. "The Role of Barnabas in the Book of Acts." *Bibliotheca Sacra* 167 (2010): 319–41.

Myers, Alicia D. *Characterizing Jesus: A Rhetorical Analysis on the Fourth Gospel's Use of Scripture in Its Presentation of Jesus*. Library of New Testament Studies 458. New York: T. & T. Clark, 2012.

Neyrey, Jerome H. "Encomium versus Vituperation: Contrasting Portraits of Jesus in the Fourth Gospel." *Journal of Biblical Literature* 126 (2007): 529–52.

———. *The Gospel of John*. New Cambridge Bible Commentary. Cambridge: Cambridge University Press, 2007.

O'Day, Gail R. *The Gospel of John*. New Interpreter's Bible 9. Nashville: Abingdon, 1995.

Öhler, Markus. *Barnabas: Die historische Person und ihre Rezeption in der Apostelgeschichte*. Wissenschaftliche Untersuchungen zum Neuen Testament 156. Tübingen: Mohr Siebeck, 2003.

Osiek, Carolyn. "The Family in Early Christianity: 'Family Values' Revisited." *Catholic Biblical Quarterly* 58 (1996): 1–25.

Painter, John. *The Quest for the Messiah: The History, Literature and Theology of the Johannine Community*. 2nd ed. Edinburgh: T. & T. Clark, 1993.

Pattemore, Stephen W. *The People of God in the Apocalypse: Discourse, Structure, and Exegesis*. Society for New Testament Studies Monograph Series 128. Cambridge: Cambridge University Press, 2005.

Pelling, Christopher B. R., ed. *Characterization and Individuality in Greek Literature*. Oxford: Clarendon, 1990.

———. "Childhood and Personality in Greek Biography." Pages 213–44 in *Characterization and Individuality in Greek Literature*. Edited by Christopher B. R. Pelling. Oxford: Clarendon, 1990.

———. "Conclusion." Pages 245–62 in *Characterization and Individuality in Greek Literature*. Edited by Christopher B. R. Pelling. Oxford: Clarendon, 1990.

———. "Plutarch's Adaptation of His Source-Material." *Journal of Hellenic Studies* 100 (1980): 127–40.

Pennington, Jonathan P. *Reading the Gospels Wisely: A Narrative and Theological Introduction*. Grand Rapids: Baker Academic, 2012.

Perkins, Pheme. *Peter: Apostle for the Whole Church*. Columbia: University of South Carolina Press, 1994.

Petersen, Norman R. "'Point of View' in Mark's Narrative." *Semeia* 12 (1978): 97–121.

Peterson, David. "Luke's Theological Enterprise: Integration and Intent." Pages 521–44 in *Witness to the Gospel: The Theology of Acts*. Edited by I. Howard Marshall and David Peterson. Grand Rapids: Eerdmans, 1998.

Powell, Mark Allan. *What Is Narrative Criticism?* Minneapolis: Fortress Press, 1990.

Quast, Kevin. *Peter and the Beloved Disciple: Figures for a Community in Crisis*. Journal for the Study of the New Testament Supplement Series 32. Sheffield: JSOT Press, 1989.

Redman, Judith Christine Single. "Eyewitness Testimony and the Characters in the Fourth Gospel." Pages 59–78 in *Characters and Characterization in the Gospel of John*. Edited by Christopher W. Skinner. Library of New Testament Studies 461. New York: T. & T. Clark, 2013.

Rensberger, David K. *Overcoming the World: Politics and Community in the Gospel of John*. London: SPCK, 1988.

Renz, Gabi. "Nicodemus: An Ambiguous Disciple? A Narrative Sensitive Investigation." Pages 255–83 in *Challenging Perspectives on the Gospel of John*. Edited by John Lierman. Wissenschaftliche Untersuchungen zum Neuen Testament II/219. Tübingen: Mohr Siebeck, 2006.

Resseguie, James L. *Narrative Criticism of the New Testament: An Introduction*. Grand Rapids: Baker Academic, 2005.

———. *The Strange Gospel: Narrative Design and Point of View in John*. Biblical Interpretation Series 56. Leiden: Brill, 2001.

Rhoads, David. "Losing Life for Others in the Face of Death: Mark's Standards of Judgment." *Interpretation* 47 (1993): 358–69.

———. *Reading Mark, Engaging the Gospel*. Minneapolis: Fortress Press, 2004.

———, Joanna Dewey, and Donald Michie. *Mark as Story: An Introduction to the Narrative of a Gospel*. 3rd ed. Philadelphia: Fortress Press, 2012 (1999, 1982). Joanna Dewey became co-author in the second edition.

Ridderbos, Herman N. *The Gospel according to John: A Theological Commentary.* Translated by J. Vriend. Grand Rapids: Eerdmans, 1997.

Rimmon-Kenan, Shlomith. *Narrative Fiction: Contemporary Poetics.* 2nd ed. New York: Routledge, 2002 (1983).

Rohrbaugh, Richard L. "Models and Muddles: Discussions of the Social Facets Seminar." *Forum* 3, no. 2 (1987): 23–33.

———. Review of Cornelis Bennema, *Encountering Jesus: Character Studies in the Gospel of John.* *Biblical Theology Bulletin* 41 (2011): 110–11.

Roth, S. John. *The Blind, the Lame, and the Poor: Character Types in Luke–Acts.* Journal for the Study of the New Testament Supplement Series 144. Sheffield: Sheffield Academic Press, 1997.

Rusten, J. "Introduction to Theophrastus." Pages 5–13 in Theophrastus, *Characters.* Edited and translated by J. Rusten. Loeb Classical Library 225. Cambridge, MA: Harvard University Press, 2002.

Schenke, Ludger. *Die Wundererzählungen des Markusevangeliums.* Stuttgarter Biblische Beiträge 5. Stuttgart: Katholisches Bibelwerk, 1974.

Schnabel, Eckhard J. *Early Christian Mission.* 2 vols. Downers Grove, IL: InterVarsity, 2004.

Schnackenburg, Rudolf. *The Gospel according to St John.* 3 vols. London: Burns & Oates, 1968–82.

Schneiders, Sandra M. "Born Anew." *Theology Today* 44 (1987): 189–96.

———. "Women in the Fourth Gospel and the Role of Women in the Contemporary Church." *Biblical Theology Bulletin* 12 (1982): 35–45.

Scholes, Robert, James Phelan, and Robert Kellogg. *The Nature of Narrative.* 2nd ed. Oxford: Oxford University Press, 2006 (1966). James Phelan became co-author in the second edition.

Schultheiss, Tanja. *Das Petrusbild im Johannesevangelium.* Wissenschaftliche Untersuchungen zum Neuen Testament II/329. Tübingen: Mohr Siebeck, 2012.

Schüssler Fiorenza, Elisabeth. *In Memory of Her: A Feminist Theological Reconstruction of Christian Origins.* London: SCM, 1983.

Scott, Martin. *Sophia and the Johannine Jesus.* Journal for the Study of the New Testament Supplement Series 71. Sheffield: JSOT Press, 1992.

Seim, Turid Karlsen. "Roles of Women in the Gospel of John." Pages 56–73 in *Aspects on the Johannine Literature.* Edited by Lars Hartman and Birger Olsson. Coniectanea Biblica New Testament Series 18. Uppsala: University Press, 1987.

Shauf, Scott. "Locating the Eunuch: Characterization and Narrative Context in Acts 8:26-40." *Catholic Biblical Quarterly* 71 (2009): 762–75.

Shepherd, William H. *The Narrative Function of the Holy Spirit as a Character in Luke–Acts.* Society of Biblical Literature Dissertation Series 147. Atlanta: Scholars, 1994.

Sheridan, Ruth. *Retelling Scripture: "The Jews" and the Scriptural Citations in John 1:19–12:15.* Biblical Interpretation Series 110. Leiden: Brill, 2012.

Shiner, Whitney Taylor. *Follow Me! Disciples in Markan Rhetoric.* Society of Biblical Literature Dissertation Series 145. Atlanta: Scholars, 1995.

Skinner, Christopher W., ed. *Characters and Characterization in the Gospel of John.* Library of New Testament Studies 461. New York: T. & T. Clark, 2013.

———. "Characters and Characterization in the Gospel of John: Reflections on the *Status Questionis.*" Pages xvii–xxxii in *Characters and Characterization in the Gospel of John.* Edited by Christopher W. Skinner. Library of New Testament Studies 461; New York: T. & T. Clark, 2013.

———. *John and Thomas—Gospels in Conflict? Johannine Characterization and the Thomas Question.* Princeton Theological Monograph Series 115. Eugene, OR: Wipf & Stock, 2009.

———, and Matthew Ryan Hauge, eds. *Character Studies and the Gospel of Mark.* Library of New Testament Studies. New York: T. & T. Clark, forthcoming 2014.

Smith, Abraham. "'Do You Understand What You Are Reading?': A Literary Critical Reading of the Ethiopian (Kushite) Episode (Acts 8:26-40)." *Journal of the Interdenominational Theological Center* 22 (1994): 48–70.

———. "Tyranny Exposed: Mark's Typological Characterization of Herod Antipas (Mark 6:14-29)." *Biblical Interpretation* 14 (2006): 259–93.

Smith, Stephen H. *A Lion with Wings: A Narrative-Critical Approach to Mark's Gospel.* The Biblical Seminar 38. Sheffield: Sheffield Academic Press, 1996.

Snyder, Graydon F. "John 13:16 and the Anti-Petrinism of the Johannine Tradition." *Biblical Research* 16 (1971): 5–15.

Spencer, F. Scott. "Women of 'the Cloth' in Acts: Sewing the Word." Pages 134–54 in *A Feminist Companion to the Acts of the Apostles.* Edited by Amy-Jill Levine (with Marianne Blickenstaff). New York: T. & T. Clark, 2004.

Staley, Jeffrey L. *The Print's First Kiss: A Rhetorical Investigation of the Implied Reader in the Fourth Gospel.* Society of Biblical Literature Dissertation Series 82. Atlanta: Scholars, 1988.

Stanton, Graham. *The Gospels and Jesus.* 2nd ed. Oxford: Oxford University Press, 2002.

Sterck-Degueldre, Jean-Pierre. *Eine Frau namens Lydia: Zu Geschichte und Komposition in Apostelgeschichte 16,11-15.40.* Wissenschaftliche Untersuchungen zum Neuen Testament II/176. Tübingen: Mohr Siebeck, 2004.

Sternberg, Meir. *The Poetics of Biblical Narrative: Ideological Literature and the Drama of Reading.* Bloomington: Indiana University Press, 1985.

Stibbe, Mark W. G. *John as Storyteller: Narrative Criticism and the Fourth Gospel.* Society for New Testament Studies Monograph Series 73. Cambridge: Cambridge University Press, 1992.

———. *John.* Sheffield: JSOT Press, 1993.

———. *John's Gospel.* London: Routledge, 1994.

———. "'Return to Sender': A Structuralist Approach to John's Gospel." *Biblical Interpretation* 1 (1993): 189–206.

Stuhlmacher, Peter. "The Genre(s) of the Gospels." Pages 484–94 in *The Interrelations of the Gospels.* Edited by D. L. Dungan. Bibliotheca Ephemeridum Theologicarum Lovaniensium 95. Leuven: Leuven University Press, 1990.

Sylva, Dennis D. "Nicodemus and His Spices (John 19.39)." *New Testament Studies* 34 (1988): 148–51.

Tannehill, Robert C. "The Disciples in Mark: The Function of a Narrative Role." *Journal of Religion* 57 (1977): 386–405.

———. *The Narrative Unity of Luke–Acts: A Literary Interpretation.* 2 vols. Minneapolis: Fortress Press, 1986, 1989.

Telford, W. R. *The Theology of the Gospel of Mark.* New Testament Theology. Cambridge: Cambridge University Press, 1999.

Thatcher, Tom. "Jesus, Judas and Peter: Character by Contrast in the Fourth Gospel." *Bibliotheca Sacra* 153 (1996): 435–48.

Thiede, Carsten Peter. *Simon Peter: From Galilee to Rome.* Exeter, UK: Paternoster, 1986.

Thiselton, Anthony C. *New Horizons in Hermeneutics.* London: HarperCollins, 1992.

———. *The Two Horizons.* Exeter, UK: Paternoster, 1980.

Thompson, Marianne Meye. "'God's Voice You Have Never Heard, God's Form You Have Never Seen': The Characterization of God in the Gospel of John." *Semeia* 63 (1993): 177–204.

Thompson, Richard P. *Keeping the Church in Its Place: The Church as Narrative Character in Acts*. New York: T. & T. Clark, 2006.

Tilborg, Sjef van. *Imaginative Love in John*. Biblical Interpretation Series 2. Leiden: Brill, 1993.

Tolbert, Mary Ann. "How the Gospel of Mark Builds Character." *Interpretation* 47 (1993): 347–57.

———. *Sowing the Gospel: Mark's World in Literary-Historical Perspective*. Minneapolis: Fortress Press, 1989.

Tolmie, D. Francois. *Jesus' Farewell to the Disciples: John 13:1–17:26 in Narratological Perspective*. Biblical Interpretation Series 12. Leiden: Brill, 1995.

Tuckett, Christopher M. "Pilate in John 18–19: A Narrative-Critical Approach." Pages 131–40 in *Narrativity in Biblical and Related Texts*. Edited by G. J. Brooke and J.-D. Kaestli. Bibliotheca Ephemeridum Theologicarum Lovaniensium 149. Leuven: Leuven Unversity Press, 2000.

Turner, Max. "The 'Spirit of Prophecy' as the Power of Israel's Restoration and Witness." Pages 327–48 in *Witness to the Gospel: The Theology of Acts*. Edited by I. Howard Marshall and David Peterson. Grand Rapids: Eerdmans, 1998.

Twelftree, Graham H. *Jesus the Miracle Worker: A Historical and Theological Study*. Downers Grove, IL: InterVarsity, 1999.

Vanhoozer, Kevin J. *Is There a Meaning in This Text?: The Bible, the Reader and the Morality of Literary Knowledge*. Grand Rapids: Zondervan, 1998.

Voorwinde, Stephen. *Jesus' Emotions in the Fourth Gospel: Human or Divine?* Library of New Testament Studies 284. London: T. & T. Clark, 2005.

Wead, David W. "We Have a Law." *Novum Testamentum* 11 (1969): 185–89.

Webb, Geoff R. *Mark at the Threshold: Applying Bakhtinian Categories to Markan Characterisation*. Biblical Interpretation Series 95. Leiden: Brill, 2008.

Weeden, Theodore J. *Mark—Traditions in Conflict*. Philadelphia: Fortress Press, 1971.

Wiarda, Timothy. "John 21.1-23: Narrative Unity and Its Implications." *Journal for the Study of the New Testament* 46 (1992): 53–71.

———. *Peter in the Gospels: Pattern, Personality and Relationship*. Wissenschaftliche Untersuchungen zum Neuen Testament II/127. Tübingen: Mohr Siebeck, 2000.

Williams, Joel F. *Other Followers of Jesus: Minor Characters as Major Figures in Mark's Gospel*. Journal for the Study of the New Testament Supplement Series 102. Sheffield: JSOT Press, 1994.

Williams, Ritva H. "The Mother of Jesus at Cana: A Social-Science Interpretation of John 2:1-12." *Catholic Biblical Quarterly* 59 (1997): 679–92.

Witherington, Ben. *The Acts of the Apostles: A Socio-Rhetorical Commentary.* Grand Rapids: Eerdmans, 1998.

———. *The Gospel of Mark: A Socio-Rhetorical Commentary.* Grand Rapids: Eerdmans, 2001.

Wright, William M. "Greco-Roman Character Typing and the Presentation of Judas in the Fourth Gospel." *Catholic Biblical Quarterly* 71 (2009): 544–59.

Yamasaki, Gary. *Perspective Criticism: Point of View and Evaluative Guidance in Biblical Narrative.* Eugene, OR: Wipf & Stock/Cascade, 2012.

———. "Point of View in a Gospel Story: What Difference Does It Make? Luke 19:1-10 as a Test Case." *Journal of Biblical Literature* 125 (2006): 89–105.

Zimmermann, Ruben, "Figurenanalyse im Johannesevangelium: Ein Beitrag zur narratologischen Exegese." *Zeitschrift für die Neutestamentliche Wissenschaft* 105 (forthcoming 2014).

———. "'The Jews': Unreliable Figures or Unreliable Narration?" Pages 71–109 in *Character Studies in the Fourth Gospel: Narrative Approaches to Seventy Figures in John.* Edited by Steven A. Hunt, D. Francois Tolmie, and Ruben Zimmermann. Wissenschaftliche Untersuchungen zum Neuen Testament 314. Tübingen: Mohr Siebeck, 2013.

Index of Modern Authors

Aichele, George, 121–22
Alter, Robert, 33–34, 56
Anderson, Paul N., 28, 65, 69
Ascough, Richard S., 178–80
Aune, David E., 32

Bal, Mieke, 2, 47–48, 60, 73, 85
Ball, David, 96, 102
Bar-Efrat, Shimon, 33–34, 47, 56–57, 73, 78
Barton, Stephen C., 121–22
Bassler, Jouette M., 148, 152–53
Bauckham, Richard, 1, 32, 43, 52, 65, 69, 136–37, 148–49, 152, 169
Beasley-Murray, George R., 137, 151
Beck, David R., 13, 19, 94–95, 136, 141, 143, 153
Beck, Robert R., 102
Beirne, Margaret M., 11, 143–44, 149–52
Bennema, Cornelis, xi–xii, 11, 15, 19, 25–26, 33, 44, 65, 75, 83–85, 88–89, 93, 96–97, 102, 106–8, 110–11, 117, 127, 133, 136–37, 142, 150, 155, 187, 189
Berlin, Adele, 4, 23–24, 33–34, 46, 49, 56, 73, 78
Best, Ernest, 5, 116, 118–19
Billault, Alain, 42–43, 45
Black, C. Clifton, 19
Blaine, Bradford B., 134, 138
Boer, Martinus C. de, 67, 160–61
Böhler, Dieter, 157
Bolt, Peter G., 165
Bond, Helen K., 70, 155–58, 160, 163, 173
Booth, Wayne, 67, 73
Bourquin, Yvan, 46, 49

Brady, David, 118
Brant, Jo-Ann A., 15, 19, 61, 92, 96, 136, 151
Broadhead, Edwin K., 116, 118, 126, 129–30
Brock, Sebastian, 175
Brower, Kent E., 134
Brown, Raymond E., 11, 67, 141–44, 148, 158–60
Bultmann, Rudolf, 143–44, 158
Burnett, Fred W., xii, 2, 15, 32, 39, 42–43, 48, 52, 55, 58, 60, 73, 105
Burridge, Richard A., 32, 40–41, 61–62

Carson, D. A., 137, 141–42, 149, 151
Carter, Warren, 156, 158, 160
Chatman, Seymour, 2, 7–9, 12–14, 17, 20, 44–46, 49, 54, 56–57, 60, 67, 73, 102
Cheng, Ling, 23–24
Collins, Raymond F., 11, 18, 104, 138, 141, 143, 148, 153
Coloe, Mary L., 143–44
Conway, Colleen M., 13, 18–19, 27, 47, 83, 92, 95–96, 142, 144, 146, 148, 155, 158, 160, 187
Cotter, Wendy J., 128–30
Cotterell, F. Peter, 149
Culpeper, Jonathan, 56
Culpepper, R. Alan, vii, ix–x, 4, 8, 11–12, 17–19, 26, 36, 64, 81, 88–89, 91, 94–95, 97, 103–4, 137, 143–44, 148, 153, 156–60, 187

Darr, John A., 4, 13, 21–24, 60, 64, 66, 68, 101, 110, 165, 187
Davies, Margaret, 11, 138
De Romilly, Jacqueline, 38, 40

Dewey, Joanna, 5–6, 10–11, 91, 100, 102, 104
Dixon, Suzanne, 179
Droge, Arthur J., 134, 136
Dschnulnigg, Peter, 129–30
Dunn, James D. G., 32, 168–69, 179–80

Easterling, Patricia E., 38, 42, 55–56
Eder, Jens, 4, 47
Edwards, James R., 122
Edwards, Ruth, 11, 145, 151, 153
Egan, Kieran, 102
Ehrman, Bart D., 156, 159
Ewen, Yosef, xii, 13, 15, 17, 20, 22, 46–47, 59–60, 62, 72–73, 82–83, 85–87, 89–90, 110

Farelly, Nicolas, 3, 16, 44, 49, 102–3, 106
Fehribach, Adeline, 11, 141–43
Finnern, Sönke, 4, 47–48, 67, 73, 82, 86
Forster, E. M., 2, 7, 9–10, 12–13, 17, 20, 22–23, 45–47, 58, 72–73, 76, 88–89
France, R. T., 128

Gaiser, Frederick J., 126
Garton, Charles, 39
Gaventa, Beverly Roberts, 101, 141, 145, 165, 167–69, 175, 180
Gench, Frances Taylor, 11
Gill, Christopher, 23, 36–39, 41–42, 51
Gillespie, Thomas W., 156
Glancy, Jennifer A., 72, 157
Goldhill, Simon, 38–39, 51, 55
Goodacre, Mark, 69
Gowler, David B., 19–21, 24, 26, 34, 37, 39, 41–43, 46–47, 51–52, 66, 82
Graham, Susan Lochrie, 5, 32, 126
Greimas, Algirdas J., 13, 44, 89, 102
Griffin, Jasper, 40
Gundry, Robert H., 115, 122, 128–30

Haber, Susan, 126
Hägg, Tomas, 42–43

Hakola, Raimo, 64–66
Hanson, John S., 117
Hanson, Kenneth C., 114
Harstine, Stan, 11
Harvey, W. J., 8, 10–13, 20–22, 24, 46, 58, 72, 88–90
Healy, Mary, 126
Hengel, Martin, 32, 171
Hochman, Baruch, 6, 10, 13, 20, 22, 47–48, 52, 57, 59, 73, 82, 86
Hooker, Morna D., 116, 121
Horsley, Richard A., 117
Howard, James M., 11, 143
Hunt, Steven A., 3, 11, 18, 26, 74
Hurtado, Larry W., 114, 116
Hylen, Susan E., xii, 3, 15, 18–19, 26, 82–83, 85, 109

Iersel, Bas M. van, 122, 128
Iser, Wolfgang, 8, 13, 22, 45, 56, 67
Iverson, Kelly R., 3, 9–10, 66, 100

Jannidis, Fotis, 4
Jervell, Jacob, 164
Jonge, Marinus de, 144, 148, 151

Keener, Craig S., 135, 141, 143, 145, 148
Kellogg, Robert, 11, 23, 28, 33–34, 53, 78, 107
Kennedy, George A., 112
Kermode, Frank, 51, 63–64
Kern, Philip H., 20
Kim, Dongsu, 134, 136, 138
Kim, Jean K., 11
Kingsbury, Jack Dean, 4–5, 102
Kistemaker, Simon J., 166, 176–77, 179–80
Kitto, H. D. F., 39
Kitzberger, Ingrid Rosa, 14
Koester, Craig R., 14, 17, 19, 36, 61, 105, 149, 152
Köstenberger, Andreas J., 137, 142, 148
Krafft, Eva, 11, 135, 144, 148, 151

Lai, Barbara M. Leung, 34
Lang, Friedrich Gustav, 179
Lawrence, Louise J., 56
Lee, Dorothy A., 71, 136
Lehtipuu, Outi, 36, 73
Lesky, Albin, 37–40, 51
Lieu, Judith M., 141, 144–46
Lincoln, Andrew T., 49, 65, 89, 103, 161
Lindars, Barnabas, 135, 148, 153
Lyons, William John, xii, 18–19, 67–69, 71

Maccini, Robert G., 11, 141, 146
MacDonald, Margaret Y., 179
Malbon, Elizabeth Struthers, 3, 6–7, 10–11, 47, 52, 58, 71, 87, 100, 119–20, 128
Malina, Bruce J., 42, 55, 60
Marcus, Joel, 115–17, 121, 128, 130
Margolin, Uri, 29, 45, 56–58
Marguerat, Daniel, 46, 49
Marshall, Christopher D., 102, 115, 125–26, 128–30
Martin, Michael W., 112
Martin, Troy W., 140, 145
May, David M., 121
Maynard, Arthur H., 133
McGing, Brian Charles, 155, 163
McKnight, Scott, 179
Merenlahti, Petri, 51–52, 64–66, 107
Michie, Donald, 4–6, 10, 91, 100, 102, 104
Miller, Susan, 5, 121–22, 125–26
Mitchell, Margaret M., 179
Moloney, Francis J., 102, 115–16, 119, 128–29, 143, 148–49, 151, 153, 158
Moore, Stephen D., 8, 44, 48, 54, 94, 102
Moss, Candida R., 124–25
Murphy, S. Jonathan, 20, 175–76
Myers, Alicia D., xii, 4, 17, 19, 25–26, 36, 60, 106–12

Neyrey, Jerome H., 85, 104, 112, 155, 157

Oakman, Douglas E., 114
Öhler, Markus, 175–77
Osiek, Carolyn, 179

Painter, John, 134, 149
Pattemore, Stephen W., 72
Pelling, Christopher B. R., 41, 51–52
Pennington, Jonathan P., 189
Perkins, Pheme, 20, 165, 167, 170–71
Petersen, Norman R., 5, 100
Peterson, David, 101, 164–65
Phelan, James, 28, 33, 53, 78, 107
Powell, Mark Allan, 49, 104

Quast, Kevin, 133–34, 136

Redman, Judith Christine Single, xii, 18–19, 26, 87, 96–97
Rensberger, David K., 157, 160
Renz, Gabi, 152
Resseguie, James L., 14, 18–19, 48–49, 67, 73, 76, 91–92, 145
Rhoads, David, 4–6, 10–11, 36, 51, 64, 91, 100, 102, 104
Ridderbos, Herman N., 134, 148–49
Rimmon-Kenan, Shlomith, 2, 8–9, 12, 17, 20, 44–46, 48, 56, 60, 67, 75–76, 102
Rohrbaugh, Richard L., xii, 32–33, 59–60
Roth, S. John, 22–24
Rusten, J., 36

Schenke, Ludger, 129–30
Schnabel, Eckhard J., 165, 169
Schnackenburg, Rudolf, 144, 148, 152–53, 158
Schneider, Ralf, 4
Schneiders, Sandra M., 11, 148

Scholes, Robert, 11, 23, 28, 33–34, 53, 78, 107
Schultheiss, Tanja, 17
Schüssler Fiorenza, Elisabeth, 11, 141
Scott, Martin, 141–42, 144, 146
Seim, Turid Karlsen, 11
Shauf, Scott, 20
Shepherd, William H., 22, 24, 26, 28, 44, 47, 53–54
Sheridan, Ruth, xii, 17, 19, 44, 106
Shiner, Whitney Taylor, 8, 10, 78, 115–16
Skinner, Christopher W., xii, 3–5, 11, 16, 19, 52, 83–85
Smith, Abraham, 9–10, 20, 36
Smith, Stephen H., 8–10, 73–75, 100, 102
Snyder, Graydon F., 134
Spencer, F. Scott, 179
Staley, Jeffrey L., 64
Stanton, Graham, 32
Sterck-Degueldre, Jean-Pierre, 179–80
Sternberg, Meir, 33–35, 47, 56, 66, 73
Stibbe, Mark W. G., 12, 19, 46, 61, 67, 89, 94, 102, 136, 142, 158, 160
Stuhlmacher, Peter, 32
Sylva, Dennis D., 151

Tannehill, Robert C., 4–5, 8, 19, 55, 95, 187
Telford, W. R., 115, 129
Thatcher, Tom, 135, 137
Thiede, Carsten Peter, 167–70

Thiselton, Anthony C., 54
Thompson, Marianne Meye, 55, 64
Thompson, Richard P., 23–24, 43, 51, 56, 101
Tilborg, Sjef van, 11
Tolbert, Mary Ann, 7, 10, 23, 25–26, 36, 50, 55, 58, 73, 114, 122, 125, 129–30
Tolmie, D. Francois, 2–3, 11–13, 17–19, 26, 46, 78–79, 88–90, 102, 138
Tuckett, Christopher M., 160
Turner, Max, xiii, 164–65
Twelftree, Graham H., 126, 128–30

Vanhoozer, Kevin J., 1, 67
Voorwinde, Stephen, 80

Webb, Geoff R., 9–10, 52, 71, 107, 128, 130
Weeden, Theodore J., 6
Wiarda, Timothy, 134–38
Williams, Joel F., 7–8, 10, 75, 100, 125, 130–31, 187
Williams, Ritva H., 140–43, 145
Witherington, Ben, 115, 122, 166, 168–69, 175–76, 179–80
Wright, William M., 17, 36

Yamasaki, Gary, 49, 90–91

Zimmermann, Ruben, 3, 11, 18, 26, 48, 82, 112

129358

CPSIA information can be obtained
at www.ICGtesting.com
Printed in the USA
FFOW04n2023070414
4749FF

9 781451 472219